Information, Opportunism and Economic Coordination

By the same author

Money Matters: A Keynesian Approach to Monetary Economics, with Sheila C. Dow (Martin Robertson, 1982)

The Economic Imagination: Towards a Behavioural Analysis of Choice (Wheatsheaf Books, 1983)

The Corporate Imagination: How Big Companies Make Mistakes (Wheatsheaf Books, 1984)

Lifestyle Economics: Consumer Behaviour in a Turbulent World (Wheatsheaf Books, 1986)

Psychological Economics: Development, Tensions, Prospects, editor (Kluwer Academic Publishers, 1988)

Behavioural Economics (2 Volumes), editor (Edward Elgar Publishing Limited, 1988)

Monetary Scenarios: A Modern Approach to Financial Systems (Edward Elgar Publishing, 1990)

The Economics of Competitive Enterprise: Selected Essays of P.W.S. Andrews, co-editor with Frederic S. Lee (Edward Elgar Publishing Limited, 1993)

Microeconomics for Business and Marketing: Lectures, Cases and Worked Essays (Edward Elgar Publishing Limited, 1995)

Marketing, Management and the Competitive Process, editor (Edward Elgar Publishing Limited, 1996)

The Elgar Companion to Consumer Research and Economic Psychology, co-editor with Simon Kemp (Edward Elgar Publishing Limited, 1999)

Economic Organization and Economic Knowledge: Essays in Honour of Brian J. Loasby, Volume I, co-editor with Sheila C. Dow (Edward Elgar Publishing Limited, 1999)

Complexity, Contingency and the Theory of the Firm: Essays in Honour of Brian J. Loasby, Volume II, co-editor, with Sheila C. Dow (Edward Elgar Publishing Limited, 1999)

Economics as an Art of Thought: Essays in Memory of G.L.S. Shackle, co-editor with Stephen F. Frowen (Routledge, 2000)

The Legacy of Herbert A. Simon in Economic Analysis (2 Volumes), editor (Edward Elgar Publishing Limited, 2001)

Information, Opportunism and Economic Coordination

Peter E. Earl

Senior Lecturer in Business Economics
University of Queensland, Australia

Edward Elgar
Cheltenham, UK • Northampton, MA, USA

Published by
Edward Elgar Publishing Limited
Glensanda House
Montpellier Parade
Cheltenham
Glos GL50 1UA
UK

Edward Elgar Publishing, Inc.
136 West Street
Suite 202
Northampton
Massachusetts 01060
USA

A catalogue record for this book
is available from the British Library

Library of Congress Cataloguing in Publication Data
Earl, Peter E.
    Information, opportunism, and economic coordination / Peter E. Earl.
        p. cm.
    Includes bibliographical references and index.
    1. Industrial organization (Economic theory) 2. Information theory in economics. I. Title.

    HD2326 .E227 2003
    330'.01'154—dc21

2002037935

ISBN 1 84064 738 8

Printed and bound in Great Britain by MPG Books Ltd, Bodmin, Cornwall

Contents

Acknowledgements

I am grateful to a number of individuals and firms for permission to reproduce in this book material that has been published previously.

Chapter 1 is a slightly revised version of an article entitled 'Scientific Research Programmes and the Prediction of Corporate Behaviour' that originally appeared in 1992 in the *Cyprus Journal of Economics* (since renamed *Ekonomia*), **5**, No. 2, December: 75–95, published by the Cyprus Economic Society. I am grateful to the *Journal*'s Editor, Professor Panicos O. Demetriades and Managing Editor, Sofronis Clerides for permission to reprint it here.

Chapter 2 is an updated version of 'The evolution of cooperative strategies: Three automotive industry case studies', which originally appeared in 1992 in *Human Systems Management*, **11**, No. 2: 89–100. I am grateful to Professor Milan Zeleny, the Editor of *Human Systems Management* (published by IOS Press, Amsterdam), for permission to reprint the revised article here

Chapters 3 and 4 are both reproduced with permission of Robert Langham, Economics Editor at Routledge. Chapter 3 is a shortened version of 'George Richardson's career and the literature of economics', published in 1998 in N.J. Foss and B.J. Loasby (eds) *Economic Organization, Capabilities and Coordination: Essays in Honour of G.B. Richardson*, London, Routledge, pp. 14–43. Chapter 4 is an updated and slightly extended version of 'Shackle, entrepreneurship and the theory of the firm', which was originally published in Stephen Pressman (ed.) (1996) *Interactions in Political Economy: Malvern after Ten Years*, London, Routledge, pp. 43–60.

Chapter 5 is a heavily revised and extended version of 'Managerialism and the theory of the firm', which was published in 1999 in P. Werhane and A.E. Singer (eds) *Business Ethics in Theory and Practice: Contributions from Asia and New Zealand*, Dordrecht, Kluwer, pp. 13–26. The copyright material is reproduced with permission from Ingrid de Boer of Kluwer Academic Publishers.

Chapters 6 and 7 both reproduce copyright material with permission of Don Lamberton, the editor and original publisher of *Prometheus*. Chapter 6 is based on an article originally published in 1994, 'The economic rationale of universities: A reconsideration', *Prometheus*, **12**, No. 2, December: 131–51. Chapter 7 is an extended and updated version of an article originally published in 1991 as 'Principal–agent problems and structural change in the advertising industry', *Prometheus*, **9**, December: 274–95.

Chapters 8 and 12 incorporate copyright material that is used with permission from Elsevier, via Jeroen Loos. Chapter 8 is a revised and slightly extended version of 'Marketing as information economics', originally published as pp. 243–61 of *Information and Organization: A Tribute to the Work of Don Lamberton*, Amsterdam, North-Holland/Elseiver. Chapter 12 is an extended version of a 1998 article 'Information, coordination and macroeconomics', *Information Economics and Policy*, **10**: 331-42.

Chapter 9 was co-authored with Jason Potts and we are grateful to Wiley for permission to reproduce it here with minor changes. It originally appeared as 'Latent demand and the browsing shopper', *Managerial and Decision Economics*, 2000, **21**, no. 3–4: 11–22.

Chapter 10 appears with the permission of Elizabeth T. Granda of M.E. Sharpe, Inc. It is an updated version of 'Normal cost versus marginalist models of pricing: A behavioral perspective', *Journal of Post Keynesian Economics*, **13**, no. 2 (Winter 1990–1991: 246–81.

Chapter 11 is a shortened and updated version of 'Liquidity Preference, Marketability and Pricing', which was originally published as pp. 271–94 of S.C. Dow and J. Hillard (eds) (1995) *Keynes, Knowledge and Uncertainty*, Aldershot, Edward Elgar Publishing Ltd and the copyright material is used here with the publisher's permission.

Introduction

This book is based on a selection of my articles and book chapters on the history of economic thought, industrial economics and Post Keynesian economics, that were originally published in the period 1990–2000. Unlike many 'collected essay' kinds of works, particularly those that have 'three-part lists' as their titles, it contains closely inter-related papers that, for maximum effect, should be read in the sequence in which they are presented. As well as having been revised in order to bring out the synergies between them, the papers have been updated in terms of coverage of the literature or to take account of recent empirical developments. They mix theoretical material and case-study analysis and deal with economic coordination both in an industrial setting and in terms of the growth of economic knowledge. Although Oliver Williamson's (1975) notion of opportunism – the guileful pursuit of self-interest based on an information advantage – is evidently an issue in some of the cases, I frequently consider the extent to which it is limited in practice both by a strategic concern with reputation and/or by an intrinsic motivation to perform in a morally appropriate manner.

One of the traditions that Edward Elgar has fostered with books based on collected essays is that their introductions should include some kind of autobiographical reflection on how the author's ideas developed and of the contexts in which the papers were written. Some authors approach this rather coyly, but I have no such inhibitions. I included an account of my road to a behavioural analysis of choice in the very first book that Edward Elgar commissioned from me (Earl, 1983b, pp. 4–11) and I am presently working on a research programme in introspective economics, the first outputs of which were Earl (2001b) and chapter 9 of this book. In the present case, the tale is a somewhat cautionary one and may contain career lessons for young scholars.

The idea for the present book owes much to an e-mail that I received from Stephen Dunn, who was familiar with many of my earlier books but had been surprised to come across the original version of the present book's final chapter during his doctoral research on Galbraith and the role of uncertainty in the theory of the firm. Dunn's e-mail carried the subject heading 'What else are you hiding from us?'. This book is a reply of sorts: it is not primarily a collection of well-known items but includes many papers that I hope readers may find interesting and thought provoking but which they probably would not encounter if conducting their research using databases that concentrate on 'core' journals and do not list book chapters.

There is a large element of 'Do as I say, not as I do' in this, for I was one of the first to write about academic search processes – in a paper (Earl, 1983a) that I allowed Alfred Eichner to include in a book after I had revised it in the light of constructive feedback from *History of Political Economy*. In failing to heed the policy implications of my own work on the business of being an academic economist, I did not merely produce the situation that Dunn's e-mail encapsulated, I also made myself less attractive in the academic labour market by producing a CV which included a list of books that was not offset by a selection of the modern currency for buying a better place in the academic pecking order, namely, recent articles in core economics journals. Rather than writing papers that were carefully targeted for the right kinds of journals and submitting them to their standard refereeing processes, I wrote papers to order, or rather casually let editors have papers that I had already written for particular occasions. In short, I published on the basis of network connections and having a reputation for being able both to write about certain kinds of things and to deliver good copy within a deadline.

The process of carving an academic career that did not follow today's rules began immediately after I graduated from Cambridge University with First Class Honours in Economics in 1977 – an achievement that would normally be followed, if one were pursuing an academic career, by a high-flyer record of papers in top journals and jobs in top institutions. By that stage, I was hooked on problems of information and knowledge and was already an admirer of behavioural and Post Keynesian approaches to economics, via reading suggestions from, particularly, Ajit Singh, Alan Hughes and Tony Cramp. However, even whilst at school (Alleyne's Grammar School, Stevenage), I had been interested in the process of structural change and the problem of economic coordination: the first two economics books that I read were not textbooks but G.C. Allen's (1959) *British Industries and their Organization*, which gave me a sense of business history, and Michael Stewart's (1967) *Keynes and After*. Moreover, of the half-dozen textbooks that I read, Alchian and Allen (1967), with its discussion of speculation in commodity markets, was the one that interested me most. In fact, my interest in competition as a process rather than a state, and in the capabilities of firms and barriers to change, began a few years before I started economics, when my geography teacher talked about 'industrial inertia' as he explained why pottery continued to be produced in Staffordshire despite the deposits of china-clay having long been used up.

I remember vividly my discovery that, for some economists, the 'theory of the firm' was the perfect competition price/output diagram rather than something rather more concerned with the firm as an evolving organization. This came during an interview with John Creedy for a place at Durham University (as a back-up in case I did not get good enough A-Level results to try for Cambridge): he was already looking rather sceptical about the range of economics books I informed him I had been reading and asked me to draw 'the diagram of the theory of the firm'. After an embarrassing silence, I had to ask him what he meant. Durham promptly rejected me, which was rather ironic given its reputation for taking those that could not quite get into Cambridge.

After graduation, I stayed in Cambridge for a further two years, reading ravenously, with little supervision and virtually no interaction with other postgraduates. (I never took up a desk in the research students' room because, if I recall correctly, in those days students were allowed to smoke there.) Instead I cultivated a strong reputation as a supervisor of undergraduates. My reading began with Loasby's (1976) *Choice, Complexity and Ignorance* – which I had noticed on display in Heffers bookshop during my final year as an undergraduate – and most of the items in its list of references, and it spread out from there via the network of citations and by seeing what was sitting close by cited works on the library shelves. I must have been one of the first, if not even the first, to pick up Williamson's (1975) *Markets and Hierarchies* in the Marshall Library and thereby be introduced to his notion of opportunism.

Early in my studies, I was summoned to be interviewed one Saturday morning by senior faculty members about my intentions/interests. My main memory of the interview was that when Frank Hahn was asked if there was anything he wanted to raise, he replied, 'No, he's an economics poet.' After eight months, I was required to submit a 'substantial piece of work', as a prelude to a thesis proposal. What I tried to submit, only to be told that I must prune it to 30 pages so that my supposed supervisor would be willing to read it, was a 150-page document entitled 'A Keynesian approach to structural change'. This was a precursor to my (1984) book *The Corporate Imagination*, that focused on problems of economic coordination in the face of uncertainty, sources of corporate inertia, non-price competition and the uptake of slack. It lacked, however, the 'corporate strategies as Kuhnian paradigms' perspective, that struck me six months later as I reflected on the fact that it is not merely scientists that cling to ideas in which they have invested. Two problems stood in the way of turning the ideas into a Ph.D. One was that no suitable supervisor was available in Cambridge. The other was that, in empirical terms, what I would have liked to do was akin to an update of Downie's (1958) analysis, but, unlike Downie, I did not have access to the kinds of raw, disaggregated performance data from firms that could only be obtained by someone working inside the Central Statistical Office.

When I told Geoff Meeks, the Assistant Director of Research, that I was thinking of giving up and turning to a career in management consulting, he raised the possibility of an external supervisor. I suggested Brian Loasby, of the University of Stirling, as the ideal person and, whilst approaches were being made, several positions were advertised at Stirling. Meeks encouraged me to apply – if nothing else, I might get a trip to Scotland to meet Loasby – and, a few months later, at age 23 and with my Ph.D. studies in disarray, I found myself with the offer of a lectureship. How different things were in those days! Several weeks after I joined the department, Sheila Dow was hired and we soon discovered overlapping interests in economic method and Post Keynesian monetary economics, that resulted in a number of enjoyable collaborative projects.

Even with Loasby's support, it took a further three years to get a topic approved in Cambridge and it was while this struggle was going on that I got on to the treadmill of being mainly focused on books rather than articles. This was in no small part as a consequence of being impressed by the ability of Mark Casson to produce a book every year and wondering whether I could do the same. The thesis that was eventually accepted in 1984, entitled 'A behavioural analysis of choice', contained elements from my (1983b) and (1986) books.

The Stirling approach to teaching economics was pluralistic and, in teaching management economics and marketing with Richard Shaw and Sue Shaw, I was introduced to the case-study method. Via the lively seminar programme, I made my first contact with Stirling alumnus Neil Kay, whose work continues to have a major influence on my thinking.

The four years and eleven months I spent at Stirling – one month short of the time that would have been sensible for superannuation purposes – were a great introduction to a lecturing career but were overshadowed by the struggle to get the Ph.D. through its various hoops, along with poor pay and, after major funding cutbacks, a lack of any immediate chance of accelerated promotion. Given the financial situation and my liking of mountainous scenery (despite having failed to make the most of what Scotland had to offer, owing to work on the books and thesis), a vacancy at the University of Tasmania looked appealing. After some initial hesitation, since the offer I received was for a three-year contract and I already had tenure at Stirling, I decided to give Tasmania a try, oblivious of the implications that the subsequent erosion of the Australian dollar and explosion of house prices in the UK would have for my ability to return to the British system.

The seven years that I spent at the University of Tasmania (1984–1991) were mostly focused, in terms of research, on monetary economics (leading to Earl, 1990) or on economics and psychology. There was little on industrial economics and the theory of the firm, aside from a growing file of correspondence with Fred Lee about the work of P.W.S. Andrews, that eventually led us to edit his collected papers into a book (Andrews, 1993). However, towards the end of the 1980s, I found myself increasingly pushed out of teaching economics, since my Post Keynesian macroeconomics and monetary theory proved an unpalatable second-year filling to a three-year sequence of courses that began and ended with units taught in an uncompromisingly neoclassical style. The consequence of this was that I ended up teaching marketing, business strategy and organizational behaviour and developing many case study resources, some of which appear here in updated form (chapters 2 and 7) or in my (1995) microeconomics text. This period also saw me moving towards the pluralistic, context-based mode of thinking about economic problems that is evident in chapter 10 (originally written in 1989) and which culminated in the (1995) text.

As with Stirling, I ended up leaving Tasmania without making the most of its leisure opportunities. Despite a CV that was dominated by books, I found myself getting short-listed for chairs. Having been marginalized amongst my economics colleagues, and with a growing vision of how economics could provide a foundation for marketing and business strategy, I accepted the position of Professor of Economics in the Department of Economics and Marketing at Lincoln University, located near Christchurch, New Zealand.

On paper, this looked like an opportune move for doing the sorts of things that I wanted to do. Lincoln University was formerly an agricultural college of some note, but was growing rapidly in the commerce area (with plenty of scope for hiring new staff) and with a head of department (the marketing professor) who had trained as an agricultural economist and taught transaction cost analysis. Three staff shared my interest in Post Keynesian macroeconomics. On top of this, Christchurch was a city with good cultural facilities, cheap and architecturally interesting housing, excellent scenery nearby and with little congestion. In material terms, the decade there was very comfortable, but stagnant house prices made departure a costly experience when I eventually managed to escape what turned out to be a most unpleasant academic environment that matched few of my expectations of what was normal in a university.

Very soon after arriving, I realized that I was not going to get time for the sort of reading or reflective thinking that I had been used to, even if I sacrificed much of my leisure. The problem was not merely that research time was limited but that it was difficult to get a sustained chunk of it; everything had to be done in small bursts, on the run. There were many reasons for this, such as a crazy timetabling system that tended to require one to teach each subject on four or five days of the week, far more contact hours per subject than I had ever known and woefully inadequate tutorial resources, quite apart from administrative joys such as having to establish and then for many years chair the Human Ethics Committee, which seemed to chew up a day every week. Any hopes that I had held of building up a group of economists committed to pluralistic thinking and with an interest in cross-disciplinary research also vanished rapidly when I discovered that I only had one vote in the hiring process and that potential supporters seemed reluctant to alienate certain powerful figures from the ruling 'mafia'. (The bullying that went on was not just implied or verbal: at one stage, when standing my ground as examinations moderator, I was even picked up by a junior colleague and thrown out of his office.) Whilst there was hostility towards pluralism from the economists, which increased as more of them came with orthodox North American training, I was also unable to win support from other business disciplines. Influential marketing and management colleagues guarded their turf carefully, such that their postgraduates often only discovered my expertise in their areas when they came to see me to discuss their upcoming applications for ethical approval. Increasingly, I wondered if this was a case of what is known in Australia and New Zealand as 'the tall poppy syndrome' in which steps are taken to cut high achievers down to normal size. The only rays of hope came via contacts that I made with social scientists in other departments, who made me welcome from the outset and with whom I developed both Bachelor and Master of Social Science degree programmes that enabled heterodox approaches to economics to continue to be taught to small classes under the 'society and business' banner after it had been pushed out of the microeconomics core.

In this context, I concluded that my best hope of maintaining a profile would be to produce the radically innovative microeconomics text and to edit books that explored things that time did not allow me to do on my own: both these kinds of work could be done in small doses during semester or in the evenings. Many of the papers that appear in revised form in this book were produced as bonuses in the midst of this, squeezed in because someone asked me to contribute something and because it turned out that I had something I felt to be worth saying and the occasion was an appropriate venue at which to say it. As a consequence, a lot more of the book editing than I had planned ended up being done in what should have been leisure time.

In the end, after being marginalized once again by neoclassically trained economists, I concluded that I really had to escape to a pluralistic environment that offered more time to think, even if it meant stepping back down the ladder for a time. In what might appear as a minor blow for the axiom of transitivity, I thus accepted a position at the University of Queensland despite having declined a position at a similar grade there at the end of 1987. Transitivity was actually not violated, though, for the working environment would now be air-conditioned – a vital ingredient during the long vacation research period – and Australian academic salaries had shot up whilst those in New Zealand had stagnated with the failure of microeconomic reform to deliver faster economic growth (cf. chapter 5). I would be working alongside my former Lincoln Ph.D. student Jason Potts, with a head of department (John Foster) who understood where I was coming from in terms of economic theory and teaching philosophy. In prospect, it felt as close as it could to being in Stirling twenty years earlier. Work on the present book commenced in my final months at Lincoln in 2001, as a closing chapter on an exhausting and frustrating decade.

Chapters 1 to 3 are linked via George Richardson's work on information and industrial organization. In chapter 1, I employ Richardson's (1960) analysis of the investment coordination problem to argue that the theory of contestable markets and the transaction cost analysis of corporate strategy imply the need for a change in economics method that their proponents mostly do not seem to have perceived: namely, a need to develop workable ways of anticipating the behaviour of actual firms if economists are to be able to anticipate industrial evolution. I then explore the possibility of modelling corporate decision processes as if firms operate in ways akin to academic sciences as depicted by Kuhn and Lakatos. Firms are depicted as behaving differently in large part because they have different corporate philosophies, different methodologies for survival in a world of uncertainty and complexity. What they choose to do depends not on their capabilities in some objective sense, but on how they see themselves and on what they are able to believe about their actual and potential competitors. If we know how the managers of a firm think, then we have a hope of forming bounded conjectures about their decisions. Though this chapter is based on a paper that was published in 1992, it originated early in 1987 as a seminar paper I wrote for my first visit to the University of Queensland at the request of Don Lamberton, whose Information Research Unit issued it as a discussion paper. It was in this early form that it had its most significant impact so far – on a University of Reading Ph.D. on entrepreneurship submitted by New Zealander David Harper around the time that I at last got around to cutting it down to the length of an article. (The pruning of the discussion paper took place after I had been doing some refereeing for *Cyprus Journal of Economics*. Its editor, George Georgiou, then asked if I had any papers on behavioural economics that his journal might consider for publication.) Harper's thesis was eventually turned into his impressive (1996) book.

Richardson's (1972) view that cooperation between firms is an important ingredient in the workings of the competitive process underpins chapter 2, which is a triple case study of quasi-integration in the automotive industry. Coalitions involving the quasi-integration of activities of rival firms come about as problem-solving devices which enable members to achieve their goals by exploiting mutual complementarities in ways that might not be possible or so cost effective if pursued by simple market exchanges or outright merger. Once in operation they tend to change the relative strength of the participants and the information that they have about each other, including information about trustworthiness and corporate capabilities. This leads to changes in the nature of the relationship and degree of intimacy between the coalition members. These themes are illustrated with reference to cooperative strategies used by General Motors, Nissan and Toyota in Australia, and the complex long-term relationship between Honda and Rover.

Chapters 3 to 5 take the coordination problem into the area of the coordination of the growth of economic knowledge. Chapter 3 is an extended case study sequel to my (1983a) behavoural analysis of economists' behaviour, which focuses on the fate of Richardson's work. The original version of it included a listing that I had assembled of the first quarter-century of 'hits' that Richardson's writings achieved in the Social Sciences Citation Index (SSCI). However, now that the SSCI is increasingly widely available in a powerful on-line format, it seemed appropriate to leave out the listing rather than update it for the present version.

Whereas the focus of chapter 3 is on the impact of a particular economist on the profession of economics, chapter 4 explores the limited impact of the literature of economics on the writings of a particular influential economist, namely, George Shackle. This chapter examines Shackle's work on entrepreneurship and the economics of the firm, which received surprisingly little attention in the intellectual biography of him by Ford (1994). Shackle's contribution here is decidedly enigmatic, missing many opportunities for integrating his ideas with the work of other authors. This is particularly the case in his (1970) textbook on the theory of the firm, but he frequently failed elsewhere to make use of ideas of Coase and Schumpeter that would have complemented his own lines of thought. The chapter also considers similarities between Shackle's views on business enterprise and what has lately become known as the 'resource-based' view of the firm, before questioning the wisdom of writing about entrepreneurship without simultaneously focusing on internalization and management. Finally there is an examination of how Shackle ended up writing about firms and entrepreneurship in a way that, in terms of modern scholarship, seems extraordinarily lax.

In chapter 5, I combine the history of economic thought and critical analysis of contemporary economic policy, with a continued emphasis on the significance of blinkered and patchy readings of relevant literature. This chapter examines links between developments in the economic analysis of firms and the rise of pro-market, managerialist policies, with a particular focus on New Zealand, the most extreme case of their application. It also links back to chapter 1 in that it begins with an attempt to characterize the mangerialist point of view as a Lakatosian research programme – that is to say, as a set of 'hard core' axioms and a set of 'do' and 'don't' rules for policy-making. After showing how a selective reading of the literature on the firm can be used to construct some kind of justification for tightening of employment contracts, funder–provider splits, tariff removal, deregulation, and so on, I suggest that more careful analysis, mindful of the notion of relational contracting, leads to recognition of the advantages of less-formal and less-adversarial ways of organizing business to achieve long-run improvements in productivity.

Several years after arriving at Lincoln University, I was belatedly asked to deliver my inaugural lecture and I decided to use the occasion to provoke some thought on how far managerialist reforms might go in the area of higher education. Chapter 6 is based on this presentation, which led to a flurry of comments from non-economist members of the University, some of whom seemed to think I might be engaged in a kind of satirical parody. It uses transaction cost economics as a framework for considering alternative institutional structures for delivering educational services. Attention is focused particularly on rival ways of coordinating the delivery of educational services and guaranteeing standards. In contrast to the present arrangement in which universities charge basically annual fees for bundled degrees, I consider costs and benefits of an extreme, market-based scenario involving freelance academics and itemized billing for specific services.

As chapter 6 progresses we begin to shift focus from managerialism towards the economics of marketing, with an emphasis on the problem of establishing credibility of products. This theme continues through the next four chapters. Chapter 7 continues to employ ideas from contestability theory and transaction cost economics – including, in passing, an attempt to explain price discrimination, not in terms of differences in price elasticities of demand but in terms of economies of scale in the transactions costs of doing large deals. Though the chapter is focused on structural changes in the advertising industry in the past two decades, many of the points made in it apply to attempts to develop global professional services businesses in areas such as accountancy, financial services, management consulting, and law. These are areas in which the quality of service is hard to judge *ex ante* and where the competitive process is shaped by the consequent tendency of clients to attach themselves to individuals that have served them well in the past, rather than to the firms for which they work. In advertising, as in the discussion of scope for increased use of the market in higher education, the extent of product bundling versus itemized billing is another major issue.

Chapter 8 was written for a festschrift in honour of Don Lamberton, my Australian mentor, who has worked tirelessly for decades to promote the case for looking at the information dimension in economic problems. His influence is felt at many points in this book, either because he encouraged me to write the papers in the first place (chapters 1, 2 and 12) or because he asked if he could publish them in *Prometheus*, the journal that he founded on information economics and science and technology policy (chapters 6 and 7).

In chapter 8 I explore the idea that marketing may be seen as the internalization of transaction costs by the supplier, which may be done particularly effectively if, via repeated transactions, the supplier can get to know the customer. I also analyse the economics of conspicuous consumption in terms of information issues: the discussion here links to parts of chapter 2 (where brand equity is a complicating factor) and chapters 10 and 11, since, in addition to affecting its status value, the cognizability of a product affects the prices that would-be entrants may be able to charge and how well it serves as a store of value.

Chapter 9 emerged from many discussions I had with Jason Potts during several brief visits to the University of Queensland in 2000. They began with an attempt to consider whether internet shopping processes – which seem to be strongly affected by network linkages and connectedness to particular nodes – are really that different from traditional shopping. This led us to consider the design of familiar shopping malls in terms of information economics. The chapter explores ways of making sense of unplanned purchases during shopping expeditions without seeing such choices as lacking any systematic foundations or as reflecting some kind of pathology. The analysis employs both introspection and inputs from cognitive science and focuses on shifts from planned search to browsing in response to promotional cues encountered whilst navigating malls that are designed to promote browsing behaviour. Browsing is examined both in terms of its socio-psychological foundations and with respect to a variety of kinds of latent demand. The economics psychology of attention is examined as are a variety of factors that bring browsing processes to a close. The chapter concludes with a discussion of the significance of the analysis in terms of the path-dependence of economic systems.

Chapter 10 is a bridge between the marketing-focused chapters and the final pair of chapters on the underpinnings of Post Keynesian macroeconomics. It examines the controversy between marginalist and mark-up approaches to pricing from the standpoints of both early organizational approaches to the theory of the firm and recent strategic thinking which considers pricing in the context of other competitive weapons in the marketing mix. How much discretion firms have in pricing will depend on the scope for competitors to copy their designs and on the propensities of buyers to engage in search and pay risk premiums when product quality/delivery is uncertain. It seems unwise to presume that the same pricing rule will fit all cases, especially as business practices are affected by changes in information technology. In principle, firms face a dynamic optimal choice of a product design/marketing/pricing strategy, but in practice complexity and uncertainty ensure that these decisions are essentially experimental.

Although chapter 11 was originally written for a Post Keynesian conference at the University of Leeds in early 1993, it was something that I had been thinking of in one form or another ever since reading extensively on Austrian economics in my last few months in Cambridge in 1979. In the process of updating it, I moved some of the material from the original paper into chapter 12. It is a synthesis of themes from Austrian, Post Keynesian and information economics regarding the ways in which prices and outputs in markets for newly produced commodities are affected by speculation and opportunities for trade in secondhand goods. At the time I wrote it, my thinking was heavily coloured by my recent experiences in the housing market and my growing sense of wonder at how far the recycling of goods in secondhand markets had developed in New Zealand after years of import controls. However, in recent years, depreciation rates have become a major strategic issue in car markets in many countries and a significant determinant of brand equity in a way that indicates just how far we still are from having a globally homogenous car market. The Toyota Camry, for example, sells over 400,000 units a year in the US and in the relatively small Australian market it sells over 25,000 units a year and maintains around half its value after three years. In the UK, by contrast, only around 1,000 Camrys are sold each year and they depreciate to about a quarter of their new price within three years. A similar fate befalls large sedans offered by Nissan, Hyundai and Kia (despite the Kia Magentis/Optima receiving quite favourable reviews in technical terms). Depreciation makes these cars very expensive to own in the UK, despite their low purchase prices relative to European prestige brands and the small numbers on the roads mean that they lack the cognizability required to achieve easy marketability. Their importers seem to be stuck in a vicious circle: if they cannot increase residual values, only the unwise will buy their cars, and hence the cars will remain relatively unknown and unappreciated by the market at large and will continue to suffer poor residuals.

Chapter 12 was originally written as a provocative piece for an intended *Economic Journal* 'controversy' section on information economics, organized by Don Lamberton. Unfortunately, one of the contributors, a very big name in the field, did not deliver his paper in time due to major commitments elsewhere, and Lamberton asked the rest of us if he could include our contributions instead in an issue of *Information Economics and Policy* (volume 10, number 3, 1998). There is a sense in which this chapter brings my thinking full circle. The work on the impact of information and uncertainty on for the question of how coordination is achieved in economic systems that most aroused my interest as an undergraduate was Leijonhufvud's (1968) book *On Keynesian Economics and the Economics of Keynes*, for which George Richardson's work was an influential source. Having begun the present publication with chapters on economic coordination inspired by Richardson's writing, I end it with a chapter that can be seen as a reflection on what New Keynesian macroeconomics seems to be failing to take account of – in particular, the work of Katona (on the impact of consumer confidence on savings behaviour) and Minsky (on speculation, layered financial intermediation and instability), as well as the macroeconomic significance of Richardson's thinking. However, chapter 12, like chapter 9, takes my concern with the process of economic coordination in a new direction, namely, that of a concern with just how chaotic and path-dependent the microeconomic foundations of macroeconomic aggregates may be, even where the latter are not affected by structural gridlocks or major failures of effective demand. Very often in life, whether in shopping malls, choosing jobs, buying houses, or trading cars, and many other cases besides, we might easily have ended up doing something different, had circumstances intervened in different ways. If we had done so, we would have had an impact, direct or indirect, on the choices of others. From a neoclassical standpoint, ripples die away and the world does not turn out markedly different if individuals jump one way or another but, from my perspective, it is far from clear that 'it all comes out in the wash'; instead, even decisions that seem at the time to be quite minor may turn out to have major long-run implications.

1. Scientific Research Programmes and the Prediction of Corporate Behaviour

All firms do not behave in the same way in similar circumstances and a theory which helps to explain why they do not is perhaps to be preferred to one which asserts that they should. (Loasby, 1967, p. 167)

1.1 INTRODUCTION

If government policy packages or corporate strategies are not to produce disappointing results, it may be necessary for their proponents to anticipate business behaviour within fairly narrow bounds. Given that such behaviour involves rejecting some opportunities in favour of others, it might seem reasonable to hope that an economist seeking to act as a policy advisor would be able to model decision-makers' opportunity costs. Herein lies a problem: the opportunities that managers and entrepreneurs elect to forego in favour of their chosen courses of action are personal constructs in the minds of the decision-makers (cf. Kelly, 1955); how, then, is the economist to anticipate corporate behaviour? An appeal to the idea of rational expectations seems weak in this context, for the expectations and scenarios that managers construct in their minds will depend on the information sets that they use and the particular systems they use for forming judgments (Boland, 1986). It is not the case that the business environment speaks for itself: business behaviour is not 'situationally determined' (Latsis, 1976). Different managers may use different rules for forming expectations and guiding action. In doing so, they may reach different conclusions about a 'given' situation. This chapter is an attempt to highlight two major areas in which an economist is unlikely to get very far without a means for getting inside the heads of corporate decision-makers, and it contains suggestions as to how this might be done.

Inevitably, the chapter involves some dramatic departures from mainstream thinking, which has sought to conduct analysis in terms that are non-specific as well as abstract. The 'theory of the firm' normally concerns a supposedly stereotypical, representative firm, depicted in terms of mathematical functions or graphs. The words accompanying these technical images seem mainly designed to justify an a priori faith in the kinds of functional forms being employed (for example, U-shaped average cost curves). Such analysis has been used to uncover equilibrium conditions before and after particular market disturbances have occurred, without recourse to information about the specific circumstances of any firms. To the extent that knowledge of magnitudes is necessary for forming judgments about the impact of firms on, for example, social welfare, the objectivist approach concentrates on working out the size of foregone triangles of consumer surplus on the basis of demand curves estimated by the economist and knowledge of best-practice accounting costs. Unfortunately, the 'costs' that one can observe from accounting data are merely the outlays that some firms have chosen to incur in preference to other un-revealed possibilities; they do not necessarily give any indication of what other firms saw as the least undesirable alternatives to their preferred courses of action.[1]

The rest of the chapter is structured as follows. Sections 1.2 and 1.3 highlight the role of managerial judgment in two contexts that have recently been the subjects of voluminous literatures, namely market entry and exit (in the theory of contestable markets associated with the work of Baumol, Panzar and Willig, 1982) and diversification decisions (in the transactions cost analysis of markets and hierarchies associated with the work of Williamson, 1975, 1985). Having opened up a major can of worms as far as the prediction of corporate behaviour is concerned, I then go on in section 1.4 to suggest that theories of the growth of knowledge and the literature on corporate culture may provide a means by which economists may hope to form bounded assessments of the possible behaviour of players in particular markets: if the economist can uncover the philosophy that provides the foundations for a particular firm's strategy, then bounded guesses about its future behaviour become feasible. Section 1.5 examines the origins of managerial philosophies. Section 1.6, which is followed by a conclusion, explores the possibilities for uncovering managerial philosophies in practice.

---

[1] For a subjectivist critique of conventional literature on the social costs of monopoly power, see Littlechild (1981); other leading subjectivist contributions to the theory of the firm are Loasby (1967), Buchanan and Thirlby (eds) (1973), and Wiseman (1989).

1.2   CONTESTABILITY AND COORDINATION

Prior to the appearance of the theory of contestable markets, mainstream economists had tended to see corporate threats to consumer welfare as varying along a market structure spectrum that had perfect competition at one end and monopoly at the other. The fewer the firms actually servicing a market, the greater was seen to be the likelihood that consumers would suffer from higher prices and reduced innovation. By contrast, the contestability literature (like that produced earlier by deviants such as Andrews, 1949, to whom due credit is not usually given) emphasizes the power of potential competition as a device to restrain monopolistic tendencies. To the extent that their markets are vulnerable to hit-and-run raids by existing producers in other markets, incumbent producers are restrained from seeking to exploit their customers. The key point of focus thus becomes the ease with which would-be producers can transfer their resources – both physical and cognitive – to and from the incumbents' line of production. If there is much scope for employing resources in new contexts, and if such moves can be made without incurring new investments in equipment, marketing and training (in other words, if sunk costs are zero), then any tendency by incumbents to set prices above the opportunity costs of would-be producers will provoke a rapid response that will drive profits down to normal levels. The prospect of such a response is predicted by Baumol *et al.* (1982) to deter incumbents from engaging in the sort of behaviour that might stimulate it.

Proponents of the contestable markets idea have conducted most of their theoretical analysis with reference to the abstract case of perfect contestability – that is, the situation in which both entry and exit are absolutely free with no sunk costs being incurred by entrants. This case happens to be convenient for formal modelling, as well as being seen to provide the basis for a welfare ideal. However, the focus upon it is something that the theory's proponents seek to justify in instrumentalist terms, as the following passage from Baumol (1982, p. 8) indicates:

> While the industry structures which emerge in reality are not always those which minimize costs, they will constitute reasonable approximations to the efficient structures. If this is not so it is difficult to account for the similarities in the patterns of industry structure that one observes in different countries. Why else do we not see agriculture organized as an oligopoly in any free market economy, or automobiles produced by 10,000 firms? Market pressures must surely make any very inefficient market structures vulnerable to entry, to displacement by foreign competition or to undermining in other ways. If that is so, the market structure that is called for by contestability theory may not prove too bad an approximation to what we encounter in reality.

With the aid of such arguments, industrial economists have been getting themselves accustomed to thinking 'as if' easy entry is the normal state of affairs.

What seems to have been forgotten in this revolution in monopoly theory (except by Wilson, 1984, pp. 226–30) is that the new literature is entirely orthodox in its focus upon outcomes of competitive battles rather than upon processes by which industries evolve and achieve some semblance of order (which it presumes they do). In equilibrium, incumbent firms recognize the disciplinary capacities of potential producers and do not misbehave themselves. No signals of potential profit opportunities are generated, so no entry takes place. Would-be hit-and-run raiders concentrate their attention on markets that are still out of equilibrium, and they make their forays into the most attractive of these. However, at no point does the new literature discuss the question of how these raiders come by the information necessary to make such decisions. Contestability theory ignores the question of coordination and what deserves to be called the Richardson Problem, after the work of George Richardson (1959, 1960/1990).[2]

Richardson's work centres on the fact that when a firm is contemplating production in a particular market it needs to have an idea not merely of the demand for the product in question, but also of the output plans of other producers. The supply policies of the latter will constrain the sales revenues and cost positions (via the extent of their complementary investments) that the former can achieve. The inability of individual farmers to outguess each other's behaviour is, of course, the basis of one of the essential set pieces of any introductory course on supply and demand, namely, the 'cobweb' or 'hog-cycle'. But most economists, unlike Richardson, never seem to stop and consider the potential for similar coordination failures outside of agricultural markets in a world where there is no Walrasian auctioneer to ensure that producers' plans are pre-reconciled.

Richardson argues that coordination is facilitated by two main factors. Unfortunately, the first of these that I will consider is called into question by the new literature on contestability, but a consideration of the second factor seems to point us in the direction of studying actual firms if we are concerned with practical policy formation. The first possibility that may prevent coordination failures is the inability of some producers who are aware of a profit opportunity to act upon it.

In agricultural markets, it is the ability of farmers to change the crops that they are growing at seeding time that opens up the possibility of destabilizing price shifts: there can be very large changes in the amount of land committed to particular crops if many farmers can grow these crops and

---

2   For a useful review of Richardson's work, see Loasby (1986); Foss and Loasby (eds) (1998) is a collection of essays in his honour.

believe it could be profitable to do so. However, if there are only a few firms who have the capacity to produce a particular good, the scope for wild lurches in its production is limited. This is because each of the firms will find it difficult to expand production in giant leaps without running into managerial problems, even if they can obtain finance to do so (Penrose, 1959; Richardson, 1964b). Moreover, if just a few firms can produce the good in question, then collusion, whether implicit or explicit, will be easier to conduct, while it may be expected to be easier for these firms to get an idea of each other's plans, whether by industrial espionage or as a result of deliberate pre-emptive announcements by first-movers in the race to acquire market share (see Porter, 1980, chapter 15).

The contestability literature is clearly at odds with this route to market coherence. Incumbents may recognize the need to behave competitively, but that does not guarantee that, if they act independently, they will produce, in total, a volume of output that can all be sold at a price that only yields normal profits. If they produce too little and build up waiting lists or opt instead to earn supernormal profits, they will make the market in the next period interesting to other producers. Even if incumbents are able to anticipate correctly the capacity level necessary to leave them with normal profits and are able accurately to guess each other's contribution to total capacity expansion, potential producers might believe that, unless some new entry takes place, the incumbents will earn supernormal profits. The incorrect appraisals by the potential producers may then tempt them into contributing inadvertently towards a glut of output.

Of course, if entry involved no new sunk costs (for example, firms might use existing sales teams and spare machinery capacity), any coordination failure would only impose a cost on consumers in terms of wrongly allocated current costs of raw materials and labour time. Such a situation is less worrying than that painted by Joan Robinson (1954) in her paper on how the entry coordination problem leads to 'the impossibility of profits'. However, if the system struggled to achieve coherence over a long period, even these kinds of errors could turn out to be very costly for consumers. Such worries become all the more acute when one notes that many products have market lifecycles. Whenever demand is expanding or contracting, ease of entry combined with costless exit would forever be opening up scope for production plans that in the aggregate implied supernormal profits or losses on current commitments. The awareness by firms of the scope for a disastrous entry could, of course, result in them holding back and leaving the profit opportunity there for the taking, with consumer wants going unsatisfied and workers un-hired (cf. the use of Richardson's work in macroeconomics by Leijonhufvud, 1968, pp. 69–70). There is no reason to suppose that, amongst those who are aware of the profit opportunity and can enter, optimism and pessimism will weigh against each other in such a way as to produce precisely the right amount of output at each point. Given this, it does not seem logical to presume that something approximating perfect contestability is to be encouraged as a means of enhancing consumer wellbeing. Static contestability theory is potentially misleading for public policy-makers.

To be on the safe side, then, we should take a dynamic view of contestability and feel drawn to Richardson's second coordination-facilitating phenomenon: the possibility that firms with the ability, in principle, to offer competitive performances in particular markets where equilibrium does not prevail simply do not see these markets as places where profit opportunities exist. They may be unaware of the scope for making money by transferring their resources to these market niches or may see better returns to using them elsewhere because, in these other contexts, they see fewer risks from competitive entry.

Richardson's analysis here depends on firms perceiving things differently, and clearly conflicts with usual tendencies of economists to think in terms of 'typical' firms. It seems to imply that we can come to no conclusions about the likelihood of chaos or coherence in a particular market unless we can model the ways in which firms judge whom their rivals might be and how seriously these perceived rivals should be viewed as threats in markets in which they see themselves as capable of operating. In turn, this requires that we can anticipate which firms might consider themselves potential entrants. In other words, to make use of Richardson's insight when considering the merits of alternative policy proposals, we need a means for anticipating the subjective opportunity costs of actual firms.

1.3   MARKETS, HIERARCHIES AND STRATEGIC DECISION-MAKING

The growing 'markets and hierarchies/transaction cost' literature spawned by the work of Coase (1937) and Williamson (1975, 1985) and integrated with themes from the business policy literature by writers such as Kay (1982) and Aoki, Gustafsson and Williamson (eds) (1990) is rarely mentioned in the same breath as the contestability literature. This is surprising, since it often is used to discuss vertical integration decisions or the use of economies of scope (synergy potential, in the language of strategic marketing). It, too, has given insufficient attention to the implications of the fact that opportunity costs are personal constructs.

This line of research focuses on ways in which transaction costs may affect which activities are conducted inside the boundaries of a firm rather than between separate firms. Contracts between transactors can be difficult to draw up and agree upon, the more so (a) the more complex and surprise-prone the environment (because there will need to be more 'fine print' to cover significantly different states of the world), (b) the smaller the number of potential buyers and sellers (since the greater is the scope for haggling without fear of being discredited or outbid by a third party), and (c) the more difficult it is expected to be to monitor and enforce the implementation of a contract. Hence the recent literature highlights three possible advantages of bringing several related activities within a single corporate whole. First, guileful behaviour may be attenuated if would-be opportunists recognize it is in their own interests to help the corporate whole. Second, the costs of specifying innumerable contingent obligations and exclusion clauses, or of arranging a succession of less complex but very short-term contracts, can be reduced by using a team of managers to direct employees hired through loosely specified, open-ended contracts. Third, internal monitoring may be easier. Attempts to expand infinitely the size of a firm in a bid to economize on the costs of using markets are, however, thwarted by the limited ability of managers to handle information.

The need for a subjective dimension to this analysis becomes obvious when one engages in case study research and discovers that companies with very different internalization strategies have successfully produced similar end products over long periods of time.

Transaction cost theory suggests that vertical integration arises because firms seek to overcome difficulties in preserving secrecy and/or obtaining reliable input supplies or downstream distribution via market contracting, and judge that it is better to incur the opportunity costs of 'doing it oneself'. These costs may include the need to learn unfamiliar skills, the greater vulnerability to sweeping environmental and technical changes and the risk that people involved with internalized activities may feel inclined to act with opportunism in the knowledge that the firm faces exit costs if it goes back to using subcontractors, distribution agents, and so on. To some extent firms can seek to get the best of both worlds by engaging in strategies of taper integration – partial do-it-yourself of a particular stage in the production process, augmented by subcontractors – and quasi integration – long-term cooperative strategies that stop short of merger (see Richardson, 1972; Harrigan, 1983).

The risks that managers construe in respect of alternative vertical (dis)integration strategies need not be identical even if they work for firms involved in producing similar products at similar volumes. Processes by which risks are assessed may be different, while whether a risk is considered at all may depend upon the actual experiences of the decision-makers or their capacities for paranoid or pessimistic thinking (cf. Kets de Vries and Miller, 1988). The indeterminacy of the vertical integration issue is neatly illustrated by the early years of the British car industry. William Morris relied very heavily on subcontracting (Overy, 1976), in contrast to his rival Herbert

Austin. The latter's revealed preference for making things in-house seems to have owed much to his early experience of being let down by suppliers whilst he worked for the Wolseley sheep-shearing company (Church, 1979). Admittedly, both entrepreneurs gradually came to employ less polar strategies, but the process of convergence took many years. In the same industry today it is possible to see all manner of differences among major players in their vertical integration strategies, with firms moving in opposite directions as they experiment with what they each see as superior ways of ensuring their growth and/or survival: General Motors is much less dependent on outside suppliers than its Japanese rivals, but even amongst the latter Honda stands out as a company that prefers do-it-yourself – for example, Honda opted to design its own fuel injection systems at a time when its rivals were using German technology produced in Japan under license.

A similar lack of 'single exit' solutions is evident when one looks at diversification strategies. Diversification is facilitated by the existence of spare corporate resources such as finance, managerial skills, factory space and workers, and unexploited marketing synergies, such as scope for using an established brand name in a new context. It may enable the firm to achieve a smoother earnings profile by hedging against temporary downturns or fatal malaises in any single product market. However, spare resources can be returned to the market instead of being used to provide a basis for new activities that may involve new risks. Surplus funds can be returned to shareholders (who might then use them to undertake their own diversification), or they might be used to purchase partial stakes in other companies, as an alternative means of hedging. Spare factory space, equipment and skills could be rented out (the firm could act as a subcontractor or engage in consultancy work for other firms, rather than seeking to compete with them), and royalties could be received in return for allowing others to use brand names and technologies. This list of possibilities goes on and on.

The transaction cost literature suggests that the options preferred will dominate by virtue of their transactional convenience: small shareholders might prefer not to have to incur the brokerage costs involved in reinvesting dividends; consultancies could be difficult to find or permit due to fears about confidentiality; licensing could result in damage to one's brand name or the loss of one's technological leadership, and so on. Once again, the possibility arises that different firms could be observed experimenting with very different strategies, without obviously getting into trouble. Kay (1982, pp. 50–1) demonstrates this point with reference to the UK soft drinks industry in 1969–70, which was dominated by three firms. Allied Breweries could be construed as aiming for synergy, with little attempt to hedge their bets: they manufactured and marketed only soft and alcoholic drinks. At the other extreme, Reckitt and Coleman were involved with a barely related mix of products: in addition to soft drinks, they made and marketed products as diverse as pharmaceuticals, mustard, shoe polish and disinfectants. Somewhere in between, Cadbury-Schweppes seemed to be exploiting the food and drink theme across a range of cakes, preserves, canned foods and convenience foods, in addition to soft drinks.

It is not hard to see why these rival experiments may be failing to reveal the strategy to adopt. A product portfolio with few linkages between activities would offer little scope for synergy, but it would be easy to organize the firm as a series of profit centres, and thereby put pressure on the various divisions to deliver strong performances. A potentially synergy-rich firm might be operating with surprisingly high outlays per unit of output, owing to the incompatibility of a 'profit centres' approach to organization with the need for a function-based organization as a means of benefiting from shared resources (see Kay, 1982, pp. 150–2). Such scenarios point to the usefulness of the transaction cost framework as a device for alerting the economist to possible modes of industrial organization and the risk/advantages associated with them. But they also highlight the predictive limitations of a methodology that provides no means for anticipating whether and how such possibilities might be judged by actual decision-makers.

1.4   BUSINESS AS SCIENCE

In suggesting that internalization strategies might be characterized as consisting of ongoing *experiments* concerned with corporate survival and prosperity, I was foreshadowing the idea that it may be useful to see business decision-making as a scientific activity. This may initially sound a peculiar suggestion in an avowedly subjectivist paper, given that, in criticizing probabilistic theories of choice under uncertainty, subjectivists such as Shackle (1988) have made much of the non-replicability of experiments in business policy. But if one takes science to mean the systematic pursuit of the ability to predict and control events then it should be a relatively non-controversial suggestion. Two issues make it particularly clear that business decision-makers' daily activities are at a deep level the same as those of scientists in the everyday sense of the word, even though they may appear superficially rather different.

First, there is the basic problem of the complexity of the puzzles with which both groups deal, and the very many ways in which they might be tackled. Both groups have to form hypotheses about the situations they need to understand in order to meet their goals (these hypotheses include conjectures about which situations are worthy of their attention). In forming their conjectures, both groups have to decide upon the level and mode of abstraction that is appropriate for their particular puzzle. Both groups would recognize that a failure to simplify far enough may result in them being unable to 'see the wood for the trees', while over-simplification may mean that they become blind to many significant possibilities. Just as one argument of the present chapter is that in some contexts economic scientists are simplifying too far when they think about corporate behaviour, so corporate decision-makers may likewise be expected to engage in debates about how far they can simplify their own tasks and the pictures they build up of their rivals, customers and general market environments. The sheer complexity of their firm's operations will mean that, at best, top-level managers are going to be working with an approximate picture of the capabilities of the human and physical resources at their disposal. They will only have an approximate idea of the outcome of any directive that they give, for they cannot be sure what will happen at lower levels in their own organizations, let alone what will happen in the market as a result of the decisions taken by other firms and potential customers.

On top of the need to simplify in order to cope with potential information overload, social scientists (much more so than physical/natural scientists) and corporate decision-makers have to build more simple models than they would ideally like owing to the impossibility or high costs of obtaining relevant information. Of course, managers in a firm do have one advantage over economists and other social scientists: in principle, at least, they have ready access to their own accounting information systems and can interview their own employees about the operations of the firm, even if in practice they simply do not have enough time or mental capacities to gather and process such information. Otherwise, though, the situations are similar, and economists and managers alike will be frequently cast in the role of external observers of firms and individuals whose behaviour they need to anticipate. In such situations, they may have to form conjectures very much in the light of past market observations, and with the aid of published statements, interviews and 'leaks'.

The second problem common to firms and sciences concerns the interpretation of available information that relates to the conjectures they are using. The two groups can be said both to have a problem of knowledge, of deciding what they know about their areas of interest and what they are uncertain about. Here they must grapple with the Duhem–Quine problem (after Duhem, 1906, Quine, 1951): in trying to find things out, they can never test hypotheses one at a time. For example, when a chemist encounters surprising results, these could be due to any one of, or any combination of, a variety of causes: faulty temperature measurements, impure compounds, dirty equipment, or even – and this is what really interests the chemist – a flaw in the theory being tested. However, to check, for example, a suspect thermometer requires the use of other instruments, which may give spurious indications of accuracy or inaccuracy, and which can only be checked themselves with the aid of yet other instruments. Likewise, disappointing corporate profits might indicate that a manager's hunches about the market are wrong, that the production department has not delivered the expected standard of product, that the sales staff have been unexpectedly incompetent at selling it, and so on. Alternatively, there might simply be something strange happening in the firm's internal reporting system. It is impossible to check these possible explanations, or any others, without taking on trust other assumptions or predictions from theories (cf. Loasby, 1976, pp. 138–9). Scientists and managers alike seem to face a problem of infinite regress every time they make a judgment.

As far as scientists are concerned, Lakatos (1970) argued that it may be useful to think of them as trying to make headway in the face of these two problems by working according to the dictates of particular scientific research programmes – what Kuhn (1962) would call paradigms. So long as they do not find themselves having to make ad hoc adjustments to keep themselves in a position to explain what they observe, they will have no inclination to change from one research programme to another. A new research programme will not necessarily be attractive even if a hitherto reliable one experiences difficulties in matching up expectations with evidence: the new one may not yet have been developed to the stage where it can deal with the same kind of range of questions as the old, even if it offers a way of coping with the particular area in which the old one seems to be failing.

Lakatos portrayed a scientific research programme as consisting of a 'hard core' buffered from the outside world by a 'protective belt'. The hard core has descriptive and normative components. The former specifies the fundamental characteristics of the scientist's view of the world, and is the means by which the Duhem–Quine problem is confronted. The scientist treats a set of propositions, which may or may not be in principle open to empirical challenge, as if they are unshakeable truths that cannot be modified in the light of evidence. The protective belt, by contrast, is the scientist's collection of propositions – 'auxiliary hypotheses' – that have been classified as potentially malleable or, as a last resort, disposable. So long as anomalous observations can be dealt with by modifying part of the protective belt without recourse to ad hoc measures or jettisoning part of it outright, then the research programme is functioning satisfactorily even though it has not achieved such perfection as to require no further development.

The normative part of the hard core guides the development of the research programme's range of compass and how it copes with potentially threatening anomalies. Lakatos called it the 'positive heuristic' (prohibitive elements in it are often grouped separately as the 'negative heuristic') and his pupil Latsis (1976, p. 16) characterized it succinctly as 'a set of imperatives which contain guidance as to how the programme should unfold, how it should be defended, what falls within and what falls outside its scope... [and] it cannot be given up without giving up the research programme itself'. The Lakatosian view of how scientists choose to develop their ideas and cope with difficulties is essentially the same as Simon's (1976) view of decision-making as a process of procedural rationality. Rather than consider myriad possibilities seriously, scientists tackle problems with the aid of sets of rules that define appropriate conducts; they use recipes for success rather than getting bogged down in thinking about alternative means to their ends.

If we extend this line of thinking to include business as a scientific activity, we can treat the nature of a 'corporate strategy' as akin to a Lakatosian scientific research programme. In doing so, an overlap with the growing literature on the concept of 'corporate culture' becomes apparent.[3] However, I believe the 'business as science' perspective goes somewhat further, for it provides a theoretical basis for the existence of corporate cultures and strategies, not merely another language for characterizing them. These writers take a far more subtle view of the nature of corporate strategy than one sees in the economics literature. For example, Lorsch (1986, p. 95) writes that

> By strategy I mean the decisions taken over time by top managers, which, when understood as a whole, reveal the goals they are seeking and the means used to reach these goals. Such a definition of strategy is different from common business use of the term in that it does not refer to an explicit plan. In fact, by my definition strategy may be implicit as well as explicit.

In Lorsch's paper the 'implicit' part of a strategy involves things which managers will bring to mind only if they realize that they are considering possible courses of action which conflict with their unwritten views of the nature of themselves and/or their firm's business; indeed, managers may not even be conscious of some of the means they use to reach particular (written or implicit) goals, and a lot of the time could be usefully thought of as being on 'autopilot'.

Many of the hard-core assumptions that managers use about the business world and their own capabilities may come into the 'implicit' category, but others are likely to be written down or verbalized within the organization. Examples of hard core assumptions could include: 'The government will not allow a company of the size of ours to go under', or 'Our geographic position

---

[3]   Pertinent contributions include Selznick, (1957), Burker (ed.) (1983), Jelinek, Smircich and Hirsch (eds) (1983), Uttal (1983), Adler (1986), Kilmann, Saxton and Serpa (1986), Lorsch (1986), Prahalad and Bettis (1986), and Kets de Vries and Miller (1988); cf. also the broader perspective in Douglas and Wildavsky (1982).

provides us with a cost advantage', or 'Major customers like big suppliers committed to the industry'. The latter two examples come from Lorsch (1986, p. 99), who, like Lakatos, portrays beliefs as being hierarchically structured with the result that, in times of trouble managers may initially act in a Procrustean way, preferring to 'bend one less-central principle than those at the core' (p. 100). A good example of some of an individual worker's normative heuristics occurs in the paper by Kilmann *et al.* (1986, p. 90): 'Don't disagree with your boss, don't rock the boat, do the minimum to get by, don't socialize with your boss, only wear dark business suits to work...' An example of a higher-level normative heuristic would be, 'Retreat up-market in the face of Japanese competition, for there they will not be able to match our quality and undercut the costs of craftsmanship through mass production techniques.' This was the rule disastrously employed by the British motorcycle industry in the late 1960s and early 1970s (see Boston Consulting Group, 1975). Another, identified by Prahalad and Bettis (1986, p. 497) in respect of Emerson Electric, is: 'Divest any business where we cannot be the lowest-cost producer in the market.'

Several questions arise once one begins thinking of managers as if their behaviour is channelled in such ways:

1. What are the origins of managers' decision-making methodologies; in other words, how do managers learn how to learn?

2. Does the use of such a framework offer the economist the prospect of an improved way of making sense of past decisions of firms and in anticipating future behaviour by them?

3. When a major change from one managerial research programme/ paradigm/strategy to another takes place in a business organization, does the process resemble that identified by Kuhn (1962) for revolutionary changes in science?

4. Those familiar with the work of Remenyi (1979) – who extended Lakatos' analysis to examine the evolution of sub-disciplines and emergence of new research programmes from within sub-disciplines – would also wish to ask: Can Remenyi's theory of core/demi-core interactions help us understand the long-term evolution of corporate strategies in cases where the original core line of business becomes peripheral or non-existent? (For example, Bendix no longer makes washing machines, and the Adelaide Steamship Company ended up little interested in shipping.)

The next two sections deal with the first two questions. I have elsewhere

(Earl, 1984, pp. 95–104) gone some way toward answering the third in the affirmative (see also Miller, 1982, Prahalad and Bettis, 1986, and Gersick, 1991); to do justice to the fourth would require a separate paper.

1.5 THE ORIGINS OF MANAGEMENT PHILOSOPHIES

In some cases, a decision-maker learns how to cope purely through a series of personally designed and possibly traumatic experiments. The decision-maker creatively constructs a representation of the problem at hand and infers a possible solution. This construction is then tried for its fit against reality and the results examined. The fit might appear, from the particular higher-level judgmental standpoint that is being employed, to be excellent, ambiguous or very bad (cf. Kelly, 1955, chapter 1). Doubtful or poor fits inspire the creation of alternative constructions and further experimentation. In due course, provided the experimenting decision-maker does not run out of resources beforehand (in the context of a business, provided that managers do not drive their firm out of business), a methodology which seems to promise satisfactory results may result.

The go-it-alone, trial-and-error route to a personal paradigm/research programme/philosophy of life/strategy is probably of far less importance than social learning of particular, preexisting doctrines (though this is not to say that all who listen to the same source of inspiration will come out of the experience with the same picture of how they should subsequently proceed, for each will have personally to make sense of what is being suggested). Just as the ways in which economists think may be in large part a consequence of where they received their formative training and the departments within which they pursued their initial research activities, so management 'styles' may emerge from particular university or business school backgrounds. For example, managers may have learnt 'The Gospel According to Harvard Business School' and see the best-selling texts by Porter (1980, 1985) as their 'bibles' for appraising markets, their own firms and their competitors. Managers' styles may also come from the experience of seeing management consultants' alternative perspectives on their firms; or, perhaps most importantly, from a gradual assimilation of their firm's established corporate culture, perhaps after an initial highly intensive induction programme.

Obviously, things could start getting unworkable if it were necessary for economists always to think of management teams as collections of many individuals, each of whom had been through somewhat different experiences and possessed unique personal paradigms. While it is undoubtedly true that, even despite the best attempts of management induction programmes, corporations are not staffed by clones, we may often be able usefully to think about an individual firm as if its top-level decision-makers all work with the same underlying philosophy, which may go far beyond what has been explicitly set down on paper in a current corporate strategy – this is what I intended in my earlier (1984) work to convey by the phrase a 'corporate imagination'. Kets de Vries and Miller (1988, p. 81) echo this view with an added psychological dimension, reporting that their 'experience with top executives and organizations revealed that *parallels could be drawn between individual pathology – the excessive use of one neurotic style – and organizational pathology*, the latter resulting in problems and poor performance' (italics in original).

In making such a simplification the co-evolutionary nature of the corporate whole and the individuals that are members of it should not be forgotten: individual creativity is unlikely in the long run to be totally swamped by prior views that 'this is how we think and what we do at XYZ, Inc.,' so the corporate philosophy will normally evolve as a result of the particular contributions of individuals, just as individual personalities will to some degree be affected by their experiences in the organization. Nonetheless, in the short run, it may be useful to think of the firm as a whole, with a particular personality of its own, and as an organization whose behaviour is in large part channelled by its philosophy despite turnover of personnel. Significant new appointments fortunately tend to be accompanied by statements in the business press by the appointees concerning any major changes of philosophy that they hope to instil.

In a firm whose goals are proving hard to meet and where the seeds of a corporate revolution are starting to germinate, the firm's corporate imagination may seem horribly confused, with a variety of different camps bickering with each other. On these occasions the competing philosophies may imply very different scenarios concerning the future development of the firm. One could well expect there to be difficulties when it came to reaching decisions about patterns of diversification. Both inconsistent behaviour and simple drift could be worth taking seriously as possibilities in this situation (cf. Kets de Vries and Miller, 1988, pp. 94–6), which could be problematic for policy-makers in other organizations.

To conclude this section and provide a bridge to section 1.6, I wish to stress that, although individual and social processes of learning leave managers equipped with philosophies for trying to cope with the uncertainties of their work environments, managers should not be thought of as possessing fully fleshed out understandings of how their area or interest works in all its complexity and of what it would be best to do in particular situations that one day may arise. They have may have judged that, in previous situations, particular routines seem to have worked; yet, as with experience in using recipes from a cookbook which does not attempt to explain the underlying chemistry involved in cookery, they may have little idea why the results were produced. Their knowledge is fragmentary and of its essence conjectural, but this will not stop them from trying to apply it to situations that often possess only questionable similarities with past experience. Unpleasant surprises may sometimes follow.

1.6 PHILOSOPHIES AND PREDICTION: SALVATION FOR THE SUBJECTIVIST?

At first sight, it might appear that if we start thinking of firms as composed of individuals who use particular collections of rules for sizing up problem environments we may end up further away from the possibility of anticipating behaviour. Despite the 'corporate imagination' argument for glossing over differences amongst the philosophies of individual managers, the 'business as science' approach may seem merely to add another dimension of complexity to analysis of the firm. However, Heiner (1983) suggests that economists could find themselves hopelessly lost were it not for the use of stereotyped rules and routines by decision-makers. Such rules reduce the range of possibilities with which we need to deal, for, in using them as substitutes for complete insights into underlying constraints and technologies, decision-makers treat unique situations as similar instead of trying to derive singular, optimal solutions for the decision problems that they pose.

If top managers in firms take major strategic decisions on the basis of broad corporate philosophies rather than in the light of an extensive knowledge of the lower-level constraints and of the internal operations of their competitors, then the economist may need only to know the nature of these philosophies in order to be able to anticipate with tolerable accuracy the behaviour of the firms that employ them. Indeed, if these rules are of a simple 'if/then' form, courses of action are being selected without any consideration of alternatives and the task of anticipating likely choices becomes simply a matter of finding out which rules might be used, rather than a matter of understanding which rules are used to construct agendas of possible courses of action and which further rules are then used to pick particular options from these lists.

Consider the position of an economist who happens to know the backgrounds of the managers of particular companies, and which 'cookbooks' they use as their 'bibles' for decision-making. Suppose, further, that the economist has access to the same information as the actual decision-makers could be expected to possess about their rivals (that is, the published reports, interviews, leaks). Then it ought to be simple enough to narrow down considerably the ranges within which particular teams of strategists might seriously expect each other's behaviour possibly to fall, and/or narrow down the directions in which they are themselves likely to wish to diversify, horizontally or vertically. It would be rather like trying to guess the kind of essay a student could write on a particular topic if one knew which source books she had consulted and which textbooks she was using. The economist might thus expect firms operating according to Porter (1980, 1985) to behave differently from firms that use, say, Argenti (1980) or Hofer and Schendel (1978), or who have picked up the message of McKinsey rather than the Boston Consulting Group.

Naturally, I would not go so far as to suggest such methods would be foolproof. For one thing, even the biggest-selling guides to practical corporate planning do require planners to make judgments for themselves: they do not come complete in every detail. Thus even if an economist knew which bibles were in use and which information inputs were being used, there would still be scope for actual decisions to differ as a result of particularly creative personal inputs or peculiarly misplaced (in the view of the economist) applications of particular notions. Knowledge of corporate philosophies and bibles may still be worth acquiring and using despite its fallibility: the key question to be asked is not whether this framework eliminates surprise, but whether the costs it involves are worth incurring given the extent to which its use reduces the incidence of significant surprises.

The picture painted in the previous two paragraphs is of course somewhat fanciful in that, in the absence of detailed case-study work, it is doubtful that economists will know details of corporate operations at anywhere approaching the level of which technical bible is employed, or even which educational backgrounds managers possess. However, workable assessments of likely corporate moves probably can be made with far less detailed information, which either involves a public report of key corporate philosophy or can be used as a basis for inferring the philosophical line now being taken. It is hard not to be struck, when reading works of business history, by the fact that it is not necessary to possess a detailed knowledge of production processes or market structures to be able to anticipate the directions in which the firms will be described as moving in subsequent chapters; nor is it that difficult to guess which moves will fail as experiments in diversification, or when firms will be forced to cease growing. For example, it may be common knowledge that firm X is dominated by engineers (and hence prone to be attracted by technical challenges with scant regard for costs); or that firm Y, having got its fingers severely burned in a previous strategy of vertical integration, is selling off some stages of its production process (and so could well be thinking of using the proceeds in horizontal expansion); or that firm Z has recently started to internalize some stages of its input-making processes after having major difficulties with its suppliers (this may be the outward manifestation of a new policy rule, such as 'we will try to guarantee our production plans by owning two-thirds of our supplies of inputs, of all forms'). Furthermore, it should not be forgotten that, just as in the case of economics texts and degree programmes, guides to practical corporate planning and to the appraisal of competitive situations exhibit considerable overlap in core areas.

In short, by combining idiosyncratic but publicly voiced philosophies with 'what every manager knows/ought to know' – what we could call the 'commonsense knowledge of managers – economists may be able to go surprisingly far in the direction of putting themselves in the minds of corporate decision-makers and hence be able to pin down quite precisely the different evolutionary pathways different firms might try to follow in the not-too-distant future. They will be aided in this work by research aimed at uncovering the types of learning techniques that are commonly used by managers to make sense of what they see going on in the market. To this end, a research agenda involving a comprehensive inventory of learning methodologies has recently been set out by Harper (1996).

1.7   CONCLUSION

When firms in a particular industry are observed to behave differently, the orthodox methodology would lead its users to seek to explain the phenomenon by saying the firms must have different endowments arising from past decisions, and therefore have different comparative advantages when it comes to operating in different parts of the objectively 'given' market environment. Identically endowed firms should behave identically. By contrast, the subjectivist position adopted in this chapter centres on the different methods of forming judgments that the firms may use, and does not focus essentially on supposed 'objective' competitive advantages or disadvantages enjoyed by the firms in particular areas. The impact of any set of policy measures can then be anticipated with reference to likely ways in which these measures may be construed by decision-makers (if indeed they are noticed at all) and on how rival decision-makers may go about construing the implications of the policies for each other, given that one firm's strategic response would have a bearing upon the kind of choice that its rivals should make.

This chapter has a reflexive dimension that should not pass unnoticed. The first two sections identified situations in which the economist's task overlaps with that of the practising manager: the central problem concerned the prediction of the behaviour of firms from an external vantage point. To the extent that practising managers are able to keep their own positions and keep their firms in business, they can be said to possess workable decision-making philosophies and heuristics for coping with the particular contexts in which they take decisions. This overlap of roles could be taken to imply that economists have much to learn from practising decision-makers about how to size up the possible patterns of behaviour of firms in a market. However, the remaining sections of the paper have noted that the techniques which firms use for appraising industries and their competitors' likely patterns of behaviour are themselves increasingly products of academic research – either in published forms, or inculcated via the efforts of visiting teams of management consultants and through management training programmes in business schools and universities.

Knowledge of the hard core of the neoclassical research programme leads me to anticipate that many neoclassical economists would choose to reject this Kuhnian/Lakatosian view of the firm as unacceptable, owing to its emphasis on indeterminacy, on the use of heuristics, and on the experimental nature of corporate behaviour. I would predict a more receptive response to the paper from those who have taken on board the new research agenda set out by Boland (1986) following a Richardson-inspired critique of the rational expectations literature.

Boland's agenda involves research into four related questions:

1. How do individuals choose their learning techniques?

2. To what extent does the choice of one technique over another imply a different pattern of behaviour?

3. To what extent does the frequency distribution of these techniques over any population affect the stability of the neoclassical equilibrium?

4. If the distribution does matter, how do we explain it without violating the neoclassical commitment to methodological individualism?

Although Boland is concerned with the scope for reaching equilibrium states, rather than with continually evolving processes and structures, and, although he is strongly opposed to attempts by behavioural theorists to replace maximizing notions with satisficing ones, his research agenda clearly exhibits a good deal of complementarity with the present analysis. It also overlaps a great deal with the even more extensive 'business as science' research agenda recently set out by Harper (1996). In economic science, as in business (cf. the discussion of the UK soft drinks industry), philosophies do not have to be identical in order to result in commitment to similar activities.

2. The Evolution of Cooperative Strategies: Three Automotive Industry Case Studies

2.1 BLURRING THE BOUNDARIES OF THE FIRM

Economists have been remarkably slow to face up to the fact that interaction between firms frequently involves cooperation as well as competition. Nearly forty years ago Cyert and March (1963) blurred the boundaries of the firm by suggesting that companies could usefully be seen as coalitions comprising not merely workers and management but also customers and suppliers of finance. These different groups could have opposing interests but, up to a point, might find it worthwhile to collaborate with each other in order to meet their own sub-goals. Since they could not know the point at which other coalition members would opt to exit, they would tend to moderate their demands on the firm so long as they were at least meeting their own aspirations. Ignorance thus opened the way for organizational slack, a means by which give and take might ensure the preservation of the coalition during periods of adversity so long as returns to continuing to be a member did not fall short of prospective returns from joining other coalitions or adopting a 'do-it-yourself' strategy.

With hindsight, it seems obvious that this view could easily have been extended to encompass coalitions between firms of the kind introduced to economists by Richardson (1972) as a means by which firms coordinate complementary activities. These include close relationships involving open-ended contracting, buy-back arrangements, shared R & D projects, joint ventures, and so on, that have come to be known as 'quasi-integration' (Blois, 1972; Harrigan, 1983; Dietrich, 1994). If we are aware of the rich array of contracting devices that firms use for coping with their business environments it should seem natural to want to go beyond the idea of the firm as a coalition and begin to think of a firm as a 'nexus of treaties' (Aoki, Gustafsson and Williamson, eds, 1990) and to keep a watchful eye out for the existence of networks and federations of companies when studying rivalry and problems of corporate accountability (Tricker, 1984). Unfortunately, in the 1960s, there was in economics no well-developed framework for trying to make sense of choices of strategies involving some form of half-way house between the internal integration of activities and impersonal trading between firms.

In seeking to draw the attention of economists to the significance of cooperative strategies, Richardson (1972) sought to contrast inter-firm co-operation and market transactions in terms of differences in their potential for dealing with problems of coordination. He focused particularly on those due to investment complementarities between multistage production processes: vertical integration might be one way of overcoming the potential for market failure, but so, too, might interlocking directorships, partial shareholdings, or the building up of trust by regular trading relationships. Richardson's contribution is significant not merely because it aims to get economists to start exploring these issues as problems of coordination but also because it never loses sight of two things: first, the fact that cooperation is a tool for use in a competitive process; and, second, that cooperative relationships between firms may be expected to change over time with changes in the competitive pressures perceived by potential and actual collaborators.

Williamson (1975, 1985) acknowledges the influence of Richardson's paper in his transaction cost-based analysis of choices between markets and hierarchies as methods of organizing activities, which has provided theorists with a framework in terms of which quasi-integration can be analysed. In the 1980s, the academic literature began to catch up with business practice (for example, see Mariti and Smiley, 1983; Contractor and Lorange, eds, 1988) and discussions began to appear in undergraduate textbooks (see Ricketts, 1987). By the 1990s, the area had become a major focus of interest, as is evident by the extent of coverage in the reader in industrial organization edited by Buckley and Michie (1996). Distinctions began to be drawn between individual joint ventures, multiple relationships between firms that constitute strategic alliances, and club or network relationships involving multiple firms in multiple relationships (Kay, 1997).

The transaction cost approach to these issues centres on two main themes. First, management teams may have fears that they could fall victim to 'opportunistic' behaviour by those with whom they choose to deal – in other words, fears that the latter will make guileful use of information advantages in the knowledge that it will be costly for the former to monitor what they are doing to ensure that it matches the terms of the contract. With incompletely specified contracts, opportunistic behaviour may involve attempts to take advantage of what has been left vague. Quasi-integration strategies of one kind or another may seem useful means of reducing monitoring costs and enforcement costs associated with 'pure' market transacting (for example, with quasi-integration, it may be easier to guarantee standards of quality control and audit the number of hours spent on particular tasks), without incurring the costs and risks that may arise if pure internalization is chosen (for example, entry to and exit from a particular stage of production or product market may be less costly with quasi-integration). Quasi-integration may also provide a different set of incentives for players to refrain from opportunistic actions (for example, with vertical integration there is a greater risk that workers will try to push their luck in the knowledge that they have a captive market for their outputs within the firm).

The second theme is that contracts are not costly just in terms of monitoring and enforcement; they are also costly to draw up in order to cover the wide variety of contingencies that might arise during their life-spans. Outright internalization of an activity replaces a particular need to have ongoing dealing with other firms, or haggling over whether or not a long-term contract covers a particular contingency, with the need to have ongoing interactions with peers and employees. However, quasi-integration may be a cheaper way of economizing on the costs of pure market contracting: satisfactory experiences in previous relatively highly specified transactions between firms may generate enough trust, enough of an expectation of mutual forbearance, to provide a basis for building plans around relatively incompletely specified long-term contracts.

Richardson's favourite example of the dealings that the British retailing chain Marks and Spencer has with its independent suppliers shows that formal short-term contracts may be combined with an implicit long-term contact. (The activities of the Italian fashion firm of Benetton have many parallels with this example: see Jarillo and Stevenson, 1991.) Marks and Spencer and their suppliers recognize that they are dependent on each other for business success. It makes no sense for Marks and Spencer to fool their suppliers in creating more capacity than they expect to use and then attempt to exploit their position when bargaining over the next round of orders, knowing they have got their suppliers into a position of vulnerability. Such behaviour might work the first time it is tried but it is not a strategy that will in the long run promote investment in assets specific to the products required by Marks and Spencer. Such investment requires confidence that Marks and Spencer will deal fairly with its suppliers when market conditions change unexpectedly and that the firm will not switch elsewhere so long as its suppliers seem able to continue to provide competitively priced sources of products that meet the exacting Marks and Spencer specifications for delivery and for the quality of its range of 'St Michael' brand of products.

2.2   THE EVOLUTION OF COOPERATION

The route towards intimate commitments between firms seems likely to involve the corporate analogue of a process that is well established in the literature on the social psychology of human relationships. Initially, people feel a need to monitor very closely that they are not being 'used' by others with whom they are interacting; much time may be spent in discussing roles and boundaries for the relationship, instead of trusting each other and getting on with enjoying the benefits of complementarity. Small-scale commitments can be used to test the other party's reliability and/or sincerity in a relatively risk-free way. However, once people feel they are getting to know the other parties well enough to know where they can trust them, they become willing to take a longer-term perspective on what they put into and what they get out of the relationship and, so to speak, extend each other 'credit' through a much looser view of give and take (Duck, 1983).

An important implication of this way of looking at relationships is that when studying the extent and nature of cooperation between firms we should consider them as part of an emerging historical process, rather than looking at them as a snapshot. The needs of managers that led them to favour particular kinds of strategies may change not merely because of changes in their external environments over which they have no control (for example, international trade policy or anti-pollution regulations); they may also change as a result of their choices of strategies changing their views about the firms with whom they have been interacting as competitors and collaborators. Experience of dealing with a firm on a relatively intimate basis may reveal information that would not have been available through trading at arm's length. This, in turn, may provide a basis for yet more intimate exchanges in which the firm embarks on, for example, a collaborative research project involving sensitive information which third parties would be keen to have. As with couples sharing private secrets, the experience of running such a project may uncover yet more information about where a partner can be relied upon and where its faithfulness can be called into question. The relationship may then take a further turn, towards or away from greater involvement.

The remainder of this chapter is an attempt to illustrate some of these themes by piecing together the evolution of a trio of cooperative corporate relationships in the international automotive business in the 1980s and 1990s. I also seek to offer support to the view expressed by Kogut (1988) that though cooperative in intent, intimate corporate relationships such as joint ventures are likely to be troubled by the underlying competitive rivalry that exists between the firms in question. (It is in respect of this competitive dimension that the analogy between social and corporate relationships must be pursued with care: though a person may pull out of a relationship if a more appealing partner is discovered, the switch will not normally be aimed at weakening the former partner. However, some social relationships certainly do break up because one party feels threatened and finds it difficult to cope with the development of the other person, for example, in terms of their assertiveness or relative social standing.) The evolutionary message of these cases may be hinted at by the fact that although there are three major relationships under consideration I will be focusing on just five manufacturers: one of the firms involved switches its partner completely during this period.

2.3   GENERAL MOTORS–HOLDEN AND NISSAN

Our first case centres upon crisis management policies embarked upon by Holden, the (then) ailing Australian subsidiary of General Motors during the 1980s. Four difficulties led this firm to search for alliances with other manufacturers in the mid 1980s. The first was that in the small car market hatchback sales were booming, whereas it had only an ageing notchback sedan (the Gemini) to offer. Secondly, GM–H had a plant for building four cylinder engines that was running with some spare capacity, despite having major contracts as a supplier of engines to GM affiliates in Europe and South East Asia. Thirdly, cars manufactured for sale in Australia after 1985 had to run on low-octane unleaded petrol in order to meet new emissions standards that required catalytic converters to be fitted: Holden's top-selling model, the VK Commodore, had an ageing engine which could not be adapted to do this and GM–H did not have the resources to develop a replacement. Fourthly, the government was seeking to make the Australian car manufacturing industry reduce its average costs by putting pressure on the five local manufacturers to halve the number of model types that they were producing and thereby achieve greater economies of scale. This was to be achieved via a mix of both 'carrot' methods – allowing firms to use credits for exports as a means to claim duty-free status for imports of fully built up cars with which they could complete their product ranges – and 'stick' methods – an intricate system in which import duties charged to local manufacturers were to be related to their sales, with any model selling less than 40,000 units per year being actively discouraged (see further, Fujimoto, 1995).

GM–H's original partner for dealing with these problems was Nissan, and the method chosen essentially involved reciprocal supply arrangements rather than any integration of the two firms. The initial contracts, from 1984–7, were aimed at grappling with the first problem without falling foul of the government's plan. Nissan Australia simply supplied versions of its Pulsar hatchback to Holden, each badged as a Holden Astra. The Astra copyright was already owned by General Motors and employed in Europe on similar-sized cars produced by Vauxhall. Nissan dealers might lose a few sales but the manufacturer hoped to benefit, like Holden, by gaining incremental sales at the expense of the other main rivals – Ford, Mitsubishi and Toyota – on the basis of brand loyalty.

The formal content of this deal was not made public. But it is likely that Nissan would have been in an advantageous position relative to Holden. To economize on transaction costs and give Holden an incentive to take seriously the task of building up a lasting presence for the Astra name, it would have made sense for Nissan to insist on a contract which specified a minimum quantity of vehicles that Holden would have to take over a particular period (if not a minimum weekly rate) and the prices which Holden would have to pay for them. Short-term flexibility for Holden would concern only the range of colours and trim specifications, the latter probably having to comprise a particular mix over the duration of the contract. Holden would then have to devise suitable incentive schemes to get its dealers to sell the cars at the necessary rate. Nissan, by contrast, would have been in a much more flexible position, for it would have been able to change its prices and output mix in the light of circumstances as they unfolded, choosing either to take profits at the manufacturing stage or through its selling arm when the cars were passed on to the dealers.

The second deal between GM–H and Nissan involved the supply, from Japan, of an advanced six-cylinder Nissan engine to power the lead-free Holden VL Commodore. Holden had looked at comparable engines from manufacturers all over the world and, despite the wide range of engines that were produced by other GM affiliates, had concluded that in terms of price and performance Nissan had the best deal to offer. Many industry-watchers saw this as a sign pointing towards a merger of GM and Nissan manufacturing operations in Australia. Little did they realize that GM–H would shortly be starting an affair with Toyota but little did GM–H itself realize what would shortly happen to exchange rates (see the next section).

The extent to which GM–H and Nissan still saw each other as rivals was evident by the fact that the contract for the Commodore engine was soon tested for its fine print. Nissan Australia was upset to see Holden advertisements that implied Holden was responsible for the engine. Their response to this seemingly opportunistic behaviour was to run a full page advertisement in all the Australian metropolitan daily newspapers in which the role of Nissan know-how was outlined and which ended by saying that 'If you're impressed by what the new Nissan engine has done for the Holden Commodore, just wait until you drive the car it was really designed for – an exciting new Nissan is coming soon!' The immediate counter-response of Holden managing director Chuck Chapman was to write to Nissan in Japan, pointing out that this sort of behaviour was excluded by their contract. Nissan Australia was rapidly ordered to fall into line (*Wheels*, 1986).

Despite this row, the relationship went on to a higher level of integrating Holden and Nissan components. After a major effort at re-engineering the original Japanese design, the 1987–91 Pulsar/Astra was given a Holden engine, despite Nissan having a perfectly adequate design of engine of its own to offer. Holden thereby enjoyed greater capacity utilization at its four-cylinder engine plant and the ability to point out to would-be buyers that its small cars were now powered by the engines that it exported for use in GM 'world cars'; Nissan could achieve its required level of local content more easily. This was clearly an arrangement that involved a new degree of contractual complexity; much more joint engineering work was required owing to the need to marry the engine with the Nissan transaxle assemblies (the Commodore transplant was relatively simple as a rear-drive chassis was involved), and to calibrate its performance accordingly.

2.4   THE BREAK-UP OF THE GM–H/NISSAN RELATIONSHIP

The era of the Nissan-powered Holden VL Commodore only lasted from January 1986 to August 1988, for with the introduction of the 1989 VN model came a switch in favour of one of GM's own engines, a US-made Buick V6. This engine was a slightly updated version of a design that earlier had been rejected in preference to the Nissan one. Its newly found favour owed much to the changes in exchange rates that had occurred during the interim and made the Nissan engine disastrously expensive for use by GM–H. At the end of 1985, an Australian dollar would buy about 180 Yen but only about 69 US cents; by the end of 1988, when the new Commodore was selling strongly, an Australian dollar would buy about 85 US cents but only about 104 Yen. Figures such as these really highlight the extent to which a system of floating exchange rates can make financial success or failure dependent on speculative acumen rather than on having an edge in terms of managerial and engineering skills or a better product (see further, Earl, 1990, pp. 128–34).

News that GM's relationship with Nissan was going to be rather short-lived broke at the end of 1987 with the revelation that plans existed for the formation of a joint venture company involving the car-making arms of Holden and Toyota (Robinson, 1987). One wonders whether Nissan were as surprised by this as most industry journalists seemed to be, for it soon transpired that negotiations between GM and Toyota had been going on for about two years (Mellor, 1988). A Toyota–GM partnership in Australia should have seemed a logical partnership right from the start, given that GM had already cultivated strong links with Toyota via the NUMMI joint venture in Fremont, California: there, in addition to producing both Toyota- and Chevrolet-/Geo-badged vehicles, Toyota's organizational skills were used to teach GM managers that a remarkable transformation in productivity could be achieved without robots and thousands of labour agreements with its unions (Keller, 1989).

Being jilted by GM was not merely costly for Nissan in Japan in terms of lost exports of engines and gearboxes. It also dramatically worsened Nissan Australia's competitive position when the contract to supply the Astra to Holden ran out in mid-1989. Buyers who might have bought a Nissan Pulsar branded as a Holden Astra did not automatically switch their brand loyalty to Nissan when the Astra ceased to be available. Nissan therefore resorted to drastic discounting of the Pulsar as a means of maintaining market share in order to avoid being 'fined' in terms of reduced import concessions for failing to meet the sales figure required for a 'viable' local product. This investment in keeping the Pulsar alive produced huge losses. In 1992, Nissan closed its Australian manufacturing operation. Nissan Pulsars currently sold in Australia are fully imported from the UK (hatchback) and Japan (sedan), while a Holden Astra is now a genuine GM Astra from Vauxhall/Opel.

2.5   THE RATIONALE FOR FORMING UNITED AUSTRALIAN AUTOMOTIVE INDUSTRIES LTD

The arrangement between (what had been renamed as) General Motors–Holden's Automotive and the Toyota Manufacturing Company of Australia represented a drastic turnabout compared with the GM–H/Nissan relationship. Although the new relationship was to involve the creation of a joint venture company, United Australian Automotive Industries Ltd, there was little sign of any immediate intention to integrate GM–HA components into TMCA vehicles or vice versa. When Nissan delivered the last Holden Astra under the earlier contract, Holden's new small car, the Nova, was simply a badge-engineered Toyota Corolla. Nissan continued to use Holden engines in its Pulsar until 1991 when an all-new model was introduced, but no attempt was made to re-engineer the Corolla transaxle to enable Holden Novas to be Holden powered and give would-be Corolla/Nova buyers a choice between hi-tech multi-valve but (at that stage, in the Australian market) still carburetor-fed Toyota engines and the simpler but more powerful larger-capacity fuel-injected Holden engine, with all that this implied in terms of their driving characteristics. Nor was there any attempt to increase differentiation by re-clothing some of the Australian-made Corolla/Nova products with body panels used in variants on the Corolla theme, such as the Japan-only Sprinter sedan that had an extra window in the rear body pillar and thereby gave the impression of a somewhat larger car.

For its mid-size model, Holden ceased production of its version of GM's 'J-car' and plugged the gap in its product range by taking the Toyota Camry and re-badged it as a Holden Apollo. To give Toyota a presence in the large family car market, the Holden Commodore was sold through Toyota dealers as a Toyota Lexcen in a slightly re-trimmed form, thereby filling a market gap between the Camry and the imported range-topping Toyota Cressida. This model was named after the late Ben Lexcen, designer of the America's Cup-winning yacht 'Australia II' in the early 1980s, but the name might have also appealed because of scope for customers to think it might have something to do with Toyota's new luxury brand, Lexus. The role of the Lexcen became somewhat vague by the end of 1992, for imports of the Cressida stopped when Toyota ceased producing the engine used in the Australian model but the Camry grew into a much larger car whose top-range Toyota versions featured V6 engines and luxurious interiors. With much of its size and power advantage thus largely removed, the much more crude Lexcen's only strong selling point within the Toyota range was its rear wheel drive, for those with boats or caravans to tow.

Although the products that initially emerged from the joint venture harked back to the early deal whereby Nissan had supplied badge-engineered Pulsars to Holden, the Australian car manufacturing operations of Toyota and General Motors were to be brought under the ownership of a single holding company. This only employed a couple of dozen senior executives to coordinate the activities of Holden and Toyota. Its creation begged the question of why the two firms did not merely enter into contracts to make cars for each other. Such contracts would been a way by which each of the partners could have had locally assembled cars for each of their three main market segments and thereby stand a chance of getting volumes of each of these vehicles up to the level required for concessionary treatment under the car industry reorganization plan. Indeed, even before the end of its contracts with Holden, this is precisely what Nissan Australia was setting out to do via a model-sharing arrangement ('Project Matilda') to produce badge-engineered variants of its forthcoming mid-range model for Ford Australia, who would supply castings and sheet metal pressings.[1] Nissan and Ford also engaged in reciprocal supply arrangements for badge engineered Nissan Patrol 4WDs and Ford Falcon utilities

Since the car plan only required the underlying platforms of jointly developed models to be common for them to qualify as a single model, TMCA and GM–HA might later have been able to move as cooperating but separate companies towards engine transplants and sheet metal differentiation without being 'fined' for having unduly low volumes. For

---

[1]   As a further sign of Nissan Australia's willingness to use contracts as a way of satisfying mutual coincidences of wants between itself and other manufacturers, it might be added that, until import duties began to come down under the car industry reorganization plan, Nissan had been party to a long-standing contract whereby it used some of its capacity for assembling 'completely knocked down' kits of Volvo cars for the Australian market.

example, the wide-bodied 1992 Camry shared much under its skin with the Japanese-market Toyota Windom, so one might have imagined flexible manufacturing techniques being applied so that more substantial differentiation occurred with Camry and Windom models, both being produced on the same production line in Australia, one as a Toyota and the other a Holden. This did not happen and integration on the engineering side only seemed to go as far as some use of Holden's research and vehicle proving centres to undertake work on the Australianization of the 1992 wide-body generation of Toyota's Camry, along with Toyota 'renting GM's styling facilities and prototype shop in order to save costs' (Fujimoto, 1995, p. 51) in the process of differentiating the brands in cosmetic terms. Australian consumers *were* actually offered the Windom, but only as an imported, luxury-trim model badged as a Lexus ES300 and selling for around twice the price of an upper-end Camry: Clearly, price discrimination with brand-conscious customers via this 'Camry in drag' (as the local *Wheels* magazine often called it) was seen by Toyota as preferable to any possibility of offering more widely differentiated mid-size Toyota and Holden models.

In trying to make sense of the move towards the joint venture we can note several ways in which its legal implications were different from the inter-firm contracting scenario just outlined. First, it must be understood that Australian car manufacturers were facing two constraints on the number of built-up vehicles they could import without paying the penal rates of duty suffered by firms such as BMW that lacked manufacturing operations in Australia: one was a basic 85 per cent local content requirement, the other was their exports of cars or components, for these could be used to generate credits for further duty-free imports. As a result of its engine exports to Europe and Korea, Holden was endowed with more export credits than it could use for duty-free car imports without undermining its car manufacturing operations, but it could not sell these credits to another company. By contrast, under the joint venture arrangement, these export credits could be applied to the combined Holden and Toyota wholesale base, enabling Toyota to import far more of its niche market vehicles on favourable terms (Mellor, 1988).

Secondly, the joint venture opened up opportunities for collaboration on pricing and product positioning that would simply have been illegal under Australia's Trade Practices Act. The shared models involved more than just re-badging, for trim and engine options were carefully selected to position most Toyota variants slightly up-market from Holden ones, effectively enabling the various models each to be offered in five or six versions against the three specification levels offered by other local producers. By finely segmenting the market between their brands in this way, Holden and Toyota could limit the extent to their dealerships were forced into cut-throat competition with each other. As market conditions changed, the relative prices and specifications of adjacent Holden and Toyota models could be adjusted without it being necessary to draw up fresh contracts. Holden and Nissan could not legally seek to coordinate the marketing of the Astra/Pulsar in this way.

A third advantage suggested by the then Holden chairman Chuck Chapman (reported in Mellor, 1988) followed directly from this ability to work out an integrated positioning strategy: since the ownership of UAAI was split 50:50 between GM and Toyota, the benefits of any action that improved the profits of UAAI would be evenly shared, regardless of what this implied for the relative standing of particular Toyota or Holden models. In principle, therefore, product specifications – such as the exclusion of V8-powered and utility versions of the Holden Commodore from the Toyota range, and the exclusion of lift-back versions of the Toyota Corolla and V6-engined Camry from the Holden range – could be decided upon without the two parent companies worrying about whether one was using a particular proposal to gain at the expense of the other.

2.6 CONFLICTS IN THE UAAI RELATIONSHIP, AND ITS ULTIMATE DEMISE

The UAAI joint venture lasted from May 1988 until March 1996, when 'after six months' study and negotiation', there was an 'amicable dissolution' (General Motors, 1996) and the local operations of the two firms were reintegrated into the global operations of their parent companies. Even at its inception, its long-term prognosis had not seemed good. A consideration of where UAAI stood in relation to its parent companies and their other subsidiaries revealed that in practice conflicts of interest were likely to lead to difficulties in the Holden–Toyota relationship. One obvious problem was that the UAAI holding company's staff were unlikely to be able to make dispassionate decisions if they had been working for Holden or Toyota for many years, particularly if they found themselves combining planning work at UAAI with a continuing part-time involvement in the running of either of its subsidiaries. Their specialist knowledge of these subsidiaries might have been invaluable in discussions about, say, which plant should be closed down and where production should be relocated, but their opinions were likely to be coloured by commitments they had made previously in these areas of the firm.

Secondly, consider the question of whose engines should power the cars. In December 1986, ostensibly as part of a financial bailout by GM in Detroit, GM-H was split into separate car making and engine making companies. The rationale for this became clearer once the joint venture was announced, for it meant that Holden's operations matched those of Toyota, which also had a separate engine manufacturing company. Initial reports suggested that the respective engine firms were to remain independent of UAAI (Robinson, 1987). This would make it inherently unlikely that there could be agreement to use Holden engines in Australianized versions of Toyota cars. If engineering the cars to accommodate Holden engines imposed costs on UAAI without increasing sales in an offsetting manner, the loss in profits would be equally shared by Toyota and Holden. However, GM could benefit in terms of a more profitable engine plant, whilst Toyota Manufacturing Australia suffered. Even if the engine transplant increased UAAI profits, differences in the strategy's overall impact upon the parent companies' interests could give Toyota cause for concern. For example, it might be that it was not merely Holden's Engine and Component Company that benefited but also that the availability of Holden-powered, Holden-badged Toyotas at Holden dealerships strengthened the Holder dealer network and the marketing arm of Holden relative to its Toyota counterpart. To avoid these conflicts of interest, UAAI needed to embrace engine manufacture, car assembly and marketing.

In practice, the main initial conflict concerned valuations to be placed on the assets of the two companies prior to the signing of the formal agreement that had been scheduled for 1 July 1991 (Hammerton and Mellor, 1991). It was only with the final signing of the contract that UAAI, in which GM and Toyota both had a 50 per cent stake, would own 100 per cent of GM–HA and 100 per cent of TMCA. Prior to this, stage one of the joint venture arrangement only involved UAAI in owning 30 per cent of these two companies, with the remaining 70 per cent shares still being owned directly by GM and Toyota, respectively. During stage one, the two companies were to put their assets into as best shape as possible, the idea being that TMCA, with a smaller asset base than GM–HA, would then make up the difference via a cash adjustment. However, this stage of the relationship lasted so long that the relative fortunes of the two players changed substantially and with them both the relative values of their assets and the implied cash adjustment that TMCA would have to pay. The original consummation had been scheduled for 1989, but the success of the new VN Commodore turned Holden into a profitable company, when previously it had been making substantial losses. To try to reduce the 'dowry' it would have to pay, Toyota put pressure on TMCA to increase its profitability, with the result that several hundred workers were made redundant as TMCA sought to rationalize its fragmented operations. The delay in signing the joint venture agreement was not merely due to arguments about asset values; there were also extensive negotiations about how tax liabilities and carry-forward losses, along with a reluctance to make commitments until the players knew of the outcome of the Industry Commission hearings into the car industry.

Ultimately, the dissolution of UAAI was in large part a consequence of something that both companies ought to have been well aware of from their joint venture experience with the NUMMI operation in California, namely, the problem of 'brand equity' (for a guide to the literature on this topic, see Dawar, 1999). A Toyota Corolla/Geo Metro produced by NUMMI costs significantly more when badged as Corolla and yet the Toyota outsells the Geo variant by a massive margin, as consumers have a strong preference for the product bearing the badge of origin. Mainstream economic theory might predict that well-informed consumers would choose the models with the price/trim/specification combination that best suited them, regardless of the brand, and then have it maintained (once out of any restrictions imposed by the warranty) by whichever dealership network offered the best service. But this in the main is not what happens and the fact that consumers operate as they do seems plausibly to be explained in terms of incomplete information, either on the part of buyers or amongst those in their social networks.

When a brand extension is attempted, as with both Holden (to Nova and Apollo) and Toyota (to Lexcen), the new model name is at an information disadvantage compared with the original name of the product. Lack of awareness of the new model and lack of any past association with it means that fewer people will actively shop for it. If Holden has a weak reputation in the small car market compared with Toyota, then selling a Toyota with Holden badges on it does not make buyers set out to look for a small Holden rather than heading straight for the perceived security of their local Toyota dealership. As well as applying to new products, it also applies to secondhand ones: trade-in prices for the brand extension version are likely to be less because dealers will anticipate that they will be harder to re-sell because of their relative unfamiliarity. Fears of more rapid depreciation make it rational even for the well-informed buyer to opt for the original brand of the product. These processes are likely to be further reinforced by the scope for social difficulties in the midst of those who are not aware of the particular details of the badge-sharing process ('You drive a *what*?'). As a consequence of the brand equity phenomenon, Toyota Camry and Corolla outsold Holden Apollo and Nova by about seven to one (Fujimoto, 1995, p. 51), with similar figures experienced in reverse for the Toyota Lexcen and Holden Commodore.

After the dissolution of the joint venture firm, Toyota phased out Corolla production in Australia and both Holden and Toyota switched successfully to a strategy of upgrading their local quality standards and exporting on a large scale, particularly to the Middle East, using imports from elsewhere in their respective global networks to fill out their product lines. While Holden revitalized its image with small and medium-sized cars by emphasizing that it was selling European GM designs, Toyota sought to compete against the much-improved Commodore by supplementing local Camry production with its larger Avalon model – essentially the recycled body and interior of a superseded US model of the same name, spliced on to the floor-pan and mechanicals of the second generation wide-body Camry. Although initially its sales were not spectacular due to bland styling and a common Australian preference that large cars should be rear-wheel drive, the front-drive Avalon soon served Toyota's sales figures far better than the Lexcen did.

2.7   ROVER AND HONDA

Compared with the cooperative strategies in the Australian car market, our third case study is of both longer duration and greater complexity. It began in 1979 with a contract by which British Leyland (subsequently Austin Rover and latterly the Rover Group) would produce Honda Ballade sedans under license for sale as Triumph Acclaims. It then progressed through the joint development and production of two new models to a situation in which Honda set up manufacturing operations in the UK and there was a share exchange by which Rover and Honda UK owned 20 per cent of each other. Three further projects followed in which Rover re-skinned and partly reengineered Honda products (Rover 200/Honda Civic, Rover 400/Honda Domani, and Rover 600/Honda Accord), along with badge-engineering of the Land Rover Discovery as a Honda Crossroad for the Japanese market. The ownership arrangements were unwound and further joint projects ceased after March 1994 when Rover was sold to BMW – much to the surprise of Honda – by its owner Vickers. However, Rover continued to pay design royalties to Honda on models that used the latter's underpinnings, two of which remained in production at MG Rover following its sale by BMW to the Phoenix consortium in 2001. During the decade and a half before the sale of Rover to BMW there was a major shift in the relative size of the two partners. Honda had originally been courted by British Leyland in the belief it would not swamp BL in the way that an earlier prospective partner, the Renault group, had seemed likely to do. By 1986, however, Austin Rover's car output of 390,000 units was dwarfed by Honda's output of 1.3 million vehicles.

The relationship began due to BL's need to get a modern product in a hurry to fill a gap in its product range (Edwardes, 1983). BL was in too precarious a financial position to develop a suitable vehicle of its own. It may appear that initially there was nothing more for Honda to gain than royalty payments and profits on the sale of components. However, we would probably be wise to note the opportunity that the deal gave Honda for learning about what BL might have to offer in the longer term. Right at the outset, BL designers revamped the seating of the Ballade and demonstrated that they could see more clearly than Honda how to create spacious car interiors within the confines of a particular body shell. The build quality and reliability of the BL Ballade then turned out to be vastly superior to anything that BL had previously produced, demonstrating that BL's poor reputation in these areas was more to do with poor design and component sourcing than shoddy work practices. If Honda had any thoughts about using the firm to assemble Honda vehicles as Hondas and thereby get enough UK content to be able to get free access to European Community markets, this was a way of testing whether it could be done without compromising Honda's excellent reputation for quality. By agreeing with BL that the Ballade would not be sold in European Community countries Honda made it easier for the license-built version to get a footing in the market and help its assembler into a more viable financial position, but it also reduced the risk of questions being asked about the quality of Ballades and, worse still, other Honda products, if BL quality turned out to be unsatisfactory.

The second stage of the relationship concerned the joint development and production of a large executive car, codenamed XX, which became the Honda Legend and Rover 800. It was Honda's first vehicle in this market segment, but was Rover's opportunity to learn how to build its bigger cars to the same sort of standards as those it was building under license from Honda. This was a more complex joint venture than anything entailed in our two Australian cases, and yet it was handled without the formation of a joint venture company. The car would be developed from the ground up, partly in the UK and partly in Japan. Modern telecommunication systems would partly facilitate this, but so, too, would a division of labour and some geographical secondment of staff. Instead of badge engineering, there would be genuine differentiation in terms of interior design, exterior style, ranges of body types (a Honda coupe, a Rover hatchback, with sedans for both brands), engines and general character. Rover 800s for the Far East would be made by Honda; Honda Legends for Europe would be made by Rover.

The contractual complexity of this venture seems potentially overwhelming, but the project would also have been difficult to administer within a single company that had internalized such disparate partners. That it worked as well as it did is probably best seen as a reflection of mutual forbearance by the two companies, rather than contracts in which every contingency had been covered in advance. If the partners were worried by the ways in which costs might be claimed by each other, they would either have needed to agree upon some formal auditing system with all the costs that this may have entailed, or rely upon intelligence picked up by their seconded workers. When it was clear that unexpectedly high costs were being incurred due to unpleasant surprises and coordination failures it is probably the case that arguments about who footed the bill were moderated by the thought that a 'go it alone' strategy would have been either much more expensive or simply impossible to fund. One press report (*Wheels*, September 1986, p. 9) suggested that the development costs that were supposed to be shared on a 50:50 basis ended up at about 60:60 due to a mixture of both obvious and unforeseen overlaps. The biggest hiccup was the discovery of durabilty problems with Honda's V6 engine barely sixteen months before the Legend's launch. The solution was a new engine block and cylinder heads; the resulting engine, being both larger and heavier required changes to the engine bay, which in turn resulted in a need for a slightly longer wheelbase and a wider front track. One wonders how the extra costs were allocated, whether Rover blamed Honda for incompetence and demanded compensation for any extra work that they had to do or whether the costs were simply added to the overall bill and put down to experience.

Other industry reports make clear the misgivings that some senior Honda engineers felt that Honda got a rather raw deal with the XX and should have had no further joint development and manufacturing projects (Kacher, 1987). With hindsight, the new head of Honda said that he doubted whether the relationship had produced any technological benefits for Honda and that it had slowed down the development of the Legend (Radley, 1990). The refusal of Rover to let Honda use its superior interior designs was one sore point. Another was the discovery that Rover had been letting Porsche do some consultancy work on alternative large engines that might one day replace Honda's V6 in up-market Rovers. It also appears that there were problems related to quality control, though quite how bad they were seen to be differs depending on which Honda source one reads – contrast Cropley (1986), *Car Magazine* (1987) and Kacher (1987). In the mid 1980s, Rover quality control may have been much improved, but it took quite some time, and a £20 million investment by Honda in a UK pre-delivery inspection centre, to get the UK-built Legend up to scratch. Akinobu Yokoyama, managing director of Honda's research and development centre, pinned the problem down to a basic difference of corporate culture (Kacher, 1987): Rover were still taking the view that their dealers could rectify faults, whereas Honda's philosophy held that a car should be 100 per cent finished when it leaves the assembly line. Yokoyama also was very concerned by the low productivity of Rover factories, despite their relatively low hourly labour costs. It is unclear whether these differences were the real reasons why the reciprocal arrangement whereby Rover and Honda produced each other's luxury models for their local markets turned out to be short-lived. Officially, it was said that it was simply not economic to continue given the low volumes that were involved – Honda assembled 1,600 Rover 800-series models and Rover assembled 3,500 Honda Legends. These small volumes also made it particularly difficult to incorporate running production changes (*Wheels*, 1988).

The subsequent evolution of the relationship seems to have been affected greatly by the changes in relative competitive strength of the two firms.

Honda's first Legend was such a success that its very different 1991 successor was developed by Honda alone and involved a move further up-market; Rover was reduced to face-lifting the original 800-series model. However, indications that Rover might be in danger of being left by the wayside were emerging long before this further down their product ranges.

Initially, there were signs that Honda saw an expanded role for Rover as a means of gaining a bigger share of the small/medium segment: with the Legend/800 on stream, Rover still found itself unable to reach its capacity utilization targets and this provided a ready means by which Honda might be able to increase its market share in Britain without breaching the 'gentlemen's agreement' that for years had been limiting its imports to slightly under 1 per cent of the UK market. The new generation Ballade that was being produced in somewhat modified form as a Rover 200 might also be sourced from Rover as a Honda for markets in mainland Europe. The same might happen with the next generation Rover 200 which was to emerge from project YY along with the Honda Concerto. Sure enough, it was agreed that Rover would produce both Ballades and Concertos. But to get 80 per cent UK content and thus qualify as a car produced in the European Community, it was necessary to move beyond having mainly Rover doing the assembling and have major components such as engines and gearboxes to be made in the UK.

Now, Honda might conceivably have let Rover build engines to its specifications for use both in Honda-derived Rovers where Rover units were not the only option given to consumers and in the vehicles assembled by Rover on its behalf. It might alternatively have moved more in the direction of badge-engineering by having Rover engines in those cars that Rover assembled as Hondas on its behalf. Instead, Honda opted for an internalization strategy, building an engine manufacturing and vehicle assembly plant of its own alongside its warehousing and pre-delivery inspection center at Swindon. It was in this operation, Honda UK Manufacturing, that Rover took a 20 per cent shareholding in exchange for 20 per cent of its own shares and £30 million in cash from Honda (Ward, 1990). (Along with the reciprocal shareholdings, a couple of reciprocal board memberships were agreed.)

This turn of events was at the time intriguing and with hindsight indicated how surprised Honda must later have been by the sale of Rover to BMW. Honda was setting itself up in a position to be a major competitor in Rover's main market and yet allowing Rover to have some involvement in its new UK operations. In trying to make sense of this aspect of the relationship we would probably be wise to remember that although Rover was a major customer for Honda's output of engines in the UK, Rover caused much disquiet within Honda by continuing to develop new generations of engines of its own (notably its modular 'K-series' designs). Honda engineers gave the impression of being at a loss to understand why Rover should do this, given its access to Honda's own excellent engines (Kacher, 1987). This apparent bewilderment might have concealed fears about the magnitude of the benefits Rover had gained from its dealings with Honda, which had provided it with the means to get back on its feet in terms of up-to-date products and improved quality. The engines were likely to have been seen as a key to Rover's strength in the future: they provided a kind of insurance that, if the relationship with Honda were to break up, then Rover could go it alone again as an independent manufacturer, but in the meantime they also gave some leverage with Honda over the terms under which engines are supplied for Rover cars. Eventually it would become tempting for Rover to cease using Honda engines in its vehicles: this would spread the fixed costs associated with its own engines over a larger output and at the same time deliver a blow to the profitability of the Honda engine plant.

By giving Rover a share in Honda's UK operations, Honda had on the one hand provided an incentive for Rover to think twice about making such an opportunistic move as it gets its strength back. On the other hand, Honda had given itself an incentive to bear Rover's long-term interests in mind. Though it fell well short of a merger, this exchange of shares seemed to produce in Honda a new outlook on the relationship: Honda's president Nobuhiko Kawamoto has said that, 'Since we exchanged shareholdings I don't look upon Rover as someone else's company. Our attitude has changed a lot. We can't just think of ourselves anymore. We have to think about them as well' (Radley, 1990). But, as we now know, all this would change when, without warning, Vickers sold Rover to BMW, the latter having little idea just how much trouble the purchase would cause them.

2.8   CONCLUSION

Organization theorists have been used to thinking about the organizational problem as if it consists of working out how to get the members of a particular coalition comprising a single firm to work most effectively together. Mainstream economists have been accustomed to thinking of firms as trying to benefit at the expense of each other unless grouping together to form some kind of cartel arrangement to restrict output and raise prices. Strategies involving quasi-integration represent a grey area between internal and market-based methods of organizing economic activities. Once we recognize the prevalence of coalitions between firms, matters of organization and inter-firm contracting acquire a further layer of complexity. Because the parties involved continue to see each other as rivals they will wish to set up contracts to safeguard their positions against opportunistic behaviour or incompetence on the part of their partners. Our case studies provide examples of such caution being entirely justified. However, relatively highly specified contracts can only cover relatively simple dealings between coalition partners, such as, in the Holden/Nissan collaboration, reciprocal uses of engines. Where more complicated exchanges are involved, such as those involving the joint development of products, uncertainty and the scope for surprises appear to militate in favour of greater contractual ambiguity and a willingness to negotiate as and when the need arises about the implications of unforeseen problems.

The contrast between the General Motors/Toyota UAAI venture and the Honda/Rover relationship is striking. If we see the long-term basis of UAAI as involving more than just a means of circumventing competition policy, it seems possible to characterize the creation of UAAI joint venture company as a way of trying to dispose of the need to make a sequence of contracts by instead making one major deal. This means that it is crucial for the partners to position themselves to their best advantage at the time the contract comes into operation. The measure apparently used by GM and Toyota for the worth of their Australian subsidiaries as pools of corporate resources was the financial state of the respective operations at the time of signing of the contract: this seems to presume that current performance is a good guide to what will be obtainable from these resources in the future.

The relationship between Honda and Rover moved to such a financially oriented level (in other words, the share exchange and the cash payment from Honda to Rover) only after over a decade of project-based contracts of increasing degrees of complexity. Over this courtship period Honda had actually helped Rover to a position of greater strength in both financial and engineering terms, as well as benefiting from having Rover as a partner. Rover no doubt had a clearer idea of the extent to which is could go it alone in the car market in the future and of the merits of having a commitment to major involvement with Honda rather than shopping around to buy in the best available parts and expertise from a range of other automotive firms – a strategy which it used in some degree even despite its relationship with Honda. The companies appear to have learnt much about each other's strengths and weaknesses, but though both made progress their relative strengths changed substantially. By formally running the relationship on a project-by-project basis (with several projects often operating simultaneously at varying stages of development), Honda and Rover had to incur the costs of repeatedly getting together at the bargaining table but kept themselves in a position to try to refashion the relationship or even abandon aspects of it in the light of changes in their perceptions of each other and their needs.

3. George Richardson's Career and the Literature of Economics

3.1   INTRODUCTION

This chapter is a somewhat reflexive tribute to, and investigation of the fate of, the work of George Richardson, whose contributions to our understanding of the processes of economic coordination have provided major inspiration for many of the chapters in this book.

Richardson's academic career is full of the kinds of achievements of which most academics can merely dream. His entry in the *International Who's Who* reveals that, after teaching economics as a fellow of St John's College, Oxford from 1951, he was promoted in 1969 to University Reader in Economics, a post he held until 1973. Between 1974 and 1988 he was Chief Executive of Oxford University Press[1] and from 1989 until his retirement he was Warden of Keble College, Oxford. His expertise as an industrial economist was recognized in his appointments as a member of the Monopolies Commission and as a Member of the Economic Development Committee for the Electrical Engineering Industry. He was also a member of the Royal Commission on Environmental Pollution (1973–4). His citation record, discussed later in this chapter, reveals that his work has been used by scholars in many countries and many disciplines. Yet, despite this, the impact of his work has been far smaller than he might justifiably have expected and, indeed, he records his disappointment in his introduction to the second edition of *Information and Investment* (1990, p. xvii). Interest in his works

---

[1]   The 1990 timing of the second edition of Richardson's 1960 book *Information and Investment* might appear to imply that it was initiated by Oxford University Press as some kind of 'thank you' to its recently retired C.E.O. but in fact the new edition was not initiated in this way. Rather, it came about as a consequence of Richardson being approached by Professor Warren Samuels, in his role as editorial advisor to reprint specialists Transaction Publishers. When Richardson checked with Oxford University Press whether this might be possible, they ended up doing the reprint instead (this information came in a personal communication from Samuels to Earl, 5 April 1992).

and those of his fellow Post Marshallians (such as P.W.S. Andrews, Jack Downie and Edith Penrose) is certainly growing but they remain unused by most economists and unknown to their students. His experience and that of his fellow deviants calls into question the dynamic efficiency of markets for economic ideas, challenging the sanguine views of Stigler (1982).

The rest of the chapter is divided into five main sections. In section 3.2, I provide an account of Richardson's path into economics and his method of operating as a scholar: this turns out to be significant for the form of his outputs and their marketability. In section 3.3, I examine the research coordination problem: the need for scholars to ensure that they are not engaged in mere reinvention or simultaneous invention of ideas. In section 3.4, I present citations evidence of the patchy impact of Richardson's work. In section 3.5, I examine critically Loasby's (1989) claims about the role of unfortunate timing in the initial reception of *Information and Investment*. Finally, in section 3.6, I consider the role that networks play as key determinants of the fates of contributions to knowledge.

3.2   RICHARDSON'S PATH TO ECONOMICS

Richardson's early career is both intriguing and paradoxical in relation to his contribution to economics. Because he was born in 1924, his university education was affected by the Second World War, as were his initial periods of employment. During the 1940s he completed a pair of two-year degrees, following each with periods of government service. His education could very easily have led him to become a physical scientist rather than an economist, for in 1942 he commenced studies at Aberdeen University and read mathematics and physics. This left him far better equipped in mathematical terms than most of his fellow economics students when he took up a scholarship to Oxford in 1947 and switched from science to Philosophy, Politics and Economics (PPE). At Oxford, his economics papers were in Economic Organization, Economic Principles, Economic Theory, and Statistics. Though the Oxford B.Phil. in PPE had been newly established in 1946, Oxford teaching was for the most part conservative rather than contemporary in its coverage (Young and Lee, 1993, p. 167). However, this was the period in which Hicks was very much in the ascendant at Oxford, and in 1952 Hicks was ranked ahead of both Robbins and Harrod for the Drummond Chair of Political Economy. By that time Hicks had became Richardson's mentor.

It was Richardson's mathematical training that led to his links with Hicks. His regular tutor in economics was Neville Ward-Perkins, an economic historian who had been taught by P.W.S. Andrews. When Richardson came to take the theory paper, Ward-Perkins initially arranged for him to be tutored by Frank Burchardt. However, after Richardson showed off his mathematical skills in presenting a paper on Keynes's theory of employment, Burchardt asked Hicks to tutor Richardson instead. Richardson recalls this rather immature display of mathematical prowess with some shame – one of his classmates remarking on leaving the seminar that if this was economics, then he wanted none of it – but he notes that without it he would not have become an economist. The irony, of course, is that much of what he was subsequently to write points away from analysing economic problems with the aid of mathematics. It leads instead to recognition of the need to become familiar with institutional details of devices that firms use to assist coordination.

Richardson's publications nonetheless have a distinctly Hicksian look to them: despite the paucity of diagrams and absence of mathematical notation Richardson's *Information and Investment* closely resembles Hicks' (1939) *Value and Capital* with its absence of section headings and only the use of occasional footnote references, mainly to classic writings. Unlike today's scholars who sometimes err in the direction of citation overkill when setting their works in the context of existing literature, Richardson and his mentor wrote about theoretical issues as if applying logic in their armchairs. Richardson's experience of being taught by Hicks was conducive to this, for the latter's method involved getting his students to read the work of great figures such as Marshall, Menger and Walras, rather than mastering a list of recent articles. In first decade at Oxford, and in sharp contrast to Andrews, Richardson did not follow in Marshall's approach of writing from a firm base in practical knowledge of business. Rather, his scholarship was based on curiosity and an eye for (what seemed to him to be) 'the obvious'. This involved much time thinking about problems in his college room or whilst walking round the college garden. When Richardson came to write *Information and Investment*, Hicks read the book in draft but provided few comments and did not discuss its central themes.

Though Hicks seemed rather distant from Richardson's own contributions, apparently regarding him as having focused too narrowly, too soon (so Richardson discovered, after Hicks had died), he did much to help Richardson to get started as an academic. He was initially unsuccessful in convincing Richardson to stay in academic economics rather than pursue a diplomatic career but, a year later, when Richardson had second thoughts and wrote to his mentor, Hicks managed to secure him a doctoral studentship at Nuffield College. Richardson was not particularly enamoured with his initial D.Phil. thesis research under Hicks and was thus happy to abandon it after only two terms, when he obtained a Fellowship at St John's on the basis of the promise he had shown. (The Senior Tutor at St John's advised him that it was no longer appropriate to read for a doctorate!) The ease with which Richardson got established at Oxford in the early 1950s is in contrast with the difficulties that Andrews had in retaining his Fellowship at Nuffield College in 1953. Hicks actively sought to prevent this, having a very low opinion of Andrews' capabilities as an economist (Lee, 1993, p. 22).

Differences between Richardson and Andrews in terms of background and relations with Hicks are perhaps significant in helping us to understand why they had almost no discussion together despite feeling they had something in common in doctrinal terms. In the 1950s Andrews had become suspicious of theoreticians and was immersing himself in empirical studies. At that stage, therefore, Richardson would have seemed to Andrews an abstract theorist. The uneasiness that Andrews felt in the company of theoreticians at least meant that there was little danger of links developing between these two Post Marshallians that could harm Richardson's standing in the eyes of those in positions of influence. Even so, having been introduced to full-cost pricing as an Oxford undergraduate, Richardson did take from Andrews the idea that spare capacity facilitates the avoidance of coordination problems since it permits firms to satisfy new demand without losing the goodwill of regular customers (Richardson, 1960/1990, p. 127).

During the 1960s Richardson's style of research increasingly came to resemble Andrews' Post Marshallian/behavioural mode. He became involved with applied studies, beginning with the heavy electrical plant industry, that led to his membership of the Monopolies Commission and provided the knowledge that eventually inspired his most influential work – his (1972) article 'The organisation of industry'. This change of research style, built on insights from his armchair theorizing, arose purely by chance. At a dinner in Sidney Sussex College in Cambridge he happened to sit next to Sebastian de Ferranti, an electrical engineering industrialist, who mentioned that the Restrictive Practices Court was about to consider a price agreement on transformers. Though Richardson knew nothing about the case, he immediately grasped the relevance of his work on coordination and remarked that there were arguments in favour of such restraints on trade, which most economists wrongly ignored (see further Richardson, 1965, 1966, 1967, 1969, 1998).

To conclude this commentary on how Richardson became an economist and how he operated as a scholar, I want to suggest that the contributions that Richardson made may have been affected by his early spells of work outside economics. Richardson himself reports that *Information and Investment* originated in a long struggle with a theoretical conundrum, his awareness of which emerged from uneasiness he felt even as an undergraduate about economists' accounts of how equilibrium states might be achieved. A modern industrial economist when presented with the Richardson Problem would tend to recognize that it may be framed in terms of the theory of games. However, Richardson's writings about the problem of investment coordination do not presume that entrepreneurs place their bets without first trying to improve the information they have about the plans of others whose actions may impinge on the outcomes of their own ventures. Another way of putting this is to say that entrepreneurs seek to gather *intelligence* by observing what rivals are up to or by exchanging information, either by mingling together or by deliberately sending signals. That Richardson should have come to view the mitigation of the problem in this way is hardly surprising when we note that Richardson's spells of government service in the 1940s included intelligence work. Just before the end of the war and soon after graduating from Aberdeen, he was sent, as a temporary naval officer, to Germany for intelligence work on radar. Subsequently he was employed as a civilian at the British Army of the Rhine headquarters, on political intelligence work and, immediately after his PPE studies, he went into the Foreign Service, having taken the entrance examination before taking his Oxford Finals.

3.3   THE RESEARCH COORDINATION PROBLEM

Academics have to grapple on a daily basis with a coordination problem every bit as complex as that upon which Richardson focused in *Information and Investment*. Rewards tend to go to those who succeed in staking claims to authorship of pioneering contributions valued highly by their peers. They may also go to those who are not first to develop particular ideas but who market their contributions in a way that better captures the attention of their peers. Physical scientists are not shy about debating in public their claims for primacy as discoverers of particular phenomena: a recent case in point is the battle between US and French AIDs researchers over the initial discovery of the HIV virus. Economists tend to be rather more reticent, or simply ignorant of potential for disputes. It is thus is left for historians of economic thought to explore possible instances of simultaneous invention or of credit going to re-inventors who, whether out of ignorance or opportunism, did not give credit where credit was due (cf. Earl, 1993).

Here is a touch of irony: George Richardson's own career as an academic illustrates well the potential for simultaneous invention of ideas and for an academic to be in the right place at the wrong time. In respect of the former we can note two examples. First, Richardson's (1972) article on the coordination of complementary investment and the subtle methods for coordinating vertical production and distribution processes appeared around the same time as a paper on a similar theme by Blois (1972). It is from the latter that the term 'quasi-integration' seems to have come into the language of economics and strategic management. Richardson had the greater richness of vision, but Blois had the buzz-phrase. Secondly, there is Richardson's (1975) awareness that he and Kaldor (1972) were thinking on similar lines about the significance of increasing returns. Richardson (1975, p. 351) notes that 'This paper was already in draft before the publication of Professor Kaldor's article "The irrelevance of equilibrium economics" in the *Economic Journal* . . . and I did not try to adapt it to take account of what he said. The arguments I put forward here are similar in important respects to those of Professor Kaldor.' Like Kaldor, he acknowledged the significance of Allyn Young's (1928) 'justly celebrated article' as a source of inspiration (1972, p. 352). To date, Kaldor's paper has attracted much more attention, probably due to its location in a core journal and because of Kaldor's fame. The profession would benefit from being familiar with Richardson's paper too, and from seeking to pull together links between the different focal points of the two contributions: unlike Richardson, Kaldor has nothing to say on the relationship between specialization and diversification in the growth strategies of firms. Both works deserve to receive more attention from those who work in the emerging literature on strategic international trade theory.

In respect of the question of primacy, we should note that, although the profession may ultimately follow Brian Loasby and myself (Earl, 1983a) and label the investment coordination problem in his honour as the Richardson Problem, he was by no means the first to recognize it. Nor was Richardson the first to write about the potentially beneficial role of market 'imperfections'. For example, discussions of interlinked expectations and the importance of frictions for the practical workings of the competitive system are to be found in the work of Clark (1923, pp. 417, 460) and Dobb (1937, pp. 206–7), though in relation to the process by which prices are changed. More noteworthy is a neglected article by Williams (1949), on the economics of structural change: its main theme is that 'dynamic competition cannot be "perfect"' (p. 124). The closeness of Williams's thinking to that of Richardson may be gauged from the following extracts:

> The fact that there are fixed factors means that capital losses inevitably follow a change in demand. Furthermore, these fixed factors, or frictions, are a precondition of the operation of the pricing mechanism. For if there were perfect mobility the emergence of a difference between price and cost in one sector would cause such a flood of resources there as to ensure losses for all. Nor could the flow back to the now prosperous deserted sectors be orderly, for with static expectations and perfect mobility (which implies that no producer has a preference or special competence for one industry rather than another) there would be nothing within the price mechanism as such to make it possible for producers to choose a profitable transfer. [to footnote] (p.126)

> [footnote] . . . he cannot rely on the law of large numbers to bring it about that too many firms will not go to one industry or another, for it is likely that industries will have need for widely varying numbers of firms. (p. 126)

> The avoidance of such a breakdown of the pricing mechanism is due to lack of

mobility, and to firms having, at any one point of time, differing degrees of mobility. (p. 127)

Problems associated with the coordination structural change and cyclical demand patterns were considered also by Joan Robinson (1954), but she did not raise the possibility that less than perfect flexibility of response might be a desirable feature. That she did not do so is perhaps surprising given her closeness to Keynes. It was Keynes (1936, pp. 239, 269) who realized, at the macro-level, that stickiness in the wage unit was essential to provide an anchor for the price level in the event of a shortfall or excess of effective demand as changes in money wages would not necessarily change the level of real effective demand and hence the demand for labour. The greater overall farsightedness of Williams's paper obviously includes the role he assigned in passing to special competences as limiting the industries in which firms will wish to participate. The competence theme resurfaces not only in Richardson's work (including his 1972 and 1975 papers) but is, of course, central to recent work on the resource-based view of the firm that takes its lead from Penrose (1959).[2]

Though scholars such as Williams and Robinson came to see the essence of the Richardson Problem before Richardson did, the case for naming it after him is that they focused on it briefly. Moreover, they failed to highlight that the coordination of complementary investment was a problem area, and they did not display his subtle appreciation of what might be included on the list of beneficial imperfections.

3.4   THE LIMITED IMPACT OF RICHARDSON'S WORK

Economists who read Loasby (1986, 1989, chapter 6) or my (1983a) paper on economists' behaviour may infer from comments therein, about the neglect of Richardson, that his publications were almost completely ignored. This inference would be somewhat mistaken but would certainly be correct in respect of research and teaching in the core microeconomic theory area of the discipline. His work challenged the wisdom expressed in the textbooks that were available as he developed his thinking, and it provided a basis for studying economics as a coordination problem, with a novel focus on institutional arrangements that facilitate coordination. But after four decades it has not become incorporated into standard textbooks.

Shortly after the publication of *Information and Investment*, Roy Harrod,

---

[2]   See Foss (ed.) (1997) for a collection of articles on the resource-based approach to the firm, which includes Richardson (1972) and extracts from Penrose, as well as many more recent papers.

in his role as general editor of the Hutchinon University Library Economics Series, commissioned Richardson to write a textbook. Richardson's (1964a) own textbook *Economic Theory* was hardly the ideal package to become a standard tool in a revamped economics paradigm. It began, like its rivals, with the logic of choice, Richardson's strategy being a very Hayekian one of going on to show that the dispersion of knowledge made it necessary to have decentralized decision-making. Unfortunately, it was too dense for the typical student and lacked the more lavish attention to matters of layout that was beginning to characterize the bloated conventional texts at the time it appeared. Instead, it was a book of intricate continuous argument in the style of introductory philosophy texts by Bertrand Russell and G.E. Moore that Richardson had himself enjoyed and was not at all the type of work to appeal to those with short attention spans.

Richardson's textbook was not a complete sales disaster, despite not taking off into multiple editions, and was translated into Spanish and Portuguese. Between it and my recent treatment (Earl, 1995, chapter 10) the only textbook on microeconomics to offer a taste of Richardson's perspective was the readings collection by Wagner and Baltazzis (1973), who reprinted his (1971) article 'Planning versus competition'. This article first appeared in *Soviet Studies* and today is of interest for those concerned with the economies of countries undergoing the transition from communism to more market-based methods of economic organization. Given this, it is interesting to note that a few years earlier, at the time of the Prague Spring, he was contacted by an economist from Bratislava, Madame Sestokova, about the possibility of translating *Economic Theory* into Slovak. The book was seen in Czechoslovakia as addressing the problem of how to move towards decentralized decision-making. Madame Sestokova visited Richardson in Oxford and, a few weeks before the Russian invasion, Richardson visited Prague and Bratislava. Once Dubcek was out of power, it seemed to Richardson unwise to write to those who had warmly hosted his visit to Czechoslovakia – letters from the West might put their positions in jeopardy. After the fall of communism, Richardson did try to resume contact and was greatly saddened to discover that Madame Sestokova and her family had fared badly in the interim and that she was seriously ill in hospital.

Though the central ideas in George Richardson's work imply a need for major reworking of textbooks, they are not fundamentally difficult to grasp. He expressed them in plain English and, particularly in his post-*Economic Theory* work, with plenty of memorable real-world examples. My experience over many years is that students find Richardson's ideas easy to assimilate compared with many of the concepts of neoclassical theory. A teacher who wishes to inspire an intermediate microeconomics class will find it far easier to do so by beginning with the economics of information and coordination rather than with the axioms of mainstream choice theory.

To see his ideas being discussed in textbooks it is generally necessary to move from the core of economics, that any student will cover, to industrial economics and business strategy. There, Richardson might have more of a feeling of success, but still considerable grounds for feeling that the profession has not made as much of his work as it might have done. The most widely read discussion of the entry coordination problem is doubtless the chapter on capacity expansion decisions in the best-seller by Porter (1980), referred to in chapter 1. Porter seems, however, to be engaging in reinvention, for he makes no reference to Richardson as he examines the problem and considers various preemptive signalling approaches for dealing with it. Richardson's vision of the significance of corporate capabilities and relational contracting is going to be absorbed by many managers via John Kay's strong selling (1993) *Foundations of Corporate Success*. Kay refers to Richardson (1972) very briefly (p. 85) as 'an early contribution', in a guide to the literature. Richardson's way of thinking will thus spread but probably without his name attached to it and with Kay's readers being oblivious of his personal links with Richardson.

It would certainly be incorrect to say that Richardson is ignored in industrial economics. He is cited in the leading British undergraduate-level texts, and occasionally in American ones, though generally without his contributions being made central to the analysis. (Clearly, there is a big difference between being merely footnoted and being discussed at length – as in Earl, 1995 – as an important contributor whose focus can be summed up as the Richardson Problem. At present, anyone who uses this shorthand term with students has to be careful to remind them of its limited currency.) Table 3.1 shows the extent to which Richardson's contributions are discussed or noted in some of the widely used texts.

If economists were as well informed as their hypothetical decision-makers it would be natural to expect to see Richardson's work on coordination receiving more attention, as industrial economics texts at the advanced level have become dominated by an interest in game theory. In fact, neither Tirole (1988) nor Martin (1993) mention it in their market-leading texts. Though Richardson had originally wanted to call his 1960 book *The Economics of Imperfect Knowledge*, anyone who hopes to see his ideas being discussed in Phlips' (1988) *The Economics of Imperfect Information* will be disappointed. One might even be so bold as to suggest that the more that industrial economics texts incorporate modern microeconomic theory focused on incomplete information, the less likelihood there is of Richardson receiving attention. Even so, there are still some occasions on which Richardson is cited in modern survey discussions at exactly the point where he might expect to be. For example, *Information and Investment* is cited in R.J. Gilbert's chapter on mobility barriers in Schmalensee and Willig (eds) (1989, p. 534). Likewise, 'The organisation of industry' is quoted by Steve Davies in his chapter on vertical integration in Clarke and McGuinness (eds) (1987, p. 84). To some extent, then, Richardson's ideas have been received into the normal science textbooks of industrial economics but they certainly have not had a revolutionary impact on the hard core of this sub-discipline. However, to the extent that modern, advanced-level texts are concentrating on surveying *recent* contributions to the field, then it is to some extent surprising that Richardson receives attention at all in these works.

Table 3.1: Citations of Richardson's work in widely used industrial economics texts

Richardson reference:	1960	1964b	1965	1966	1967	1972
Cited in (with page no.):						
Pickering, 1973	295/324	115/309	278/323		295/324	
Devine *et al.*, 1976	407, 436, 445		436, 445	436, 445		
Hay and Morris, 1979	412	303, 393–4	173, 593	173		57, 593
George and Joll, 1981				173		
Reid, 1987	65, 69, 213					
Scherer and Ross, 1990	299			295, 309	311	
Greer, 1992				408		

Kuhnian historians of science would look to textbooks for evidence of a scholar's revolutionary impact. By contrast, present-day academic audits of research productivity focus on success in being published in 'core' journals on the basis that it is much more difficult to have works accepted in these journals and that articles published in them are likely to be cited in subsequent works. All of Richardson's English-language articles were in high-ranking journals but that did not guarantee that they would be rapidly picked up and frequently cited. It is somewhat difficult to study the citation pattern of Richardson's work before 1969, for it was not until that year that the *Social Sciences Citation Index* (*SSCI*) commenced publication in its present form. A complete listing of citations of Richardson's works recorded in the first quarter of a century of the *SSCI* reveals that Richardson was cited around seven times times a year on average, 186 times in all (including only two self-citations), with the lion's share of the citations being *Information and Investment* (50 times) and 'The organisation of industry' (83 times). The *SSCI* listings provide a fascinating picture of how his work has been used.

Richardson has been cited in most major economics journals and by many eminent economists, including Nelson, Scherer, Scitovsky, Teece and Williamson, but these 'core' citations, most of which are to *Information and Investment*, only account for a small fraction of the total. Many citations are not in English-language journals or are in journals outside of economics, in disciplines such as marketing, strategic management, geography and sociology. This is particularly the case with his (1972) paper. Richardson's work is not yet famous in the sense that most teachers and students of economics have heard of it, but that has not prevented it from being discovered and used by scholars working outside of the core of economics. So far, I have only been able briefly to examine the lists of works cited by some of the articles that cite Richardson and which I had not previously seen. The initial impression is that these papers tend not merely to cite Richardson but also relatively underused works by other scholars such as Malmgren and Hirschman, that I stumbled across myself in the late 1970s when first searching for contributions that might augment the Richardson perspective. But there were many works listed with intriguing titles that were unfamiliar to me. I hope that readers will use *SSCI* listings to uncover and explore these works further and develop a clearer picture of the extent of thinking by other neglected authors, completing the augmentation process.

3.5 WAS DEBREU THE CAUSE OF THE FAILURE OF *INFORMATION AND INVESTMENT* TO TAKE OFF IN THE 1960s?

A variety of interpretations can be offered for Richardson's failure so far to have a major impact on the core of economics, despite being surprisingly successful in being noticed in an interdisciplinary sense. According to Loasby (1989, p. 99), Richardson's great misfortune was that his critique of general equilibrium analysis appeared just after Debreu's (1959) exposition of an abstract economic model in which complete contingent claims markets 'solved' the coordination problem, for Richardson's prose lacked the hard scientific appeal of Debreu's mathematics. This view can be challenged.

For Loasby's view to be correct, it would seem to require that economists in the early 1960s were actually worried about the coordination problem, and that Debreu was indeed praised for his solution to the problem around the time that Richardson's work appeared. This being so, mainstream scholars would have no need to search for alternative perspectives that might remove their uneasiness. Contemporary reactions to both Debreu and Richardson provide evidence to the contrary and may indicate how the profession at large was prone to construe particular contributions and choose between theories. Before we consider the content of the reviews it is worth noting that book reviews in professional journals are the academic equivalent of quality signalling devices in other markets. Such devices include reports of restaurants in good food guides, credit ratings by agencies such as Standard and Poor's, and admission to trade association membership. In other words, they are devices of the kind that Richardson has sought to emphasize in his work on coordination.

Debreu's book was not widely reviewed beyond the American journals. There were no reviews in *Economica*, the *Economic Journal* or the *Economic Record*, while the review in *Econometrica* is in quite difficult French and so would have been relatively insignificant in the English-speaking world. In the four reviews that I have unearthed, Debreu was generally praised for his innovative technical exposition but the reviewers did not appear to be cheering him for showing how general equilibrium and uncertainty could be made compatible. On the contrary, either the issue was not highlighted or he came in for criticism for his abstractions and failure to use examples. In the *American Economic Review*, Hurwicz correctly predicted that the book would have a major long-term impact. However, he commented that, in relation to Debreu's fifth and sixth chapters (on existence and optimality of competitive equilibria, respectively), 'One's understanding of the problem would have been greatly deepened by examples lacking equilibrium due to the failure of one or another of the assumptions' (1961, p. 416). Hurwicz had little to say, however, about Debreu's treatment of uncertainty, merely mentioning that this was introduced in the seventh chapter. In the *Southern Economic Journal*, Harrell hardly went further, simply ending his purely descriptive review by saying that, 'In the last chapter a revised definition of a commodity leads to a theory of uncertainty which is normally identical with the previously elaborated theory of certainty' (Harrell, 1960, p. 150). Much more critical is Baudier (1961), in *Econometrica*, who noted that the cost of Debreu's concern to state his purpose precisely is that he gives readers no indications of the implications of the theory about which they must themselves form judgments. Baudier then commented that

> The consequences are, however, to my way of thinking, too important to pass by in silence and too numerous to be counted. Let's mention this one: the last chapter introduces the possibility of 'commodities' of a new type for which there is no market (at least in general) and therefore the prices of those 'commodities' could not be held as given by economic agents who don't even know them. Thus one of the conditions of applying the theory of equilibrium to the real world collapses. (Baudier, 1961, pp. 259–60; my translation, with assistance from Pascal Tremblay)

Similarly, in the *Journal of Political Economy*, the young Frank Hahn (1961) praised the *Theory of Value* as a technical achievement but criticized it in three significant ways: first, for proceeding implicitly 'as if' the non-existence of contingent commodity markets does not matter; second, for leaving no role for money; and, third, for having nothing to say about what happens in an economy when conditions are insufficient to produce an equilibrium. That Hahn should have reacted in this way is ironic given his later spirited defences of the Arrow–Debreu approach as a benchmarking tool for policy diagnosis – arguments that Richardson (1960/1990, pp. xxi–xxii, in the 1990 edition) finds utterly unacceptable.

None of the reviewers of the first edition of *Information and Investment* made any reference to Debreu's contribution. Nor did any reviewer note another point that would be obvious to modern-day economists, namely, that Richardson might have done well to relate his work to the literature that, by the late 1950s, had appeared on the theory of games. Morgenstern, one of the co-founders of game theory recognized as long ago as 1928 that the attainment of economic equilibrium could not be explained in terms of existing theory in cases where an agent's choice of a plan of action required knowledge of plans of other agents (see Borch, 1973, p. 67). Rather, the reviewers focused on the *overly theoretical* nature of the book. In other words, Richardson's marketing problem seemed to be one of getting economists to agree that there was *actually* a problem of coordination worth worrying about. It seems unlikely that, in 1960, he would have better satisfied his reviewers if he had made the most of his mathematical training and set out the coordination problem in Debreu's style. His reviewers appear merely to have wanted the kinds of down-to-earth examples that he was to use so effectively in his later writings.

Potential readers of the book can hardly have been encouraged by the observation of Power (1961, p. 761) in an otherwise perceptive and favourable review in the *American Economic Review*, that

> The method of the book is essentially armchair reasoning with only occasional reference to empirical studies . . . Readers may find the concluding section of the volume disappointing in the light of earlier bold statements about the omissions of conventional theory.

The first comment is an accurate characterization of how Richardson had worked, but the second is somewhat unfair: its intended implication seems to be that the book does not offer much to fill the gap that it exposes.

Lesley Cook (1964, p. 168) begins her *Economic Journal* review by suggesting that the title, *Information and Investment,* is slightly misleading' and that the book is 'a theoretical examination of the effects on investment of uncertainty resulting from inadequate information'. The book is surely better characterized as a critique of conventional theories of the workings of the price mechanism and an alternative analysis of how allocation mechanisms work in the face of incomplete knowledge. Richardson may well have been wiser than his publisher in wanting to call the book *The Economics of Imperfect Knowledge*. (Hicks, as one of the Delegates of Oxford University Press, had been unwilling to accept that title, remarking to Richardson that it would demonstrate an imperfect knowledge of economics.) While also broadly favourable, Cook's review can only have damaged the book's impact by suggesting that, 'He is largely concerned with problems related to the cobweb theorem.' Conventional theorists seem to be predisposed to view the cobweb theorem as affecting only agriculture and the construction industries. Thus they would have been inclined to agree with Cook when she argued that Richardson was probably exaggerating the importance of the coordination problem when he applied it to investment decisions in general. (Such an inclination would have been particularly likely if they had just read Muth's (1961, pp. 330–4) now-famous work on rational expectations. This highlights the empirical limitations of cobweb models and tentatively argues that the rational expectations hypothesis has superior predictive capabilities – even though Richardson (1959, p. 233) had already called into question any notion of rational expectations.) The fact that Richardson's book was four years old before this review appeared could hardly have helped its chances with, particularly, British economists who had not noticed it on its publication *if* they had in the meantime tuned into the message of Debreu. (I could find no review of it in *Economica*, merely one by Laurence Harris (1965) of Richardson's (1964a) textbook. Harris does note Richardson's focus on the restrictive nature of the perfect knowledge assumption but gives no clue regarding the nature of the problem that Richardson has in mind. He goes on instead to criticize the text for being too brief and superficial and for lacking any discussion of method or suggestions for further readings.)

Cook argued that an orderly process of market adjustment through sequential market entry would have seemed much more plausible, especially if he had chosen to analyse the problem in disequilibrium terms rather than with comparative statics. In fact, Richardson (1960, pp. 51–2) *had* presented an examination of sequential entry but had noted difficulties for entrepreneurs in assessing precisely how much capacity rivals had already commissioned, the more so the larger the number of firms participating in the market. Cook further failed to explain to potential readers that Richardson's aim was not to demonstrate, as Joan Robinson (1954) wished to do, that the coordination problems causes chaos and 'the impossibility of profits'. Rather, he was more concerned to show how such problems may be avoided in practice and thereby to put readers in a better position to appraise the implications of competition policies based on conventional theories which neglect the information structures that help markets to function.

John Grant's (1962) review in the *Economic Record* echoes the sentiments of both Power and Cook. He claimed that

[T]he book is not wholly satisfying, because the argument remains on a purely theoretical plane throughout. The reader cannot fail to wonder about the magnitude of the problem under discussion in the real world. Some empirical research would not only have made the book more interesting but may also have increased the author's contribution to economic analysis.

The line of thinking here seems to be that the price mechanism in practice does not appear to produce chaos, so Richardson is worrying about a problem that does not really matter and that therefore it is safe to continue with conventional theoretical analysis. The reviewers seem blind to Richardson's key point: the traditional theory has a logical flaw and chaos is avoided – insofar as it *is* avoided – because supply decisions are reached in ways fundamentally different from those posited by traditional theory. This being so, it is conceivable that attempts to make the world resemble the traditional theoretical world more closely in terms of the competitive rules of the game might result in inferior patterns of resource allocation. Such a 'second best' world might function in a more chaotic manner and/or entrepreneurs in general could become more hesitant about investing. Thus, even without any buttressing from Debreu's make-believe world of complete contingent commodity markets, the traditional theory seemed to have been quite acceptable to Richardson's reviewers as an 'as if' approximation of how the world works.

In taking issue with Loasby here on the impact of Debreu's success on the reception of *Information and Investment* I am not denying that the timing of its release might have been more fortuitous. Indeed, there are several reasons to believe that the market for Richardson's message has ripened steadily since 1960. It also seems likely and that the book would have fared far better had it been published around 1972, with the title that Richardson originally intended and including material from his 1972 article, which is logically linked with it (see Foss, 1994a, on the relationship between Richardson 1960 and 1972):

1. One might expect traditional theory to look less plausible when the 'golden age' of economic growth came to an end and excess capacity creation would no longer rapidly tend to be rendered non-problematic by ongoing demand growth. During the golden age, interest in investment coordination problems tended to centre on the question of which firms should exit from markets suffering from chronic excess capacity due to changes in global competitive conditions. Examples include traditional staple industries such as cotton textiles (see Miles, 1968) and wool textiles (see Wool Textile EDC, 1969). There was also some interest the possibility of dysfunctional defensive investment (Lamfalussy, 1961). Richardson, however, had not focused on exit games under conditions of gross immobility of capital and human resources. Nowadays, with

frequent periods of recession and new investment occurring despite chronic over-capacity in many modern industries (for example, the motor vehicles industry), it is not easy to dismiss Richardson's work as empirically insignificant.

2. Those who were less enamoured with the price mechanism doubtless learnt a lot more about the nature of the coordination problem in the decade after *Information and Investment* appeared. Attempts at indicative planning, such as those of the UK Labour Government in the late 1960s, and the 'balanced versus unbalanced growth' debate in development economics may have aroused a greater recognition of the issue of coordination. Planners became painfully aware of complementary aspects of investment as well as of the difficulty of ensuring the right amount of investment in any one sector if directives were not to be given to individual firms and communication between them was not allowed. It is easy to see why Richardson's (1971) timely article 'Planning versus competition' was so swiftly reprinted in Wagner and Baltazzis (eds) (1973). Had his 1960 book not already been published, Richardson's (1969) report on collusive tendering in the UK's heavy electrical engineering industry would have made a powerful empirical addition to it. This embraces both the complementarity problem (a surplus capacity problem due to the electricity industry expanding rapidly in keeping with the National Plan, only to find that most of the rest of the UK economy did not), and the question of whether market imperfections might enhance dynamic efficiency.

3. It was around 1972 that the so-called Crisis in Economic Theory really seemed to break out, with widespread criticism (for example, Kaldor, 1972) of the kind of abstract and institutionally implausible research that Debreu's work had helped to foster.

Had Richardson's work attracted widespread attention during the early 1970s, it is conceivable that a good deal of subsequent work on industrial economics would have been done differently. In particular, those involved with the development of contestability theory would have had reason to be rather more cautious in advocating the removal of entry barriers in industries such as passenger aviation and financial services that have since suffered from severe adjustment problems (see further Earl, 1995, pp. 305–9).

3.6 NETWORKS, INSTITUTIONS AND ACADEMIC SEARCH PROCESSES

The volume of potentially relevant material that academics might find worthwhile to read is typically enormous relative to the time they have to read it and the capacity of their libraries to stock it. This makes it seem inappropriate to try to make sense of the fate of particular contributions to knowledge in terms of a perspective which sees academics as if they know not merely which kinds of ideas they like but also where to find them. Some economists in the 1960s may indeed have been deterred from reading Richardson (and even Debreu) by contemporary reviews. Some may have seen his work and decided not to read it because it did not fit with their growing taste for technical rigour. However, it is unlikely to be the case that most economists currently working have sized up Richardson's work with the aid of such reviews and have decided not to read it in detail, or, like his reviewers, have read it and decided not to take his ideas on board. A more plausible hypothesis is that most economists are simply unaware of his contributions and use search processes or move in social circles that are not conducive to discovering what Richardson has had to say.

In the analysis of life-cycles of consumer products it is commonly recognized that social factors play a major role in determining how much attention potential buyers pay to new products and whether or not they experiment with them. The same seems to hold in academia and, as with consumer markets, some people may have more influence than others. Two conditions are required for networks of personal contacts to have a far smaller role to play in shaping the esteem attached to particular contributions to knowledge. The first is that researchers habitually search for relevant materials with the aid of indexing and abstracting systems in the manner that libraries nowadays try to inculcate among students. The second is that such systems cover older works as well as recent contributions. However, I suspect that until recently very few academics made great use of such potential as existed for systematic search, with the result that networks were of vital significance. Many university librarians are yet to work out how to release the resources required to subscribe to superb electronic databases such as the Web of Science electronic version of the Social Sciences Citation Index and pay for the growth in inter-loan requests whose use these tend to generate.

When the bulk of Richardson's work appeared there were relatively few economics journals with which to keep up to date. However, this was also a period in which indexing systems were poorly developed and economists were not accustomed to making extensive use of abstracts (the *Journal of Economic Abstracts* commenced publication as late as 1963 and only turned into the more extensive *Journal of Economic Literature* in 1969). It is also probably fair to say that it was only in the 1970s that the Harvard system of referencing really caught on and made it far easier for potential readers to get a flavour of a work by examining its bibliography. In terms of presentation and layout, the reprint of *Information and Investment* was remarkably uninviting to the casual browser of the 1990s. As already noted, Richardson's works were typical of their time: the world of infrequent references scattered around in footnotes and of a notable absence of the use of section headings in chapters and papers.

Prior to the age of information and the development of sophisticated indexing systems, some scholars who became aware of Richardson would have done so either by serendipity (for example, stumbling across his books or articles whilst looking purposively for something else that happens to be physically adjacent). Others would have discovered them to a greater or lesser extent with the aid of networks. Seven main types of connections promote the discovery of contribution to knowledge, and some of them can be illustrated by reference to tales of 'routes to Richardson' reported to me by contributors to the colloquium held in Richardson's honour in Oxford in January 1995:

1. *Being a pupil or colleague of the author in question, or a student with an intellectual lineage traceable back to the author.* For example, given their associations with St John's College Oxford, it should be no surprise that Richardson has influenced both John Kay and Leslie Hannah. John Nightingale's lineage, by contrast, links Oxford and Australia. Richardson was one.of a number of authors (including Penrose, Downie and Andrews) whose recent works were discussed by Don Lamberton in a final year undergraduate unit taken by Nightingale at the University of New South Wales in the mid 1960s. Lamberton had recently returned to Australia after meeting Richardson when working on his D.Phil. at Oxford.

2. *Seeing a work that cites the author, or at least cites a work that cites the author.* For example, the writings of Loasby (particularly his 1976 book) introduced the name of Richardson to myself, Nicolai Foss (who discovered Richardson around the same time also from the citation in Leijonhufvud, 1968, pp. 69–70), and Richard Langlois. In turn, Richard Arena reported that he first saw Richardson being mentioned in Earl (1983b). It is, of course, common for academics to prime their markets (or assert their property rights) via preliminary publications, such as articles and discussion papers foreshadowing their major works whilst preemptively staking their claims as market leaders in particular areas of research. Richardson's articles from the 1950s pave the way directly to his (1960) book in intellectual terms. He also certainly helped his readers

discover his earlier work by his own citations (oddly enough, in his 1972 paper, his footnote reference [p. 891] to *Information and Investment* lists it as published in 1961, not 1960!). Though he did not engage in forward citation, his Oxford colleague Malmgren (1961) helpfully discussed his work in the *Quarterly Journal of Economics* at a very early stage. This should have helped stir up interest among potential readers in America who were not regular readers of *Oxford Economic Papers* or the *Economic Journal*. Malmgren's work, which has recently been reviewed in a useful article by Foss (1996), unfortunately seemed to suffer much the same initial fate as that of Richardson.

3. *Being taught by someone familiar with the author's work despite not being a direct or indirect pupil of the author.* For example, Mark Casson commented that 'I think Richardson (as well as Coase, Penrose, etc.) was on the undergraduate reading list at Bristol, and I used to read the things on the list. So I never "discovered" any of these writers – I was simply directed to them. Hence I never regarded them as particularly unorthodox.' Neil Kay was introduced to Richardson's work as a pupil of Loasby at Stirling University. Gavin Reid used Richardson's (1964a) text as a second year undergraduate at Aberdeen University in 1966–7 when looking for a short, clear conspectus of basic economics. However, Reid thinks that J.N. Wolfe, a close friend of Richardson, introduced him to *Information and Investment* in the early 1970s when he was a graduate student at Edinburgh University.

4. *Meeting with the author, or with other scholars familiar with the author's work, at conferences and/or meetings of professional societies or during the author's periods of sabbatical travel.* In this connection we might note that Richardson's impact in North America ought to have been greater given that *Information and Investment* was in part written whilst he was on a Rockefeller Foundation fellowship. As he noted, this left him free to 'indulge in stimulating conversations with colleagues at Harvard and the University of California at Berkeley' (Richardson, 1960, p. xv).

5. *Receiving a word of mouth recommendation from a colleague.* For example, Paul Robertson believes that he first heard of Richardson (1972) around 1986, from Dick Merrett, a fellow business historian in Melbourne, who had just read it for the first time himself.

6. For academics in the future, the *Internet* is likely to become the ultimate networking device for affecting the spread of new ideas (see further, MacKie-Mason and Varian, 1994, and Goffe, 1994 – references to

which my own attention was drawn via an e-mail from Don Lamberton).

7. *Publishers' mailing lists and catalogues, and their use of particular 'names' to endorse their products.* For the second edition of *Information and Investment*, David Teece and Oliver Williamson provided supportive comments: the fate of the first edition might have been very different had it come with a foreword from, say, Hicks (who had read it in draft) or Shackle. In future, on-line reviews, indexes of books and contents listings (such as those offered by Amazon.com) may have a major role to play in enabling academics to decide what to order without being overwhelmed by printed catalogues, so choices of titles and contents designs will become even more important. This being the case, we should all take note of Richardson's view that his publisher's favoured title *Information and Investment* was unfortunate, since it led to the work being catalogued in libraries alongside books on the Stock Exchange (see his preface to the 1990 edition, p. xvii).

The existence of so many potential linkages is significant given the danger that any one link will be of limited effectiveness. If academics are working under pressure they may not register signals as they encounter them, or may not bother to act upon them. My own route to Richardson illustrates this graphically. In 1977, as a postgraduate student inspired by the discussion in Loasby (1976), I read Richardson (1972) for the first time. I immediately realized that I had encountered it before, at high school in 1972. The trouble was that, in giving us such memorable examples from 'the latest *Economic Journal* that has arrived from the town library', my teacher had not mentioned Richardson by name as the author. Later, on re-reading Leijonhufvud (1968), a work that had played a crucial role in getting me hooked on the economics of uncertainty, I noticed for the first time the footnote references to Richardson (1959), in precisely the part of the book that had made such an impact. Later still, when collating old subject outlines I discovered that my final year industrial economics reading list from Alan Hughes's lectures at Cambridge included *Information and Investment* but somehow I had not followed it up at the time.

Whether or not recommendations or citations *are* followed up may depend considerably on the availability and anticipated quality of the work in question. Certainly, in using the *SSCI*, I was struck by the obscurity of many of the journals in which Richardson has been cited (I was not been able even to track down the full names of some of them, let alone get access to copies). Since Richardson's articles appear in major English-language journals, they are relatively easy to obtain at a moment's notice in older libraries, as are his books. Yet all of them might well be dismissed as 'too old and out of date' by current scholars unless they are discovered via more modern secondary sources of note in which their virtues have been extolled at length.

To conclude this section I would like to emphasize that when a scholar has to go to some trouble to obtain a work, learned societies have a major role to play in determining whether it will look sufficiently attractive in prospect to seem worth chasing. They may also help to determine whether it gets discovered in the first place. It is rare for such societies to insist that members conduct their research in a particular manner, unlike trade associations who may debar from membership anyone whose standards of work do not meet with association norms. Even so, their ability to control what gets presented at their conferences or what gets published in their official journals means they have a major gatekeeping role in respect of the marketing of contributions to knowledge. A further aspect of this professional control is the ability to determine which journals are abstracted in the society's abstracting publications. This is important not merely because articles published in unlisted journals have a smaller chance of being discovered. It also matters because librarians, concerned to see that their investments are thoroughly used, may refer to the places in which a journal is abstracted as criteria for deciding whether or not to agree to take out a subscription. Any economics journal not abstracted in *Web of Science*, *ABI-Inform* and the *Journal of Economic Literature* is likely in future to have a hard time attracting both subscriptions and high-quality papers from authors who are keen to see that their work is widely read.

Mere publication of an article signals to the academic community that it has been through a pretty stiff competitive refereeing process if it is published in a dominant professional grouping's generalist journal. Different signals about the height of refereeing hurdles and about the likely style and content are emitted if it is published in a sub-disciplinary or heterodox journal. (It is probably fair to suggest that when Richardson published frequently in *Oxford Economic Papers* in the 1950s and 1960s, this journal was much less of an international organ than it is today.) Commercially published journals serve a similar signalling role, and, of course, many of these are associated with academic societies or networks. Firms that publish a large number of journals of high quality have an incentive to maintain their standards as they add new journals to their catalogues, for fear of damaging their overall images and hence the subscriptions they can command. editorial boards of reputable academics signal the standards that are being targeted even if no learned society sponsors the journal. Likewise, in respect of book publishing, catalogue branding is extensively used to signal the type of book to potential purchasers. Most publishers run a variety of imprints and under any particular imprint they may also include a number of series of books of particular kinds, each edited by academics with reputations as expert in the fields in question.

3.7 CONCLUSION

Richardson's work on economic organization and coordination has been widely used despite so far failing to become part of the core of microeconomic theory. It also provides valuable perspectives for viewing the operations of academia, encouraging us to look for networks and other institutional devices that assist academics to reduce coordination difficulties. The risk that academics will unwittingly reinvent each other's ideas or pursue dysfunctional lines of inquiry owing to their ignorance of particular contributions is reduced to the extent that they can search systematically with the aid of subject and citation indexes, abstracts and book reviews or contents listings. In the past, haphazard methods of research and weaker networking/indexing made it all too easy for scholars to to be unaware of works that they would have welcomed or that would have forced them to rethink their ideas. It was not wise to presume that if a contribution to knowledge was of a high standard this would necessarily be swiftly reflected in its rate of citation or number of copies in circulation. Now, in the new Millennium, we are entering a world in which information technology will permit scholars to operate in a far less haphazard manner as they attempt to discover and screen contributions for their likely usefulness. Much screening will take place on-screen and ideas will be able to spread far more rapidly so long as they have been judiciously titled and summarized. Even so, older contributions or contributions in obscure journals may remain at risk of being neglected.

ACKNOWLEDGEMENTS

I would like to thank Michael Brooks for many useful comments on an earlier version of this chapter, which has also benefited from comments by Fred Lee, Brian Loasby, Nicolai Foss and an anonymous referee, and from correspondence with George Richardson himself (who provided some very useful autobiographical notes).

4. Shackle, Entrepreneurship and the Theory of the Firm

4.1 INTRODUCTION

Though George Shackle's subversive thinking is yet to make an impact on mainstream economics, his (1961, 1972) analysis of the role of time in economics and his critique of probability, if not his possibility-based theory of choice under uncertainty, have been widely accepted as core ideas within Post Keynesian economics. His ideas have also been taken up in practical terms by some strategists that engage in scenario planning (see Jefferson, 1983). Many modern-day researchers in the area of entrepreneur-ship have been influenced by his work, particularly those close to the Austrian school. In contrast to the previous chapter, therefore, my focus here is not on the extent to which economists failed to pick up Shackle's ideas. My intention is rather to show how Shackle himself failed to grasp opportunities for integrating his thinking with the work of other authors who had complementary ideas. In the course of uncovering opportunities that he took up or missed I aim to contribute to this process of integration. This chapter also serves to fill a gap in the critical analysis of Shackle's career, since his work on the role of the entrepreneur and on the theory of the firm received surprisingly little attention in the major intellectual biography by Ford (1994).

The chapter is divided up as follows. Section 4.2, is an examination of missed opportunities in Shackle's (1970) textbook on the theory of the firm. Section 4.3 explores potential linkages between Shackle and Coase, while in section 4.4 I contrast the attention Shackle gave to Cantillon's work with his tendency to ignore Schumpeter. Section 4.5 is an examination of the similarities between Shackle's views on business enterprise and what has lately become known as the 'resource-based' view of the firm. In section 4.6, I attempt to pull together threads from the preceding ones and question the wisdom of writing about entrepreneurship without also focusing on inter-nalization and management of activities in the sense associated with Coase. Prior to the conclusion, section 4.7 examines some possible reasons for Shackle's failure to follow his research through to reach similar conclusions.

4.2   SHACKLE'S GREAT MISSED OPPORTUNITY

Shackle was given the opportunity to present his perspective on firms in the first of the Allen & Unwin 'Studies in Economics' series of textbooks. This series was edited by Charles Carter, who had been a sympathetic but critical reviewer of Shackle's contributions to the theory of choice under uncertainty (see, for example, the papers by Carter reprinted in Earl, ed., 1988). The blurb on the back of the soft-cover edition of the resulting book, *Expectation, Enterprise and Profit* (1970), promised a work that even three decades later sounds excitingly different and relevant:

> Production is a complex system of inter-necessary activities, such that the existence of each activity is necessary to that of the system as a whole, which itself ensures the continuance of each individual activity composing it. In such a system resources must be committed to specific technological purposes long in advance of the ultimate sale of goods to the consumer, or durable equipment to the investing businessman. The problems of such a system rest on the *durability* of the instruments it uses. These are so complex, sensitive and powerful that their huge expense can only be recouped if they can be used for many years. Yet when the decision is taken to invest in them, those years of use are in the future and its conditioning circumstances are *unobservable* and *unknown*.
>
> The firm is the essential institutional means, in Western economies, of confronting this problem of uncertainty. Professor Shackle's book is centrally concerned with the nature and mode of the firm as a means of policy formation in the face of uncertainty. It includes also an explanation of the classic maximizing problems in the *absence* of uncertainty, which form the subject-matter of the traditional theory of the firm. (Rear cover of Shackle, 1970, italics in original)

The book is certainly different from standard texts, but it offers readers only a very selective coverage of pre-1970 contributions to the theory of the firm that highlighted the problems of complexity and uncertainty. Inter-connectedness is addressed with reference to Leontief matrices, and the marginalist optimizing analysis is precise and lucid, as is Shackle's introduction to discounted cash-flow analysis. However, as far as the analysis of uncertainty is concerned, the material is almost exclusively drawn from Shackle's own potential surprise theory of choice, and his model of bargaining is the only contribution to be confronted with Edgeworth's work in the chapter on interdependent decision-making.

This is an extraordinarily narrow examination of the relationship between uncertainty and business decision-making compared with what would have been perfectly possible had Shackle made use of literature published in the preceding fifteen years. Shackle neglected the work of the Carnegie School (Simon, 1957; Cyert and March, 1963) on the use of rule-based procedures for coping with uncertainty and complexity. He employed neither the Post Marshallian analyses of market behaviour and the growth of firms offered by Andrews (1964) and Penrose (1959) nor Richardson's (1960) work that explores the significance of market 'imperfections' for helping decision makers to cope with uncertainty and interdependence. These omissions are indeed odd even though such contributions were by no means part of the established wisdom in the economics of the firm. Shackle had far less excuse than other economists for ignoring such works. He knew Andrews well (both had worked as researchers under Phelps-Brown in Oxford in the late 1930s). His complete neglect of the Carnegie school is despite his having visited Pittsburgh for a conference on uncertainty (the proceedings of which were published as Bowman, ed., 1958). Whilst there he met Herbert Simon (see Augier, 2000) and shortly afterwards he published a review of Simon's *Models of Man* (Shackle, 1959) in the same volume of the *Economic Journal* as Richardson's subversive (1959) paper on expectations and interdependent decision-making.

Don Lamberton had already recognized connections between such works, and with Shackle's work. With Andrews as a mentor, Lamberton was working on his doctorate at Oxford around the time that many of these new contributions appeared. He met Shackle, who was visiting Oxford, over an evening dinner before a student seminar at Nuffield College in 1959 and thus began an intermittent flow of correspondence that continued through the rest of Shackle's lifetime. After returning to his native Australia in 1960, Lamberton developed and taught at the University of New South Wales a course based around recent evolutionary and information-based approaches to the firm. Though he did not integrate these contributions into a textbook he did explore some linkages in his (1965) doctorate-based monograph on profits (which Shackle personally had recommended to Blackwell for publication). Although it was many years before textbooks began to appear which actually offered what Shackle's one had merely promised (Ricketts, 1987; Earl, 1995), a very obvious indication of linkages Shackle might reasonably have been expected to explore by 1970 materialized much sooner. This came in the now-classic monograph by Loasby (1976), himself a pupil of Charles Carter. Loasby not only employed ideas from the Carnegie School and Post Marshallian economists along with Shackle's thinking, but the rear of the dust-jacket of his book was an advertisement for seven of Shackle's own books that had been published by Cambridge University Press.

At the time Shackle's textbook appeared, he was not castigated for failing to grasp the opportunity to link his own work with that of recent knowledge-related contributions to the theory of the firm. Devletoglou reviewed the book in the *Economic Journal* (1973) and criticized Shackle for not using the book as an occasion for exploring the micro-foundations of macroeconomics and what these might imply for policy. However, he otherwise seemed inclined to reinforce Shackle's view that a theory of the firm should focus on the problem of doing business calculations in the face of uncertainty and on the role of the entrepreneur. As Devletoglou observed (1973, pp. 545-6),

> If uncertainty were entirely absent, and every individual in perfect knowledge of the situation, there would clearly be no occasion for anything in the nature of responsible management or control of production activity. Even marketing transactions in any realistic sense would not be necessary, and the flow of raw materials and productive services to the consumer would be entirely automatic.
>   ... the problem of forecasting becomes a significant part of the organization of the firm – with responsibility for such forecasting and organization centering on a unique class of producers, *i.e.*, the entrepreneurs.

These remarks should be kept in mind during the next section, as should the reference on Shackle's cover to the firm as the 'essential institutional means ... of confronting this problem of uncertainty'. I relate Shackle's vision not to heterodox writings on the firm from the 1950s and 1960 but to the earlier work by Coase (1937) on the nature of the firm.

4.3   SHACKLE AND COASE, MONEY AND ENTERPRISE

It seems most useful to begin an analysis of the relationship between Shackle's vision and Coase's work on the nature of the firm by noting that in his writings on macroeconomics Shackle gave considerable attention to money as an institution that facilitates coping with an open-ended choice environment. A persistent theme in Shackle's work is that investment spending can dry up if those who might make finance available, and/or those who might undertake spending on capital items, lose their nerve and decide to avoid commitment. Assets that might have been purchased today may be cheaper tomorrow in the event that pessimistic expectations turn out to be justified. When the future seems capable of going in a number of directions, each of which carries different implications, decision-makers can wait and see by holding liquid assets.

Shackle's view of liquidity (1988, pp. 236–7) brings together uncertainty and, in the jargon of modern industrial economics, 'asset-specificity'. General-purpose metal-machining equipment is liquid compared with, say, the highly specialized tooling that Henry Ford's engineers developed for producing the Model-T car. Even so, it is still very risky to own, rather than holding one's assets as money: circumstances may lead customers away from metal-based products towards, say, those of ceramic or plastic materials. By keeping liquid, a decision-maker sacrifices opportunities to achieve higher earnings streams – Ford's Model-T-specific machinery enabled the Model-T to be produced for lower outlays than general-purpose equipment would have made possible – and risks finding some assets more expensive to obtain at a later date. On the other hand, liquidity enables the decision-maker to reduce risks of capital loss.

Such perspectives on liquidity, which focus on the possibility of surprising discontinuities in the unfolding of economic events being the causes of changes in the market values of particular assets – what Shackle (1974) called kaleidic changes – are independent of the other key element of theories of money, namely, transaction costs. Shackle never used transaction cost terminology but it is clear that his broader theory of liquidity embraced their role, and that he saw costs of using markets as part of the problem of uncertainty, the waiting for relevant data to come in. For example, in speaking of a preference for liquidity in cases where people have received income and discontinuities and where carrying costs are not problematic, he writes of

> [T]he trouble of deciding what to buy, of finding suitable specimens of it, and the prospective trouble of finding for these specimens a buyer when some consumption goods shall eventually be needed. The key word in this sentence is 'finding'. *To find* has a meaning inseparably connected with another, that of *not knowing*. The clue to to meaning and nature of liquidity lies in its avoidance of the trouble arising from not knowing (Shackle, 1972, p. 215, emphasis in original).

Even in the absence of fears of kaleidic changes in long-term relative values, transaction costs militate against most physical assets being held as stores of value. The problems of finding and disposing of assets may be expected to increase with their specificity. This is a key reason why an equity shareholding in a company, which is not attached to ownership of any particular item legally owned by that company, will seem relatively liquid in normal times. One can, of course, conceive of patterns of corporate ownership in which shareholders actually owned particular assets and rented them out to firms or received profit dividends in proportion to the fraction of the firm's total assets that they owned, but the transactional barriers to such arrangements are obvious.

Given Shackle's analysis of the role of money, along with his emphasis on uncertainty and, implicitly, transaction costs, it would have been appropriate for him to consider Coase's (1937) 'The nature of the firm' in two of his books. He might first have discussed it in his famous (1967) examination of the development of economic theory in the period from 1926 to 1939, and then developed Coase's ideas in his 1970 text.

According to Coase (1937, p. 389), 'the distinguishing mark of the firm is the supersession of the price mechanism'. From a neoclassical perspective, his focus seems to be on the decision regarding whether or not to bring a marginal transaction inside the boundaries of the firm as a determining factor in the size of a firm. This was not what struck me when I first read his article as an undergraduate, not long after picking up Shackle's (1967) message about the significance of uncertainty in economic systems. Rather, from the Shacklean perspective, what stands out in Coase's portrait of the firm is that it is an institution in which resource owners provide services on the basis of *loosely specified* contracts, with the nature of the services they are to supply being decided by managers as events unfold.

Coase himself does not focus on contractual ambiguity. In the space of a few lines (1937, p. 391) he simply observes that it is important to note that the essence of a contract by which a resource owner agrees to obey the directions of an entrepreneur is that it should only state the limits to the latter's powers. Even so, contractual incompleteness is actually an essential precondition for his discussion of the coordinating and directing role of managers. If contracts of employment were fully specified, workers would know precisely what to do once they knew what the state of the world was. In reality, although managers may sometimes have to take decisions about what the state of the world should be seen to be, their broader role consists in allocating tasks so that employees do not pull in conflicting directions. (A third managerial role, as monitor – ensuring that what they have decided needs to be done actually gets done – is now prominent in the modern principal–agent literature, but was not central to Coase's seminal contribution.) Managers are seen as worth paying for to decide on and direct firms' operations where markets seem too costly to use to programme activities in a world of uncertainty.

There would be no need to hire managers and assume the risks that go with contractual ambiguities if comprehensive contingent claims contracts could easily be devised and implemented along the lines imagined in the Arrow–Debreu models of general equilibrium systems. But such contracts cannot be devised in a complex universe where surprise remains a possibility even if one has thought long and hard about what might happen, and where novel products and production processes are often being devised. Likewise, there would be no need for managers if activities could be arranged seamlessly by a series of short-term contracts without parties having continually to stop what they were doing in order to negotiate new deals or, if nothing had changed, to sign extensions of contracts that had just expired.

Open-endedness is the characteristic that particularly stands out when we start likening firms and money as institutional devices for making uncertainty less of a problem. Liquidity provides freedom to manoeuvre that highly specific assets do not and, as Foss (1994b, p. 47) notes, it is the flexibility of the firm as a contracting system that forms part of its rationale. It is the flexibility of, for example, employment contracts that enables transaction costs to be saved as business conditions change. Unfortunately, Shackle never drew the connection and he made no reference to Coase's article.

The fact that firms and money would both have no role in the zero transaction cost, closed-choice world of general equilibrium theory did not go unnoticed in Shackle's lifetime. In the mid-1970s both Goodhart (1975, p. 4) and Loasby (1976, pp. 165–6) commented on this point. In his Nobel Lecture, Coase himself later observed that 'I know of only one part of economics in which transaction costs have been used to explain a major feature of the economic system and that relates to the production and use of money' (Coase, 1991, p. 231). It is indeed puzzling that Shackle himself did not recognize the overlap between the theories of money and the firm and give attention to Coase on a similar scale to that which he lavished on the small group of scholars whom he cited with predictable regularity. As a postgraduate student at the LSE in 1937, Shackle would certainly have been reading *Economica* – he had himself published in this journal in 1936. Moreover, he had been working on the integration of macroeconomics and the economics of the firm in relation to the causes of the onset of trade-cycle downturns (see Shackle, 1938). He thus should have been ripe for becoming a rapid convert to and publicist of Coase's way of thinking, just as he had been captivated by Keynes's writings.

4.4   SHACKLE, CANTILLON AND SCHUMPETER

When the transaction cost programme took off in the late 1970s/early 1980s, it became, via the work of Williamson (1975, 1985), even more focused on the difficulties that specific assets pose in a world of uncertainty. The possibility of unpleasant surprises looms large in Williamson's writings, via his focus on opportunism as a barrier to mutually satisfactory dealings. Shackle might have been expected to appreciate this line of thinking, given that it also implicitly recognized another of his favourite topics, namely, creativity (for example, in respect of interpretations of what might legally be done within the wording of a contract). But Shackle did not choose to comment on how transaction cost economics related to his own work. Instead, he devoted considerable attention to trying to publicize the early writings of Richard Cantillon (1755) on entrepreneurship (see Shackle, 1988, especially chapter 4).

Cantillon's vision of the entrepreneur is of someone who makes commitments to take delivery of goods at a price known today with a view to selling them in the future at a higher price, which cannot presently be known. This picture can easily be related to the activities of roving merchants in the eighteenth century. On their travels, they bought cottage industry produce in the hope of selling it for a profit in the towns. Cantillon would have had no difficulty in recognizing similar kinds of entrepreneurs in the late twentieth century. Into this category would come those traders from former communist countries of eastern Europe who buy goods at duty free stores in the Persian Gulf to sell in their home countries. Also in this category are used-car dealers in New Zealand who regularly visit Japan to purchase heavily depreciated but low-mileage vehicles for resale to relatively impecunious private buyers in New Zealand. Such kinds of entrepreneurship are based on alertness to opportunities – the factor most stressed by Austrian writers such as Kirzner (1973) – and skill in valuing assets in different settings and bargaining over buying and selling prices.

Given Shackle's interest in the creative potential of human imagination and the role of surprise as a force for opening and closing opportunities, it is strange that he should focus so much on Cantillon's contribution. It portrays the entrepreneur often as little more than an arbitrageur or, at best, an intermediary who risks being left with unsold stocks or having to sell at a knockdown price. This is a very different vision from that associated with the work of Schumpeter (1934, 1939) and his (1943) theory of business dynamics in terms of 'creative destruction'. Cantillon's entrepreneur is not the residual claimant to the proceeds of innovation based on creative thinking and skill in engineering, design or marketing. The Schumpterian entrepreneur, by contrast, is proceeding into unfamiliar territory and faces major uncertainty on the cost side as well as on the revenue side, for many false trails and disappointments may be encountered before a vision can be turned into reality. Schumpeter's vision of the entrepreneur is a far more heroic image than that of Cantillon in relation to the microeconomics of the firm and the macroeconomics of employment. Schumpeter is talking about enterprise as an activity involving investment and employment, whereas Cantillon's view is applicable to those 'paper-shufflers' of the mid 1980s who earned their titles as 'entrepreneurs' in the tabloid press essentially by buying and selling existing assets, not because they had creative vision.

Shackle's early failure to acknowledge Schumpeter's work on business cycles is readily explicable in terms of timing, for his thesis on business cycles was published in 1938. Its republication, in 1968, provided a ready opportunity for Shackle to reflect on Schumpeter's contribution, but he did not do so in the new introduction that he added. Moreover, even in his later work, Shackle barely mentioned Schumpeter's contribution (for example, there is a fleeting comment in Shackle, 1974, p. 75, about Schumpeter being referred to by Keynes, 'as summarized by Wesley Mitchell', for his analysis of fixed investment). This is despite the compatibility between Shackle's kaleidic perspective and Schumpter's notion of 'creative destruction', and despite the fact that, for both authors, the clustering of innovations can initiate macroeconomic cycles (see further, Ford, 1994, chapter 6).

4.5   STRATEGIC MANAGEMENT AND THE RESOURCE-BASED VIEW OF THE FIRM

Despite his apparent enthusiasm for Cantillon's narrow vision of the nature of entrepreneurship, Shackle certainly did write about investment decision-making with reference to opportunity costs faced by managers in terms of how they use their time, and about firms essentially as established entities rather than newly created operations. Even in his early writings, Shackle (1938) was keen to present decision-makers as struggling in managerial terms to find a way forward in the face of uncertainty. Decisions that take the firm into new territory necessarily increase uncertainty and lead to hesitation and to periods of consolidation, particularly if investment is a crucial experiment that involves indivisibilities rather than gradually working up from pilot operations. Despite his lack of a Coasian perspective, he was thinking in terms of the individuals or teams of people who decide which risks to take as being the same people who have to take senior decisions concerning the management of projects previously embarked upon. As he put it (Shackle, 1938, p. 99),

> Since any conception of the future can be informed only by inference from the immediate and recent past, it is natural that a businessman should feel his way by desisting for a time, before embarking on further addition. An important addition to plant constitutes a change in the basis of his calculation, rendering his inferences as to future conditions and possibilities for his own business more difficult and insecure for the time being. Moreover, a considerable increase in the scale or scope of his operations will make at first a far more than proportional increase in the time and nervous energy which he must devote to mere management, as distinct from the planning of further progress.

This perspective is at odds with steady-state models of corporate growth that were subsequently proposed by scholars such as Marris (1964) but it provides the basis for Shackle's 'investment bunching' view of macroeconomic cycles. It has much in common with Penrose's (1959) *The Theory of the Growth of the Firm,* for it does not suggest firms have a long-run problem of diseconomies of size even though their growth profiles may exhibit 'plateau' phases. Note that Shackle's use of the word 'scope' in this context means diversification, exactly as in the modern literature.

Penrose explicitly argues that an increase in the pace of growth and hence in the size and/or scope of a firm cannot simply be achieved by hiring more managers to reduce the decision-making burden on existing managers. The problem is that it will take time for new managers to get to grips with the problems and resources of the firms they join and hence to become effective members of the management team. A more general statement of this problem is that it applies to the firm's stock of human resources in general. In other words, the activities that firm can take on at any moment and perform in a competent manner are constrained by the pool of experiences it can call upon and what it has been doing in the past. For example, we would not expect IBM suddenly to be able to switch successfully into car production from computers, nor Ford vice versa, even if the relevant physical assets could readily be bought and sold. The activities of producing cars and computers involved are very different in terms of the know-how they entail (see also Richardson, 1972). This is a theme that has become a core notion in an interdisciplinary research programme known in evolutionary economics and strategic management theory as the 'resource-based view of the firm (for a survey, see Mahoney and Pandian, 1992, which is reprinted in the excellent reader edited by Foss, ed., 1997). It is precisely this view that seems to underlie Shackle's writings about the nature of the firm:

> The firm's practical problem is not to start with a clean slate and survey the entire range of technological and market possibilities, for using its abstract total value of resources, that the world presents. At any moment when policy or plan is being formed, the firm is a going concern engaged in a particular skein of activities, equipped with certain plant and staffed by men with certain skills and experience. The question to be answered . . . is how to use these assets. (Shackle, 1970, pp. 29–30)

The recent emphasis on the firm's existing stock of resources arises from recognition that, contrary to the assumptions of neoclassical theory, much knowledge about production functions is not merely expensive. Rather, it is something that can only be picked up from experience of working with others who already have know-how but cannot readily articulate it. Firms with different histories will therefore have different prospective production costs in respect of a particular product because their degrees of competence differ. Perceived relative competence hence may have a major role in determining which activities a management team chooses to internalize. By contrast, the Coase/Williamson view of the nature of the firm takes our attention away from production costs and leads to a blinkered focus on the costs of fixing up deals and ensuring that one is not short-changed by opportunistic outsiders or employees (see further, Foss, 1992).

The question of 'how to use these assets' is one that simply will not go away in a Schumpeterian world where innovation and upgrading of rival products is continually taking place, making counter-attacks necessary in order to keep capacities utilized. Learning by workers and their managers also keeps expanding the output potential of existing assets as well as making time available for planning and coping with additions to the firm's stock of assets. But Shackle did not make these themes explicit in his (1970) text or highlight them elsewhere. From within economics it was left to Neil Kay (1984) to fill this gap, integrating Schumpeterian and Shacklean perspectives from the standpoint of an approach to the firm which seems to be of the transaction cost variety but which on closer examination turns out to be solidly Penrose-inspired.

Kay sees managers as worried by visions of sudden product obsolescence, the more so the more that they are operating in industries where technological change has been a regular feature of the competitive environment. Such managers are aware of their inability to foretell the future and expect to have to deal with unpleasant surprises. The problem then is how far they should try to insure their operations against sudden changes in the rules of the competitive game by taking on activities that use existing resources in conjunction with new assets involving new requirements in terms of competence. Such anxieties may limit the extent to which managers will seek to maximize synergies arising from competence in established markets and technologies. Instead, they often seem to prefer to venture into new technologies and markets where at first they will be somewhat out of their depths and vulnerable to competition from those with greater experience and specialization in these new activities. Kay argues that advantages of 'sticking to one's knitting' are commonly sacrificed because of the risks of 'having all one's eggs in the one basket' – unless it is judged that a synergy-based strategy offers a better way of weathering the sorts of surprises that might arise. (If there is a residual market in a collapsing industry, it may indeed pay to concentrate on getting synergy by concentrating purely on a related set of products for that market. In doing so, one might out-compete those who hedged their bets by diversifying as the shrinking market became more price competitive. However, precautionary diversification would have been the more sensible route for, say, the specialist slide-rule manufacturers whose ranges of products were rendered comprehensively obsolete by the technology that gave rise to the pocket calculator.)

Shackle's impact would no doubt have been greater had he sought to bring the work of scholars such as Penrose and Richardson into his writing about the nature of business activity. This logically would have led him, like Kay, in the direction of studying how strategic choices of diversification and vertical relationships can be used to make uncertainty bearable, and away from road to economic nihilism that clearly troubled many of his readers. However, there is also no doubt that those who teach strategic management may benefit from studying what Shackle has to say about the business of thinking about the future, which may be summarized as follows.

Once managers have imagined possible sequels to decisions the next question is how seriously they should take them. In Shackle's analysis, the proposed thought-strategy is to look for reasons for disbelief – that is to say, for other events that might prevent the taking place of the imagined outcomes if they are not themselves prevented from coming about. This strategy must eventually founder in a complex chain of infinite regress. Uncertainty will thus remain and with it the need to judge just how much to sacrifice by way of guarding against worrying prospects, however precisely they have been imagined – control and flexibility may both be sought-after in a world of uncertainty but both come at a price. Feelings of pessimism or optimism about the prospects of particular projects seem likely to depend on the ranges of ideas that managers entertain and their personal systems for assigning degrees of disbelief. These ranges must be finite if boundaries are to be placed on possibilities and a basis for action settled upon. What managers will be able to imagine depends on the mental *elements* that they have at their disposal to combine in an alphabetic manner (Shackle, 1979, p. 21). Moreover, these elements need to have an emotional dimension, the ability to arrest the attention by virtue of their attractiveness or alarming connotations, for otherwise they are likely to end up being shunted to the back of the decision-maker's mind. If particular elements are missing from managers' thought-schemes then the managers are likely to be blind to threats and opportunities that could be construed with reference to these elements.

4.6   ENTREPRENEURSHIP AND INTERNALIZATION

Shackle's failure to include Coase in his own repertoire of elements for constructing economic analysis becomes all the more frustrating if we examine how Coase's work relates to Cantillon and Schumpeter and the resource-based view of the firm. In his article on the nature of the firm, Coase defines an entrepreneur as 'the person or persons who, in a competitive system, take the place of the price mechanism in the direction of resources (Coase, 1937, p. 388, footnote 2). The Russian 'entrepreneur' who acts as a market maker is consistent with Coase's definition as well as with Cantillon's, for otherwise there is no coming together of supply signals from duty free stores in the Persian Gulf with the latent demand from residents of Moscow. Coase's definition would also be consistent with a labelling as an 'entrepreneurial team' members of property development firm that subcontracts all the operations involved in designing, erecting and selling an estate of new homes or a major skyscraper complex. The complementary nature of the stages involved in construction projects makes it unlikely that grand schemes will take shape in physical terms unless there is an individual or team who can stitch together a diverse collection of contracts and orchestrate the delivery of the services involved.[1] This is precisely the sort of

---

[1]   See Earl (1996) for a detailed discussion, in the light of Coase and Richardson, of Sabbagh's (1989) excellent case study account of the construction of Worldwide Plaza in New York.

example that Shackle might have been expected to use to illustrate 'inter-necessary' activities in his (1970) textbook whilst showing how such complementarities can be dealt with in practice.

There are, however, many conceivable institutional devices for dealing with complementarities of this kind and a fundamental gap in Shackle's writing is that, unlike Coase, he never examined ways in which problems of knowledge in business affect the division of business activities between firms. These problems are particularly significant in the case of new products. In many cases, problems of knowledge are such that it is impossible to turn an entrepreneurial vision into reality without getting involved in managing many activities that might, in principle, be contracted in the market (see Langlois and Robertson, 1995). Much of Coase's use of the term 'entrepreneur' is actually in the context of what we would nowadays call the business of *management*. That is to say, he refers to the coordination of activities that have been internalized within a single legal entity via loosely specified contracts, as well as monitoring the timely delivery of services that have been ordered by rather more precise, inter-firm contracts.[2] Normally the management role is discussed as if the firm under consideration has been in existence for some time and the issues of interest are precisely which activities have been internalized and why managers are not attempting to handle even more. However, it is easy to see scope for market failure that may lead an entrepreneur to create a multi-activity firm in order to exploit the opportunity to fill a market gap or deliver an innovative product that seems present.

One reason why an entrepreneur may opt to coordinate a variety of related activities is that s/he may find it impossible to find anyone who shares her/his vision. A classic example here is of the author who sees a market for a book but continually receives rejection letters from the publishers to whom s/he sends the manuscript. Here, publishers are in effect intermediaries who are refusing to take Cantillon-type risks over the manuscript in question. Possible solutions to such a market failure are self-publication or paying a ('vanity') publisher a risk premium to handle the production and marketing of the book. The self-publication route need not involve the creation of a Coasian firm, for typesetting and printing can be handled by subcontractors, as can warehousing, order processing and publicity. Such an author may even be able to find other authors, with established reputations, who think the book is of high quality and are prepared to endorse it and thereby help potential buyers (in the first instance, bookstores) cope with the 'experience good' nature of such a product. For such a venture to succeed, the

---

[2]   In the case studied by Sabbagh (1989), there is evidence of both kinds of entrepreneurial activity in Coase's sense, for the property developer farmed out the construction coordination task to a construction management company.

entrepreneurial writer needs not only to be justified in her/his faith in the product but also competent in choosing reliable, cost-effective subcontractors and in raising finance to pay for services ahead of sales. (As a related aside it should be noted that the entrepreneurial skill of many publishers includes the ability to judge, based on experience in the industry, how many copies a book may sell, not just how few. Most academics that serve as referees for publishers are prone to underestimate potential sales of books they regard as publishable propositions, even if they themselves are experienced authors. Though each book is to some extent a new product, knowledge of how many copies of somewhat similar books were sold may be invaluable in sizing up the viability of a proposal.)

Problems with property rights over knowledge may mean that the product will only reach the market if the entrepreneur gets into the business of producing and distributing it rather than selling to others the right to do so via a licensing or franchise arrangement or by subcontracting these tasks. The entrepreneur may be reluctant to get subcontractors involved for fear that they may steal the concept or produce a profitable variation on it. The trouble is that before a subcontractor can even make a confident estimate of the price at which a particular service can be performed it is necessary to spell out its specification in detail, but once this has been done, the cat, so to speak, is out of the bag.

This is very close to Arrow's (1971, p. 74) paradox regarding scope for failure in markets for information. As Arrow points out, to know whether information is worth buying, we need to know what information we are going to get, but once this is explained to us we have no need to buy it. The Arrow paradox promotes internalization in cases where the gap in the market simply concerns a failure to supply an existing type of product in a particular territory. Here, it is unlikely that an alert person will be able to capture the bulk of potential profits by selling the information about the market opportunity to an existing supplier who presently focuses on other territories. The latter will be unwilling to pay for the information without having a good idea of what the information is, but once thus alerted in general terms may see no need to pay handsomely to get specific details from the former. This is a very acute version of the more general problem that Lachmann (1976, p. 59) has noted for entrepreneurs: it is impossible to exploit a gap in the market without running the risk of drawing the attention of other, less alert businesses to its presence.

Silver's (1984) contribution to the resource-based view of the firm provides my final example of how problems of knowledge may lead entrepreneurs to engage in 'do-it-yourself' production and/or distribution. It centres on problems in articulating a novel vision to subcontractors in technical terms and/or convincing them that it will make good business sense. On Silver's analysis, path-breaking projects will tend to involve considerable vertical integration. Once their ideas are tried, tested and spread widely, pioneering entrepreneurs may later find their integrated businesses having to deal with competitors who can rely more on subcontractors, each of whom is keenly competing for business (contrast, say, Henry Ford's early operations with Japanese followers such as Toyota; cf. Langlois and Robertson, 1989, 1995).

Pressures for entrepreneurs to engage in 'do-it-yourself' early in a product's life will be increased if production necessitates new investments characterized by asset specificity. Subcontractors might only be able to complete their contributions to the process of production and distribution if they invest in specific capital items (dies and moulds, for example, or training workers in special skills). If they do not share the vision of the entrepreneur it may be difficult for the entrepreneur to realize her/his vision without paying for such investments on behalf of the subcontractors. Alternatively, the entrepreneur might have to pay much higher fees to the subcontractor to insure against the risk that production will be abandoned long before the capital items have generated an acceptable rate of return (cf. the passage quoted earlier from the cover of Shackle, 1970).

The point here is related to the book example, where the author could not convince conventional publishers that her/his proposed book could profitably find a market. It is also an inverse of the Arrow problem. In this case the entrepreneur is not worried so much about opportunistic behaviour by subcontractors with whom s/he discusses the project. Rather, the worry is that subcontractors could make a mess of things because it is impossible to show them the vision of what needs to be done without first doing it in practice. Given that even the entrepreneur may have a somewhat incomplete vision of how the new concept is going to be made to work, there may reasonably be expected to be considerable learning by doing, such as frequent adjustments to specifications as the product is debugged and the production process fine-tuned. Such adjustments may be cheaper to coordinate if activities are internalized, rather than each change needing to be the subject of a fresh contract, which might also entail payments of penalties if existing contracts have to be torn up.

To sum up this section we can say that, given his interest in problems of knowledge associated with multi-stage production and distribution systems, there is much that Shackle might have been expected say on the relationship between entrepreneurship and internalization. These two phenomena go hand in hand, the more so the greater the value of resources required to turn an imagined venture into reality and the more difficult it is to find other parties with whom risks can safely be shared. In the absence of easy access to venture capital, the best way for someone with entrepreneurial capabilities to make things happen is by being achieving a position as an influential visionary within an existing firm that has already assembled a formidable pool of resources. Otherwise, one must simply begin with a small-scale venture and gradually grow one's own firm (as Akio Morita did with Sony) or run the risks associated with trying to sell access to one's ideas via licensing, franchising and so on. The choice may come down to perceived capabilities: there is no guarantee that people who can see unexploited market opportunities or who have new visions for products or marketing will possess the managerial talents required to make a success of coordinating the activities they opt to internalize.

4.7   MAKING SENSE OF SHACKLE'S SCHOLARSHIP

Though justifiably praised for its eloquence, Shackle's writing is typical of an old-fashioned style of scholarship that does not involve the use of copious footnoting or Harvard referencing and massive bibliographies. In writing about the business predicament, Shackle cited a far smaller range of sources than the refereeing process would nowadays permit, and he continued to be able to do so late in his career even after modern scholarly and citations styles had become established. It is unfortunate that he failed to draw connections that now seem obvious between his oft-repeated lines of thinking and themes central to works by other writers who, like Shackle, were not prepared to accept the deterministic paradigm. In this section I consider how he ended up being so selective in his use of other scholars' works.

Historians of economic thought can savour a veritable feast of Shacklean delights in the extensive archives that he deposited at Cambridge University Library, a catalogue of which has been compiled by Cann (2000), with an accompanying guided tour by Littlechild (2000). The latter also notes the existence of a catalogue of other papers and offprints once held by Shackle. There is a further smaller archive at the University of Liverpool. Until historians of economic thought have made a careful study of the Shackle papers, we can only make conjectures regarding the extent to which simple ignorance of particular works can account for his neglect of them. As noted in chapter 3, any academic is likely sometimes to fail to make use of relevant ideas owing to bounded rationality, or even to fail to cite contributions despite being familiar with them. The risk of this must increase in the case of academics that spend a lot of their time writing rather than reading.

A clear picture of Shackle's academic life emerges from Ford's (1994) biography and from the details that Littlechild and Cann provide of the Shackle collection in Cambridge. It is of a man who spent a huge amount of time writing not only for publications but dealing with correspondence from hundreds of academics from all over the world, including a veritable who's who of the great economists of the twentieth century. Ford (1994, pp. 12–13) and Littlechild (2000, pp. 332–7) emphasize that he wrote in a slow, methodical manner and that, in his reading, he returned to classic sources time and again, annotating them carefully. His style of work was definitely the antithesis of some modern researchers who frantically scan abstracts for the latest relevant contributions whilst presuming that anything over five years old is out of date.

Shackle's failure to pick up the work of Simon and other behavioural economists on decision-making in the face of bounded rationality clearly did not arise from ignorance. Possibly it reflected instead Shackle's disappointment that Simon would not incorporate his general philosophical critique of subjective expected utility (SEU) theory. In a note reviewing Simon's (1983) *Reason in Human Affairs*, Shackle (1985, p. 246) wrote that 'Simon dismisses SEU, not on the ground of its being meaningless (as I would) but because no human mind could encompass the task of construction.' He seems to be saying here that fundamental uncertainty is a different kind of problem from bounded rationality. This is a line of thinking to which Dunn (2000) has recently given thoughtful support. Certainly, as regards investment decision-making, the difficulties associated with solving the Richardson Problem arise essentially because of the interdependence amongst firms, not because the problem is inherently tricky to make sense of in general terms. To put is another way: the need to outguess each other's behaviour is a problem of infinite regress that is not solved by extra cognitive processing power. (So, too, it might be noted, is the problem of searching for information that makes optimization logically impossible in the face of uncertainty.) But it is a moot point whether uncertainty regarding future innovations is really a consequence of bounded rationality, arising because managers cannot anticipate creativity that goes on in rival institutions.

It is possible that Shackle did not recognize potential intellectual synergies because his style of academic research was so different from authors whom he failed to cite. Consider how he differed from Coase. In the 1930s Shackle was operating very much as an armchair theorist and writing in a technical manner, whereas Coase was following in Marshall's footsteps and anticipating the behaviouralists' strategy of using empirical inquiries as a means for provoking theoretical activity (cf. Coase, 1991, p. 234). It is also unclear whether, much later in his career, Shackle would have been particularly happy with Coase's work and extensions of it had he examined them. It is legitimate to read much of Coase's analysis as being firmly within the closed neoclassical style of thinking, even though his argument about the rationale of the firm implies a commitment to an open-ended view of economic systems. As Foss (1994b, pp. 46–7) has pointed out, the Coasian manager is depicted as dealing with a given set of inputs and outputs in a transaction cost-minimizing manner, and analysis in the 1937 paper is conducted in comparative static terms. A similar tension is evident in the work of Williamson (1975, 1985), who is arguably the most influential of Coase's followers (see Foss, 1994b, pp. 52–7).

It is interesting to note that, as the transaction cost analysis of the firm has taken off, it is the static elements in Coase's analysis that have been taken on board. Neoclassical contributions have had little to say about ways in which managerial decisions about what to make the subject of very loosely specified contracts may be affected by concerns about the possible emergence of new production processes and products. A popular area of interest, for example, is vertical integration, the make-or-buy decision, and managers are typically portrayed as having a good idea of the kinds of games that subcontractors might engage in, given the extent of asset specificity involved in the production process. Possible technological obsolescence is not a prominent theme in such work, and neither is the possible strategic use of surprise, in Shackle's sense (1972, pp. 422–6), to rewrite the rules of the game. For Shackle, by contrast, the secret of success is novelty and the ability to outflank business rivals by surprising them through being able to imagine and implement things of which they could not conceive. The focus of neoclassical transaction cost economists contrasts sharply with that of Shackle-inspired contributors such as Kay (1984, particularly chapter 5), who focuses on ways in which management teams' choices of activities and methods of organization may be shaped by worries about vulnerability to technological change.

It is easy, when seeking to understand Shackle's scholarship, to give insufficient consideration to strategic aspects of Shackle's approach to his writing. His extraordinary personal humility and philosophical approach to the subject could make him appear as someone most unlikely to be engaging in the strategic use of rhetoric. However, although Ford's intellectual biography highlights Shackle's generosity and Christian humility, it also shows how Shackle was exceedingly resistant to changing his own theories (Ford, 1994, p. 482). Ford also reveals some of the diversionary tactics Shackle used to uphold his position in the face of critics (*ibid*, pp. 102–4). He argues that Shackle 'surely has exaggerated his all-embracing contention' (*ibid*, p. 432) that Keynes only really saw in 1937 what the central message of the *General Theory* really was. Behind the humble exterior there lurked a man with a vision of economics to sell and his skills as a writer, so frequently remarked upon, had rhetorical uses as well as having the properties of eloquence and lucidity.

To understand his method of writing, I think it is vital to keep in mind the frequency with which he quoted (for example, 1967, p. 135) Isaiah Berlin's use of the Archilochus line, 'The fox knows many things, the hedgehog knows one big thing', in distinguishing different approaches to science. An examination of Shackle's career reveals him as seeming to believe it worth operating as a hedgehog rather than a fox. He had a handful of key messages he wanted to convey about the nature of economics and the human predicament and he sought to get his messages across by citing a select band of authors whose work seemed especially useful towards that end.

Shackle's lukewarm reception to the idea of bounded rationality as a basis for criticizing subjective expected utility theory is worth reconsidering mindful of his motivation to interest others in his own critique and alternative theory. The investment decision may indeed be non-probabilistic in nature, for if managers misjudge the actions of those engaged in competitive and complementary investment, then they may not get a further chance to take a better decision regarding the problem at hand. If things go badly wrong they may be out of a job and/or the competitive environment may have changed irreversibly due to their own actions and those of others. However, regardless of whether fundamental uncertainty is capable of being reduced in theoretical terms to a problem of bounded rationality, Shackle would have been on tricky ground if he accepted Simon's perspective with enthusiasm. The problem is that the non-probabilistic decision environment might result in behaviour that is better described in the terms outlined by Simon and his colleagues – in other words, based upon simple rules – than in terms of Shackle's potential surprise model.

Cantillon is someone upon whom Shackle could lavish praise for his early writings on entrepreneurship, *not* because Shackle was setting out to study entrepreneurship in all its facets but because he saw employers' uncertainties about future revenue streams as being central to Keynes's theory of employment in a monetary economy. As Shackle (1974, p. 9), put it,

> The employer is Cantillon's merchant, who signs contracts to obtain the means of production at known prices in order to sell, when it shall have been produced, a product whose price, when he makes these contracts, he does not know. How then can he know what an extra man's work will be worth to him? He cannot know, or he would have no claim to be called an enterpriser, and that is the point.

Given his desire to make this basic point, Shackle could have felt uncomfortable if he had pursued some of the theoretical complementarities considered in this chapter.

Consider once again the links between the theory of money and the theory of the firm. An enthusiastic embrace of Coase's insight about the nature of the firm would have had unfortunate rhetorical connotations for Shackle's writings, given his desire to push the line that macroeconomic systems are inherently prone to kaleidic instability. The flexibility provided by money contributes to instability by enabling holders of money *not* to signal what they will ultimately spend it on and when they will spend it. By contrast, the flexibility that vague employment contracts offers to managerial decision-makers may be more likely to contribute to the resilience of the economic system, as Loasby (1976, p. 166) points out. This point is amplified the more that it is in the long-run interests of managers and employees to be flexible and to pull together – rather like the population of a country in a wartime fight for survival. In such a situation, planned coordination and the issuing of directives can be a far more effective system for getting things done than would a market-based approach of using new price incentives to encourage people to fix up new deals. As firms become larger and less prone to have all their eggs in the one basket, their managers can think more in terms of the long haul and be less prone to hair-trigger reactions to changes in the state of the news. Suppose the news is of a change in the pattern of current demand rather than in its total volume. If so, managers who coordinate the use of modern flexible production methods increasingly can be quite insulated to surprises that would be disastrous for enterprises based around specialization to produce a specific design at least cost.

Here, then, is a paradox. For all his criticism of neoclassical equilibrium theory, Shackle can best convince his readers about the significance of the kaleidic perspective if he sets it out alongside the textbook neoclassical theory of the firm. In the textbook treatment, relational contracting is conspicuous by its absence, as is strategic diversification, with financial markets ever prodding for short-term profits via their interest in the latest quarterly results. Economic kaleidics has less rhetorical appeal if one's mental stereotype is the Japanese method of corporate organization, with lifetime employment relationships, incestuous cross-ownership patterns and close ties with banks. Such institutional devices facilitate long-term investment planning and business can be conducted with an absence of perennial worries about take-over raids. If things turn sour, they enable restructuring to be achieved largely without corporate resources having to be returned to the market and without workers being made redundant and having to search for new positions (see Dore, 1986).

Similar problems would have arisen for Shackle if he had sought to consider what lessons the management literature might have in respect of precautionary tactics and institutions by which business decision-makers seek to make uncertainty less problematic (my words here echo those of McQueen, 1994, pp. 43–4). A well-run firm is developed with a view to its being a long-lived institution for coping with uncertainty rather than an operation whose managers become bewildered by an infinite array of possibilities and thus end up flailing incoherently or paralyzed. It can be argued that much of the writing in the management area presents problems for Shackle's Cantillon-inspired vision of the entrepreneur as an agent who heroically shoulders uncertainty. Many of the policies and tendencies of managers seem decidedly unheroic and positively aimed at reducing the riskiness of investments. By way of example, in addition to the hedging diversification strategies of the kind discussed by Neil Kay (1984), consider the following:

1. The use of short-term payback periods in investment appraisal. This is essentially a simple decision rule of the kind emphasized by Simon, which simply ignores the more distant future rather than trying to ask what possibilities might eventuate and how seriously they ought to be taken.

2. The suggestion by Cyert and March (1963) that, rather than facing up to uncertainty, managers often select strategies based on 'uncertainty avoidance' or attempts to achieve a 'negotiated environment'.

3. The widespread suggestion in the strategic management literature that firms should only venture into territories in which they have reason to believe they have a *sustainable competitive advantage*, such as a product, production process, supplier system or distribution system which others will find it very difficult to copy. For example, John Kay (1993) makes a very strong case for the competitive role of what he calls 'architecture', in other words, a distinctive collection of relational contracts that enables highly flexible responses and effective exchanges of information. More generally we can say that the over-riding theme of the resource-based view of the firm is that firms should keep to areas where they have distinctive capabilities.

4. If relational contracting is not enough to manage supply chains, firms with the capacity to acquire or develop appropriate capabilities can use vertical integration to achieve greater *control* wherever it would be problematic to obtain replacement up-stream inputs, down-stream demand or distribution services. Neil Kay (1997) has recently suggested that vertical integration is driven by the concerns regarding the difficulty of replacing of suppliers and/or customers who cease to deal with a firm, rather than by asset specificity. In a sense, this involves a return to the perspective offered in Galbraith's (1967) *New Industrial State*, a work that also emphasizes how advertising might be used to manage demand. To reinforce this line of thinking one can turn to recent work by Dunn (2001) on the significance of Galbraith's writings for the Post Keynesian theory of the firm, which complements Dunn's (2000) contribution on fundamental uncertainty and its role in the theory of the firm.

These lines of thinking lead to a view of strategic management as an activity aimed at bringing uncertainty within narrower bounds in order to reduce the vulnerability of a firm's asset base to losses of value (Beckett, 1996). It is more in the nature of cautious risk management than the taking of courageous, all-or-nothing leaps in the dark that involve placing the entire firm in jeopardy.

4.8   CONCLUDING THOUGHTS

Shackle managed to write much about the business predicament without writing much about entrepreneurship and business institutions along lines that would have been possible on the basis of works available during his lifetime. Towards the end of his career he sought to publicize the writings of Cantillon. His reasons for doing so seem, however, to be based less on an interest in how firms do in practice cope with uncertainty than on his desire to highlight the speculative nature of business and scope for macroeconomic instability. Within his writings there are, nonetheless, fragments which suggest his view of firms had much in common with some of the most up-to-date writing in the area, for he saw firms as ongoing organizations that comprise pools of resources more suited to some tasks than others. For all his interest in Cantillon's view of business as a speculative activity, he did not see enterprise in the mainstream way as simply as the hiring of factors of production 'off the peg' to produce a particular set of outputs in a specific way. Unfortunately, he largely left it to others to write an economics of the firm in which knowledge, creativity, uncertainty and prospects for surprise are central themes. His failure to shoulder this task himself has made it easier for critics to condemn his philosophy of economics as nihilistic. This is in contrast to the constructive approach of scholars such as Loasby (1976) and Kay (1984). They lead the way in writing about firms by interweaving Shacklean themes with ideas from industrial economics and strategic management, seeking to identify ways in which uncertainty and fears of unpleasant surprises can be prevented from paralyzing choosers into inaction.

Shackle's work on the firm has aroused most interest in relation not to the function and forms of firms but to the problem of choosing between rival investment schemes once conjectures have been formed concerning their possible gain and loss outcomes. However, one can also benefit from reading the transaction cost and resource-based literatures on the firm from a Shacklean standpoint. Shackle's work is not merely a powerful source of the message 'beware of the possibility of discontinuities and the dangers or irreversible commitments', it also leads to the conclusion that a firm is limited in what it may be expected to try to do not merely by its physical assets and past knowledge of using them but also by the particular standpoints from which its decision-makers gather information and view the world. However, some of Shackle's own messages are somewhat tempered by reading his contributions in the light of related literatures. On the one hand we have his vision of the entrepreneur as someone who heroically shoulders risks. On the other, there the vision of the entrepreneur as someone who may be acutely aware that projects will only be worth embarking upon if the degree of contestability of the market in question can be carefully managed to ensure that business risks fall within acceptable bounds.

5. Managerialism and the Economics of the Firm

5.1   INTRODUCTION

Unlike physicists, economists operate in a reflexive relationship with their subject matter. That is to say, their ideas can have an impact on the workings of the system that they are trying to understand. In turn, changes in how the system works may provoke economists to rethink their views of how it works, leading to further changes as policymakers are influenced by their writings. In this chapter I explore the impact that the writings of economists have had over the past two decades on how policymakers that oversee corporations and public sector agencies set out to make their organizations perform more efficiently. This period has seen a remarkable change in the managerial ethos in many countries. In most cases, it was instigated by right-wing politicians or by agencies such as the International Monetary Fund. In the most extreme case, New Zealand, however, sweeping reforms began in 1984 under 'labour' politicians that were desperate to find a way to stop a slide down OECD per-capita income rankings and into rising indebtedness. The second half of this chapter includes a reflection on this extreme case.

The managerialist world-view that constitutes the new microeconomic orthodoxy can be framed in terms of a Lakatosian scientific research programme (Lakatos, 1970). It has as its hard core the following axioms:

- People are basically selfish and will only undertake actions that are in the social interest if they stand to benefit sufficiently themselves.
- People tend to be untrustworthy and operate in an opportunistic manner; if they believe that, because of an information asymmetry, they can get away with something that is in their personal interest at the expense of others, then they will do so.
- Workers lack an intrinsic motivation to perform to the best of their capabilities.
- Innovation and high productivity levels only thrive if there is sustained risk of losing one's position to more dynamic competitors.
- There is considerable slack to be taken up in economic systems that have

been insulated for a long time from the pressures of hotly contested markets.

- Without gross inequality of incomes, the mass of the population will not be sufficiently motivated to take the risks necessary to elevate themselves in terms of income and wealth.
- It is not necessary for managers to have experience in performing the tasks that they oversee, for generic management skills, such as those obtained via a reputable MBA programme, can be applied to problem-solving in general.
- There is no need to build relations between workers and managers or organizations and their 'customers' on a humanistic basis (contrast with Lutz, 1999); all that matters for the success of such interactions are the costs and benefits that the parties to a transaction perceive.
- Microeconomic policies need to be supplemented by a strong macroeconomic policy that is concerned above all with the control of inflation, for in an inflationary environment the efficient working of markets is impeded by the noise that the non-simultaneous adjustment of prices to inflationary pressures introduces into decision-makers' information sets.

Policy-making based on these axioms largely reduces to the application of simple 'do' and 'don't' rules such as:

- Impediments to international competition, such as tariffs, quotas, non-tariff barriers and limits on parallel importing should be removed.
- Impediments to employers' freedom to terminate employment contracts or bargain with individual workers should be removed.
- Wherever possible social welfare-supporting activities formerly undertaken by the State (such as the provision of housing, healthcare and education) should be returned to the market, and benefits should be cut to discourage claims by those who could work if they really had to.
- The advocacy of actions/purchasing/funding of outputs should be separated from the administration of actions/provision of outputs.
- Organizations should subcontract the supply of inputs to specialist outside agencies where possible, and/or or failing that, they should introduce internal markets; no supplier should be able to presume that they have a captive market and customers should indicate this by periodically calling for fresh supply tenders from anyone who wishes to put in a bid to be a supplier.
- Managers should be hired on short-term contracts that include performance-related bonuses as a major part of the total remuneration.
- Marginal income tax rates should be cut, particularly for higher incomes

to provide better extrinsic motivation to work hard and take risks.

- Organizational restructuring should create environments in which workers vie with each other for the rewards of being more productive, beginning with a downsizing of the labour force in which existing employees are required to compete for a smaller number of revamped jobs.
- Government departments should be corporatized and, once running as commercial entities, they should be privatized.
- Performance should be audited frequently and those whose performance is not in the top league should be denied access to further resources.
- Output that cannot be quantified should not be considered as output for audit purposes.
- No resources should be allocated to activities that have not been justified in terms of a business plan.
- Let managers decide what workers should do, and when, rather than the workers whose wellbeing is affected by such decisions.
- To ensure that a corporate or bureaucratic entity has unity of purpose in its competitive struggle for survival and resources, it must have a mission statement and corporate plan.
- To ensure that politicians and reserve bankers do not seek to pursue their own ends to the detriment of the performance of the economy, the former need to be legally constrained to act in a fiscally responsible manner and the latter must be hired on the basis of short-term contracts that require them to meet particular anti-inflation performance standards via their monetary management and enable them to operate without political interference.

Most academic economists will be familiar enough with many of these elements of managerialism from their own workplaces, where they observe, for example:

- Growth in the number of senior-level managerial positions relative to academic and general staff.
- Widening of the pay differentials between senior university managers and operational staff.
- Increased use of short-term contracts and adjunct/sessional staff.
- Increased pressure to fund operations from competitively raised research grants, industrial sponsorship, or full-fee-paying international students.
- Shifts away from a ludic to a banausic learning focus (cf. Holbrook, 1995a, 1995b) – that is to say, away from a focus on learning for intrinsic interest, towards a 'learning for the real world', craft-oriented delivery focus.

- Increasing corporatization, via the development of mission statements (often at faculty 'retreats'), shifts in the style of the workplace décor and expected dress standards, and the use of slick PowerPoint lecture presentations whose highly scripted nature limits scope for profitable improvization in response to student questions and whose set-up costs, in contrast to the now-frowned-upon chalk-and-talk mode of teaching inhibit changes when next the subject is taught.
- The McDonalization of teaching, at least at the introductory level, in which students are processes in huge numbers with the aid of highly dehumanizing programmed teaching systems and do not build up any kind of relationship with their lecturing staff (see Ritzer, 2000).
- An emphasis on well-defined and immediate results, with a pressure to publish articles in journals with high 'impact factors' and a positive discouragement to work on long-term book projects, or the refusal to grant sabbatical leave unless there is a plan of definite measurable outputs against which performance can be assessed, rather than allowing sabbatical leave as an opportunity for wider reading and reflection.
- A progressive increase in student/staff ratios coupled with students increasingly being self-funded by part-time jobs that conflict with the needs of full-time study, leading to greater pressures on teaching staff in terms of inputs or to dumb down grades in order to maintain student numbers and, thereby, academic jobs.

The change towards a much more hotly contested working environment, less based on humanistic considerations or long-term employment and trading relationships looks particularly extraordinary as a measure of the power of proponents of this point of view when one notes how radically it contrasts with the world of Japanese business during its period of ascendancy, from which very different policy lessons might have been learnt. It also is at odds with emerging thinking in the literature on relationship marketing and supply-chain management, which has a distinctly Marshallian flavour in its focus on the development of goodwill. The obvious question, then, is how did this perspective get developed?

In sections 5.2 to 5.5 of this chapter, I attempt to make sense of the emergence of managerialism in terms of the influence of academic writing. I do so with an emphasis on how the messages in particular leading contributions to economic theory, such as those from Coase, Hayek, Baumol, Williamson and Leibenstein, were not properly grasped by those who set out applying. In sections 5.6 to 5.8 I then critically examine the impact of managerialism, with special reference to the New Zealand case. The pro-market lobbyists and designers of public policy can be charged not only with displaying a lack of insight when reading such authors. They also seem unaware of – or have failed to absorb the implications of – other, well-conceived writing in the very same area, that points towards very different perspectives on the nature of business management and productive relations. Ideology appears to limit both what these powerful people read and how they interpret it; wider reading, with a more open mind, leads to a much more pragmatic view of the roles of markets and managers. The same can be said of some critics of managerialism, and I begin by discussing charges that Herbert Simon is responsible for the change in ethos, after which I present my own interpretation of it.

5.2   HERBERT SIMON'S ALLEGED ROLE

From the standpoint of public administration research, Dennard (1995) and Davis (1996) have blamed Herbert Simon for what they characterize as a neo-Darwinian view of management. Central to their case is the suggestion that Simon's work (particularly his 1945 *Administrative Behaviour* and his 1957 *Models of Man*) reduces management and work generally to information processing and problem solving, removing any analytical interest in the human side of workplace interaction. This perspective can be challenged on a number of counts.

First, if we take Horn's (1995) *The Political Economy of Public Administration* as an exemplar of the interaction between academic research and policy-making at the highest level – since it is based on Horn's 1988 Harvard doctorate and was published while he was Secretary to the New Zealand Treasury – it is clear that Simon's work is completely absent from the discussion or references, which is dominated by the transaction cost approach. It was also clear to me from my time in New Zealand that few of that country's other technocrats or pro-business lobbyists would have encountered much of Simon's thinking in any local training they received in economics. Thinking at the Treasury in the 1980s and early 1990s was notoriously dominated by economists trained at the University of Canterbury, whose economics department was thoroughly neoclassical in its approach.

Secondly, as I have argued at greater length elsewhere (Earl, 2001a, pp. xvii–xviii), there is no basic contradiction between taking a rule-based view of human thinking and the view that people have emotions that affect how they choose and feel about particular situations. The key point is that the rules we use to choose, like those in a Lakatosian scientific research programme, exist in the context of a hierarchical structure: workers have principles that they use to guide their lives and get very hot under the collar when they find themselves in situations at odds with these codes of conduct.

Thirdly, as Augier (2001, pp. 328–9) points out, Simon emphasized the significance of altruistic behaviour and suggested that economists needed to pay more attention to the way in which employees come to identify with the goals of the organizations for which they work. Moreover, the central influence on Simon, when he wrote the doctorate that eventually became his classic (1945) book, was Chester Barnard's (1938) *The Functions of the Executive*, which argues that authority in organizations is something granted by workers insofar as they respect the leadership of managers. On this analysis, authority is not something that a chief executive officer can get by hiring more managers to order and cajole workers into offering higher productivity levels if this would take them beyond their zone of tolerance.

Whilst Simon's analysis may thus have been unfairly blamed for providing foundations for dispassionate neo-Darwinian managerial styles, I think that his satisficing perspectives provide a useful way of making sense of how workers have ended up accepting the burdens that this style of management entail. Not all notions of what is acceptable are immutable principles, though on some occasions workers do resign 'on principle', objecting to what they are being asked to do. In many areas, workers may judge what they should tolerate from their bosses with the aid of external reference standards. Hence, if, for whatever reason, employers in other firms succeed in getting away with increasing their demands on workers, then those employed in other organizations may count themselves lucky if demands on themselves are cranked up rather less, even though they would have objected vehemently in the absence of any precedents. As a close friend and fellow academic ruefully remarked to me, whilst talking about his early-retirement strategy, 'We have accepted increasing pressures just like the proverbial frog that does not jump out of a cooking pot when the temperature is gradually cranked up to fatal levels, even though it would have jumped out immediately had the pot been hot when it was first placed inside it.' Or as my (former) head of department remarked when I lamented the lack of time for serious reflective scholarship, 'The world has changed; you can't say "Stop the world, I want to get off".'

5.3   FREE MARKETS AND TRANSACTION COST ECONOMICS

The rolling back of the State, with the corporatization or privatization of public sector business activities, has taken place on the basis that the market mechanism is the supreme device for ensuring the best allocation of resources. This point of view pre-dates Hodgson's (1988) argument that markets emerge as sets of transaction cost-reducing social institutions so that, compared with a situation of institution-free bilateral exchange, buyers and sellers can locate each other relatively easily and identify deals that are unlikely to have large opportunity costs. It is a point of view that often seems oblivious to the fact (stressed by Hodgson) that even though markets reduce transaction costs, they do not eliminate them: the deals that are done in markets *still* entail costs of search and appraisal, contract negotiation and implementation, monitoring, and possibly even litigation. There is every reason to suppose that yet other institutional arrangements might be able to reduce such costs still further.

Coase

As we have noted in earlier chapters, it was Coase (1937) that first raised the issue of the costs of using markets, as part of his attempt to make sense of the nature of the firm. The underlying assumption of his analysis is that incomplete contracts are a means of economizing on transaction costs. Instead of incurring the costs of either a succession of short-term deals or designing contracts that might contain masses of redundant fine print and yet still fail to cover what actually eventuated, entrepreneurs might coordinate production and distribution by having open-ended contracts that only vaguely specified how resources would be used. Such arrangements are exemplified by employment contracts, of the sort that used to be offered before the contemporary managerialist credo led to increasingly detailed job descriptions and performance measurement criteria. These were far cheaper to organize than contracts whose designers attempt to set out in great detail what is to be done and when it is to be done. Anything not explicitly ruled out by an incomplete contract might be done, so such a vague contract can cover all manner of unforeseen events. As a simple example, note that a modern university run along managerialist lines might have a harassment policy directive running to many pages, whereas, in the past, the following one-liner would suffice: Members shall behave in a civilized manner at all times. (As Alan Singer pointed out to me, The Queen's College, Oxford has used this rule for hundreds of year without any attempt to specify the meaning of 'civilized'.) The cheapness of vagueness comes, of course, at another cost, and Coase himself presented this cost in terms of the managerial resources needed to ensure that the firm's resources are used effectively.

In Coase's vision of the firm these costs of management had to be incurred to give direction that might otherwise be provided (in a market system) by a changing array of relative prices. It must be understood that Coase was writing not long after the Soviet system had been put into place as a means of producing without relying on the market, as well as in the light of visits to factories in the US where he saw managers actively engaged in problem solving. Workers change tasks not because the relative rewards associated with different tasks has changed but simply because the boss, having decided on a solution to the problem at hand, asked for the worker to change task. Put differently, persuasion was with words (backed up with positional power), not money. Furthermore, to the extent that the past repeats itself and effective solutions to past problems have already been identified within a firm, the workers may not actually need to be told what to do by a manager. So long as they know what the state of the world is (which may not necessarily be something that requires a manager to pronounce upon), they can apply the appropriate and trusted routines to the problem in question. So long as there is a collective memory in the firm, all this can be done without any need for anybody to write down a complex set of 'if this, then that' contingent management procedures or clauses in employment contracts.

Hayek

Coase's analysis fits well with that of Hayek (1949) on the limitations of planning systems compared with the market: central planners could not possibly know everything that is known somewhere in the market, on which knowledge private actions might be based. The central planner's task involves altogether too big a jigsaw to piece together. Worse still, it is a jigsaw that may change faster than the planner can impose any order upon it. At best the planner might have to work with far more simplified, rough and ready models of the system than those possessed by individual specialist agents. The power of this view was to become increasingly evident as the Soviet economy matured and the system of material balances, that had worked remarkably well in the early days, became ever less able to handle the growing complexity of the productive system, particularly one with multiple technologies (see Ellman, 1971).

5.4   CONTRACTUAL INCOMPLETENESS AND DISCRETIONARY BEHAVIOUR

The classic pontifications on rivals to the market (such as firms and central planning) are driven by concern for the avoidance of chaos and the attainment of orderly economic growth and prosperity. But Coase's analysis left the path open for a very different and more cynical perspective: contracts that do not specify much may result in rather little being delivered.

Sure enough, in the early post-war period, the possibility that workers might exploit weaknesses in their employment contracts and actively resist attempts to increase productivity seemed quite real. *Pro*-business sentiments were neatly captured in 1959 in a satirical British film *I'm Alright, Jack*, which featured Peter Sellers as Fred Kite, a communist shop steward seeking to protect his covertly card-playing colleagues from the activities of the time-and-motion studies officer. The British Disease infected Australian and New Zealand workplaces via migration of activist trades unionists who fought for feather-bedding work arrangements and were able, by working to rule, to bring factories and transport systems to a standstill by choosing to exploit the deficiencies of what was written down explicitly in the employment contract, as well as what was not included.

Baumol

If one looks at the changing literature on the economics of the firm and the emergence of an economics of discretionary behaviour, such popular mythology concerning shirking workers actually seems to play far less of a role than a recognition that managers, too, might have their own sub-goals to pursue. In the late 1950s a series of new theories of the firm began to appear in which managers pursued objectives that might conflict with shareholder welfare, and possibly that of workers and customers. Initially, Baumol (1959) portrayed managers as sales-revenue maximizers who would push sales beyond the profit-maximizing level, by charging lower prices and spending more on advertising. The Baumol firms produced a profit-sacrificing volume of output and in the process generated higher levels of turnover that would enable managers to award themselves higher remuneration. However, Baumol presumed that the output levels were achieved at the lowest costs possible and with no mention of shirking by workers (for further discussion, see Loasby, 1989, pp. 101–11).

Williamson

A few years later, the ethics of managerial behaviour and their implications for corporate governance began to surface in the work of Oliver Williamson (1964). He had been a graduate student of Cyert and March and contributed a chapter to their (1963) book in which they abandoned maximizing behaviour for the pursuit of *satisfactory* outcomes and portrayed the firm as a coalition of competing interest groups/individuals with their own sub-goals. In his doctorate, Williamson presented a model of discretionary managerial behaviour in which managers optimized their overall benefits from working for a particular firm within the cozy confines of a relatively weakly contested product market and a capital market that was rather thinly populated with takeover raiders: *managers* might deliberately sacrifice profits in pursuit of pet projects or lavish spending on office accommodation, corporate expense accounts and so on. This view of managers as self-serving set the tone for Williamson's work on firms and corporate governance for the next three decades.

Cyert and March

In Cyert and March's own work there was much more of a focus on problems of knowledge than was evident in Williamson's early writings. Of particular significance were the related notions of satisficing – picked up from their colleague Herbert Simon – and organizational slack. In the face of uncertainty about what was feasible, and about how far to search for a better outcome, people were presumed to bring their decision processes to an end once they had found a strategy that looked sufficiently likely to deliver an outcome good enough to satisfy the target on which they were presently focusing. They were also assumed to be prone to engage in incoherent behaviour at times due to pursuing targets sequentially rather than in an integrated manner that was mindful of interdependencies. These targets would be based on what experience had demonstrated to be feasible, which might be well short of what could be achieved with rather more industrious searching (and design). Actual performance in excess of aspiration levels would tend to lead to upward adjustments of targets. However, this would occur only after a lag during which it had been confirmed that the unexpectedly good results were not merely outliers. Emerging gaps between aspirations and attainments (and ignorance of how far any other player in the organization was prepared to go in sacrificing attainments) tended to result in people holding back from pushing their luck (in terms of making demands on other members of the corporate coalition) unless they were finding it difficult to meet their own personal objectives. This ignorance-driven restraint on the pursuit of sub-goals tended to give the firm a measure of organizational flexibility, for weathering tough times. In good times, managers might not dare to reduce dividends or raise line speeds in order to obtain more retained resources to spend on their remuneration packages or pet projects. In tough periods, however, they might risk these policies. In so doing, they might succeed in generating investment funds or keeping prices competitive and hence keep the firm afloat whilst continuing to meet their personal aspirations.

For those, such as mainstream economists, who were not used to focusing on the impact of complexity and partial ignorance on decision making, the notions of satisficing and organizational slack were all too likely to conjure up visions of firms in prosperous or protected economies as rather casual and unstressed places, on whose report cards management consultants would naturally want to write could do better with a bit more effort. The focus on sub-goals can lead the analyst to cast *anyone* involved with a coalition comprising a firm – whether as a supplier of physical or financial resources, or as a customer – as being prone to play deviously and to make foggy the issue of the minimum terms required for their continuing membership of the coalition. Unfortunately, it opens up a pathway for suggesting that what businesses may need is a tougher environment that will encourage them, rather as the fear of being hanged concentrates the mind wonderfully, to raise their productivity levels.

Such a suggestion completely misses several key messages from the work of Cyert and March. Even the firms that lead in terms of productivity are satisficing and are likely to contain organizational slack, since their decision-makers are contending with problems of incomplete knowledge. The presence of slack, as Hirschman (1970) was later to reiterate, is vital for enabling organizations to recover from environmental surprises and relative lapses in performance: give-and-take enables organizational coalitions to be preserved in tough times, rather than members having to incur the transactions costs of attaching themselves to new organizations, following any fragmentation of existing arrangements. Moreover, unlike many subsequent economists, Cyert and March never argued that slack is a bad thing just because it results in consumers paying more than the minimum possible price. On the contrary, in their analysis, affluent customers might let workers, shareholder and managers enjoy a better deal by paying nearer the maximum they are *willing* (and hence able) to pay, all the while remaining unclear how much lower the price charged for the product might be without jeopardizing the firm's long-run existence. Ignorance thus affects the distribution of income, possibly in an equitable manner. As far as members of a corporate coalition are concerned, there may be some suspicion that organizational slack exists, somewhere, but the situation might nonetheless be one of Pareto efficiency, in which no coalition member can benefit without someone else in the coalition making a concession.

Downie

The particular view of organizational slack presented by Cyert and March (expressed formally in terms of the difference between the sum of returns enjoyed by coalition members and the sum of their respective transfer earnings) rather diverts attention from another form of slack involving a potential Pareto improvement, namely, slack due to technological or managerial ignorance. This was rather more the slack that Downie (1958) seemed to have had in mind when he wrote his book *The Competitive Process* .

Downie investigated how tendencies towards industrial concentration (which he called the transfer process) might be offset by an innovation process. In many respects it was a formalization of Schumpeter's notion of creative destruction: the economy progresses as one firms problem-solving activities caused problems for others, that might eventually become acute enough to provoke action. Downie saw the presence of slack as dynamically efficient even if it entailed sub-optimal short-run performance, because it tended to keep alive rivalry between alternative business paradigms (instead of producing a world in which someone ended up with a monopoly). Unfortunately, Downie's book went largely ignored within economics, outside a small circle in the UK and Australia. It was not referred to by Cyert and March, nor by other US writers to whom it would have appealed, such as Nelson and Winter (1982) (see further, Nightingale, 1997, 1998).

Leibenstein

For economists with narrowly orthodox training, the idea that economic systems contain slack, which competitive pressure might reduce is actually unlikely to have come via Cyert and March, unless they picked it up in an industrial economics segment on 'new theories of the firm'. Rather, it is likely that the impetus towards the view that workplace pressures could be stepped up to the benefit of the consumer came from Leibenstein's (1966) classic paper on what he termed X-inefficiency. Prior to this paper, industrial economists had typically discussed efficiency lapses in terms of prices being pushed above social opportunity costs due to monopoly distortions. Leibenstein's suggestion was that consumers were actually getting a far worse deal than this, because the analysis had presumed that costs were as low as could be achieved, when it might well be the case that costs were padded out to levels far higher than necessary. He suggested three reasons for this:

(i)   The production function is not fully known by firms, who might discover more possibilities if they conducted time and motion studies (as in Taylorist or Fordist 'scientific management'), called in consultants or engaged in benchmarking or other comparative performance measures.
(ii) The market for management works imperfectly (the best managers might not be ending up in the firms that most needed their services).
(iii) Employment contracts are vague, leaving workers with discretion about the amount and quality of effort they provided.

Point (i) obviously relates to Downie, whom he did not discuss – thereby failing to pick up Downie's dynamic perspective on the benefits of slack in terms of allowing for long-run persistence of competition and to the work of Cyert and March on satisficing. Point (iii) links to Coase, whom he did not discuss, either – thereby failing to register the benefits of contractual vagueness in a world of unexpected change and high transaction costs (see Loasby, 1976). Point (ii) has been little discussed, yet if seen alongside point (iii) it should lead one to consider the possibility of attributing major differences between the actual and potential performance of firms to their managers' inability to motivate their workforces through transformational leadership and design of good jobs (cf. Barnard, 1938), rather than detailed performance contracts.

Although Leibenstein's attempts to proclaim a new kind of inefficiency were criticized by some leading economists (most notably Stigler, 1976, to which Leibenstein, 1978, is a reply), his view of inefficiency has a much more ready appeal to policy-makers than the traditional allocative inefficiency notion. It seems closer to familiar lay ideas of inefficiency based on management incompetence and indolent workers. It gives them reasons to be tough on monopolies but it also points towards practical policies such as calling in consultants, hiring more managers, formalizing work procedures and tightening up job contracts.

5.5   DIVIDE AND RULE

The relationship between the modern New Right/technocratic policy package and the modern economics of the firm has also been affected by the use that some economists made of the research of pre-eminent business historian Alfred Chandler. Like Downie (of whom he seems to have been unaware), Chandler portrayed the growth of firms as discontinuous – each firm's history has obvious 'chapters' – and as driven by problem-solving activities. A firm's strategy for growth may work for a time, but non-incremental organizational rethinks are sometimes necessary.

Chandler
The thesis of Chandler's acclaimed (1962) book *Strategy and Structure*, in simple form, is that initially a firm can get by without much of a formal organizational structure, but, as it gets larger, it eventually runs into control and coordination problems and is forced to consolidate its activities. The management typically introduce a formal functionally based structure, before embarking on the next major growth phase, involving diversification. Eventually, an increasing number of projects and regions becomes difficult to administer, even in terms of a functionally based structure (it may be very hard to separate out costs and revenue streams for individual product lines) and the firm reorganizes around a strategic planning headquarters and a set of mini-firms-within-the-firm, based on products or regions.

Aspects of Coase's analysis of the firm are shared here, as well as of Downie's thinking: managers can only handle so much and may need to use the market – albeit perhaps an internal capital market – to make larger volumes of business activities sustainable. However, what *also* clearly emerges in Chandler's work, based on meticulous case-study investigations of Standard Oil, General Motors, Du Pont and Sears Roebuck, is the highly *political* nature of the process of change within organizations. Here, we again see echoes of Cyert and March's sub-goal concept, together with a rather cynical view of empire-building, perk-seeking managers. The same idea again found expression in Williamson's writings of that same time (see below). Chandler clearly saw that organizational structures may be used instrumentally, by individuals, to assist in building their own empires. For example, in a U-form corporation, functional specialists are only too willing to apportion blame for poor performance to other functions. A divide-and-rule strategy within an M-form corporation forces divisions to compete energetically as rival teams.

The seemingly superior properties of M-form organizational structures were picked up rapidly both by management consultants (McKinsey's consultants in particular adopted this philosophy and applied it to many UK firms) and by industrial economists. Williamson (1970) used this theme as the basis for a book and a number of empirical studies were conducted, both on Chandler's 'structure follows strategy' thesis and on tests of the empirical superiority of M-form structures (see, for example, Channon, 1973; Armour and Teece, 1978; Steer and Cable, 1978; Teece, 1981; and Thompson, 1983). Less well advertised was the work of Cable and Dirrheimer (1983, p. 60) who provided the main empirical anomaly. They reported a West German finding of a reduction in profitability for some years following reorganization with no clear sign of an eventual upturn. They suggested that this could well reflect the significance of institutional differences, such as the high level of owner-control and heavy involvement of banks in strategy formation, in the large German companies.

Williamson

Chandler's *Strategy and Structure* provided a key theme that was employed in a stream of articles and books by Oliver Williamson, in which he further developed his 1964 model of discretionary managerial behaviour. (This model had been based on the Ph.D. that Williamson was writing at about the time that Chandler's book came out.) In 1975, Williamson produced his best-known book, *Markets and Hierarchies*, which is the key intellectual foundation for much of the modern thinking on economic organization and restructuring policies. The book can be seen – although Williamson's claim-staking activities, distinctive jargon and referencing/indexing policies somewhat obscure this – as a synthesis of (i) Coase and Hayek on transactions costs, information and the limits to the market, the firm and the state; (ii) Cyert and March and Leibenstein on non-optimizing behaviour, complexity, sub-goal pursuit and slack; and (iii) Chandler on the significance of internal markets and organizational structure.

In putting forward his synthesis of these ideas, Williamson performed a service by re-launching Coase's hitherto mainly neglected (1937) work on the nature of the firm. But he also did Coase a disservice, by diverting the attention of readers away from issues of coordination and towards the idea of guileful exploitation of information advantages by self-serving individuals, or corporate bodies, that he labelled as opportunism. This was a logical extension of the cynical view of executives that Williamson had worked with in his doctorate-based (1964) book on discretionary behaviour. Accordingly, the general presumption in *Markets and Hierarchies* is that economic agents are indeed prone to look for opportunities to get away with taking advantage of situations in which they find themselves. They are typically devious at someone else's expense, if they judge they can get away with it. A rather similar presumption also pervades the highly influential principal–agent literature, which was derived from work published almost simultaneously by Jensen and Meckling (1976). With their focus on just how widespread sub-goal pursuit might be in situations of what Williamson called 'information impactedness', both of these literatures provided a basis for policies that set out to make the operations of organizations more transparent via formalized operating procedures and objectively measurable performance standards.

Williamson's perspective is best illustrated with reference to the dilemmas that arise in the economics of vertical integration, the area to which his work has been particularly applied. The corporate strategist must choose between using external contractors or using internal resources to do the same task (or else use taper integration, a combination of the two policies). A do-it-yourself (make, don't buy) strategy may limit a firm's flexibility and its workers may be aware that they can threaten to disrupt production processes and leave dedicated assets idle, as a means of extracting more of the corporate pie for themselves. Here, the workers exploit issues that were left vague in their employment contracts. If secondhand asset markets were perfect and outside supplies readily contractible (or if it were easy to replace recalcitrant staff) such opportunistic bargaining stances from internal suppliers would not be viable. However, if external markets were hotly contested and buyers and suppliers became proficient in writing their contractual obligations down in detail, one might as well use external contractors.

Baumol

The analysis in *Markets and Hierarchies* came prior to the contestable markets revolution in the analysis of competition policy, led by Baumol, Panzar and Willig (1982) and considered in chapter 1 of this book. Initially, therefore, Williamson's analysis of vertical integration was seen as suggesting a case *for* the do-it-yourself (make) strategy, despite its hazards. First, people with conflicting interests could be made to pull together, by making them part of the same business unit. Second, managers could ensure supplies of the do-it-yourself product beyond the normal contracting horizons, in a situation where it was expensive to engage in litigation to force external contractors to deliver. Third, internal activities were likely to be easier to audit and monitor. However, with the emergence of the contestability literature, and consequent heightened awareness of the power of potential competition, the scope for outsourcing without running into supplier opportunism soon seemed much better.

This was a remarkable about-face for Baumol, who over two decades before had opened up the idea of discretionary behaviour within organizations via his model of sales revenue-maximizing managers. Now, he was showing that, in practice, the pursuit of sub-goals was likely to be limited so long as impediments to changing suppliers were removed. This argument was actually nothing new: Andrews (1964, pp. 50–3) had critically discussed the original Baumol model at an early stage and pointed out that its predictions depended on a the presence of a well-defined downward-sloping demand curve and the associated absence of potential competition. However, Andrews' own analysis of the competitive process combined an emphasis on the power of potential competition (as a restraint on the earning of supernormal returns), with an analysis of the development of buyer–seller goodwill relationships (as determining relative market shares). The latter dimension was absent from the Baumol-inspired literature, where any form of trading relationship would be seen as an impediment to the power of potential competition. The policies that this literature in turn inspired took a similar stance. But to Andrews, as to Richardson (1972), such relationships seem to play a vital role in enabling both suppliers and customers to reduce uncertainties that would otherwise make it harder for them to plan their activities and have the confidence to make expensive investment commitments.

5.6   MANAGERIALISM AND THE NEW ZEALAND ECONOMY

So far, I have tried to undertake a rational reconstruction of the intellectual basis of managerialist thinking, with an emphasis – like that in chapters 3 and 4 – on the difference that wider reading and different preconceptions can make to the interpretation one forms of particular ideas. A more cynical view may also hold the key to the rise of managerialist mode of thought:

> [T}he prevailing faith that market flexibility will set the economy back on track reflects at best an extreme ignorance of the dynamics of capitalist development and at worst a means for those with economic and political power to open up more avenues for free marketing that permits them to extract value from the economic system without contributing to the value creation process (Lazonick, 1990, p. 331).

These words, by the author of *Competitive Advantage on the Shop Floor*, were not written with New Zealand in mind. Even so, they serve well to provide a critical perspective on what went on in New Zealand in a decade and a half of managerialist, free-market reforms, during which economic growth was erratic and income distribution became markedly less than egalitarian.

New Zealand had once been a prosperous but insular society in which subsidies and protection from global competition permitted an egalitarian ethos amidst what looked, in terms of international productivity benchmarks, to be a state of widespread disguised unemployment. In this 'prosperity consensus', as James (1992) has labelled it, the work environment could be low in stress, whilst the wages of relatively unskilled workers, engaged in producing (often merely assembling) domestic supplies of internationally tradable goods did not get pushed down to the corresponding levels found in developing nations. At the same time, there was a view of New Zealanders as diligent, hard-working people who would give anything a go with minimal resources and a colonial pioneer's ability to improvise solutions.

Tax rates were high, rather as in Sweden, but the implicit tax cost of the system was higher still. Instead of paying taxes that might explicitly be spent on transfer payments to the unemployed, New Zealanders who were working in areas that were capable of survival without tariff protection ended up paying higher prices for the outputs of protected sectors. The overall cost of such a strategy in terms of material living standards is actually far from clear. For example, locally assembled products such as cars did indeed have high prices but actually motoring was much less expensive than it superficially seemed. Vehicles depreciated at a very slow rate and were kept running by an army of mechanics and suppliers of reconditioning services well past the age at which they would have been scrapped in other economies. Thus the country may have had an older fleet of vehicles but nonetheless it enjoyed one of the highest vehicle ownership rates in the world.

The New Zealand economy in the 1950s and 1960s came to be likened to a capitalist Poland or an economic bumblebee that flew when it should not have been able to do so, but at that time discussions about its sustainability tended to focus on the absence of scale economies in a domestic market that was minute by the standards of many other OECD nations.

With the entry of the UK, into the European Community and the major oil price shocks of the 1970s, the interventionist system became unworkable even from the viewpoint of politicians on the Left. Accordingly, in the period since the election of the Labour government in 1984, the New Zealand worker has been subjected to rhetoric and reform-based views about the benefits of competition and market forces (see James, 1992; Massey, 1995, and Jesson, 1999). The core axioms and associated policy heuristics of managerialism that I outlined in section 5.1 were essentially a summary of the thinking of the reformist Labour government and its National and Coalition successors, as well as from the business press and, most of all, the Business Roundtable.

5.7 CONTESTABILITY IN NEW ZEALAND

Prior to 1984, New Zealand had hardly been a paragon of strong potential competition, with many state-sanctioned monopolies and distorting regulations designed to protect certain suppliers. For example, prior to the reforms, NZ Rail's life was made easier by considerable restrictions on the operations of road freight transport. As the contestability revolution took hold, public policy-makers increasingly recognized that divide-and-rule and competitive tendering could be used, both in internal markets (as when different business units within a firm battle for the right to provide a service being purchased by another part of the organization) and in external markets. If entry into, say, the trucking business were freed up, a logging company might no longer employ drivers and own its own logging trucks but, instead, it could put trucking work out to tender to rival trucking companies or, better still, to a multitude of individual self-employed owner-operators. Likewise, a public utility, such as the now-privatized and largely foreign-owned Telecom New Zealand, might cease providing operator assistance services in-house. If they were lucky, the operators that it fired under reformist labour-market legislation that permits easier retrenchments of staff might end up working for third-party contractors who specialize in providing such services. The latter, in turn, would know that they risked being dropped in favour of credible alternative suppliers that offer to do the same job for less. Trucking services are as vital for a logging company as operator services are for a telephone company, but they involve different capabilities from forestry management. These kinds of services can safely be purchased from specialist outside contractors, so long as the latter have strong incentives not to let their customers down.

Accordingly, within New Zealand, much public policy effort was devoted to promoting contestability and facilitating the vertical disintegration of supply chains. Policies aimed at increasing the strength of competitive pressure and the division of labour, by changing incentive structures and enhancing contestability by such means as deregulation and tariff removal have been developed and implemented, ostensibly in the name of the final consumer. Yet the final consumer in this analysis is often precisely the same person who is the target of the policies the person presumed to be likely to shirk and generally operate in an opportunistic manner if not motivated by fear of losing a paying task to another potential provider. Put differently, the only *undisputed* net beneficiaries of these policies are the independently wealthy, who no longer need to sell their labour services and who are further presumed to have accrued *their* wealth by merit, rather than guile. There is no sign that policy designers have seen or considered the wider implications of Martin's (1978, p. 282) suggestion that estimates of X-inefficiency due to tariff protection have been prone to ignore the benefits of protection in terms of the joys of a relatively quiet life in other words, that welfare depends not just on what or how much is produced, but on *how* output is produced.

5.8 THE LONG-RUN COSTS

In the New Zealand case, as Hazledine (1998) and Dalziel (2002) have demonstrated, the wave of reforms has not been accompanied by any conspicuous sustained leap forward in the rate of economic growth. If anything, the reverse has occurred. Moreover, the reforms have produced a nation of far greater inequality and a people rather punch-drunk with all the change, especially the tendency of many newly promoted managers to operate without much of a humanistic perspective. The overall picture is precisely of the kind exposed by John Ralston Saul in *Voltaire's Bastards*, his (1993) critique of the rationalist managerialist ethos: high-level technocrats now operate like control-hungry parents who set about beating their offspring into submission, rebuking them until they get their acts together. Despite all that was possible in the era of 'fortress New Zealand' in terms of economic growth, it is now presumed that the population cannot and will not work effectively without tighter contracts, formalized procedures and measurable performance objectives all linked to a mission statement

Such a failure of managerialism should not be a source of surprise. I have already noted some of the dangers, in terms of lost flexibility and costs of redundant content, of trying to pin down worker tasks by finer and finer detail in employment contracts that go directly against the grain of what Coase perceived as the essence of the firm. Many New Zealanders are very familiar with these costs, having given time to writing out or trying to make sense of increasingly formal job contracts and increasingly having to deal with more formalized, bureaucratic ways of doing business, to ensure that everything they do is accountable (I speak from experience!). In the long term, the damage to flexibility may come from a different source: declining standards of industrial relations (despite the threat that failure to fit in with the growing demands of employers will lead to a non-renewal of employment contracts). As Saul (1993) stresses, the technocrats engaged in implementing the managerialist philosophy tend not be very widely read and in consequence act without regard to the lessons of history. One possible lesson they ought to be learning comes from the work of William Lazonick (1990, 1991), which is greatly influenced by Chandler's analysis of the development of the modern business enterprise, but does not come to the conclusions reached by Williamson, Baumol and their followers in favour of divide-and-rule policies based on the promotion of greater contestability.

Lazonick's work on industrial leadership and structural change focuses on the loss of industrial leadership from Britain to the United States, and from the United States to Japan, during the twentieth century. He finds that the ability of firms to embrace new technologies and products depends very much on the attitudes of their workforces – attitudes that British and American managers mistakenly alienated. Lazonick argues that worker attitudes depend on whether they have 'good jobs' or 'bad jobs'. If workers have bad jobs, industrial relations will be poor, even if the typical outcome is that the workers are ejected from their bad jobs and replaced by others. Put simply, a job that is a source of misery and poor morale is not a job one will be motivated to try to keep, particularly if life is bearable on the dole. If he were to study New Zealand, Lazonick would doubtless recognize an increasing swing towards bad jobs. The rolling back of the New Zealand's welfare state might appear to make the possession of at least a bad job something that is essential; but emigration, particularly to Australia, has been an attractive alternative for many, myself included (and, as the Australians say, 'Would the last Kiwis to leave New Zealand please turn out the lights before boarding their trans-Tasman flight!').

Let us be clear about the essence of the distinction between good and bad jobs. It centres on the difference between *relational* and *un*committed contracting, a difference that has its origins in work on industrial organization by Richardson (1972). Richardson noted how some firms develop commitment on the part of suppliers, by giving repeat business to them in close consultation with them and by *assisting* them if necessary (as in policies of constructive engagement) rather than periodically putting work out to fresh tender or engaging in vertical integration (see also Richardson, 1998). This cooperative approach to the business of adding value and adjusting to changed conditions is not based on any explicit, detailed contracts, nor formal promises; but on the development of an atmosphere of trust and commitment that promotes what transaction cost economics (which has been slow to pick up Richardson's work) would call *consummate* rather than perfunctory cooperation. The relational vision is very similar to the picture of Japanese business brought to Western readers by writers such as Adams and Kobayashi (1969) and Dore (1986), before Lazonick published his historical thesis. Relational thinking also has more recently been developed for the management audience by economist John Kay (1993), who argues forcefully that business success depends on concentrating on doing the things for which one has a capability, and on developing one's business architecture, by which Kay means a network of relational contracts. (Subsequent ideas about transforming other entities, rather than offering them take-it-or-leave-it choices, may also be found in Singer (1996) and Hampden-Turner and Trompenaars (1997).)

Relational contracting with labour entails providing workers with good jobs: a long-term career path in the one firm, where they are treated as valuable assets whose skills and insights count. In such a firm, managers invest in workers' skills without fear that the latter will then move elsewhere and use them to the benefit of another employer, whilst they set out to enhance intrinsic motivation by job enrichment and the like. By contrast, a worker with a bad job is treated as disposable and replaceable (if you won't do this, there are many more who will), rather like an inanimate item of physical capital. The worker with a bad job is not someone whose heart is in doing the job well, particularly if growing levels of monitoring signal that the worker is not trusted; indeed, the mind of the worker might well be entirely preoccupied with thoughts of how awful the working relationship is and how to escape from it.

Academic jobs past and present illustrate well the contrast between good and bad jobs. Once, they were highly relational. After being hired on the basis of references from within a relational network and/or granted tenure after a probationary period, academics were largely left to get on with their jobs as professionals, with minimal monitoring, until they retired. In return, a great many academics happily worked long hours on the basis of intrinsic motivation rather than brilliant salaries. There were, to be sure, occasional cases of career failures in the form of academics that rusted out under this low-stress system; but that may have been a small price to pay, given the low cost of operation of the system and its ability to induce commitment. Now, those new to the academic game or brave enough to switch employers, often find themselves subject to frequent performance appraisals, or with employment contracts so short (in the name of leaving the employer with flexibility because of funding uncertainty) that it becomes necessary to start looking for a new job on the Internet between preparing classes almost from the moment the latest contract has started. Bad jobs and loyalty do not go together.

In the short term, managerialism's adverse motivational and labour relations effects on productivity might well be masked by productivity improvements consequent on increased pressure at work. However, such an improvement is unlikely to be sustainable in the long run if it imposes undue stress levels and ultimately illness or exhaustion on workers (for a case study, in the context of the application of managerialism to Australian schools, see Carr, 1994). Chronic high-pressure work environments are not remotely conducive to reflective thinking about ways of doing things better: fire-fighting gets in the way of designing more fireproof structures. As any organization theorist would inform, but rather few economists seem to be aware, burnout is disastrous for relationships with customers. Typically, the quality of the interaction declines: even if frazzled employees still manage to offer service with a smile, the chances that they will make serious mistakes are increased by relentless pressure. Damage-control and inquisitions following such mistakes then add further to stress. The task of replacing those who quit due to burnout imposes yet further costs. These include severance pay, substantial hiring costs and the time taken for new appointees to reach the previous performance standards through on-the-job learning (including learning about the corporate culture). Tacit knowledge is often required to do a job effectively, particularly where it is centred on intellectual accomplishments and human relations. But this, by definition is not something that can be written down in an employment contract or manual (see further the discussion of the concept in Nelson and Winter, 1982). On top of this are all the costs in terms of new managers to enforce the whole philosophy (documented for the New Zealand economy in general by Hazledine, 1998, chapter 12). Accordingly, managerialist efforts to reduce X-inefficiency (slack) in the short run may have disastrous long-term effects on efficiency and effectiveness. Whilst some politicians might even welcome this outcome in the case of higher education as a means of pushing public sector universities towards extinction, the wider argument about managerialism applies equally to any knowledge-based or customer-focused entity, in the public or the private sector.

5.9   CONCLUSION

The approach to achieving increased productivity that has been adopted in New Zealand and (though normally to a lesser extent) elsewhere focuses on doing business in an increasingly formalized, accountability-conscious manner, as well as on separating purchaser and provider roles along the value chain and making markets as contestable as possible. It is clearly possible to use the literature on the theory of the firm and industrial organization to construct a coherent but by no means compelling justification for managing in this rationalistic, technocratic style. It is a style of management that has been thoroughly criticized and satirized by John Ralston Saul in his best-selling writings and widely broadcast radio presentations, which were extensively aired in New Zealand during 1997 after he visited the country. Even so, it has served well the short-run interests of those running the reforms, both those at the top (managerially and financially) and the extra layers of managers that it requires (see Hazledine, 1998).

The likely long-term consequences of such policies are highly debatable, since the justification for them is constructed by applying a particular set of blinkers that leads to the neglect of the relatively informal literature on relational contracting and of contrary lessons from business history. Some employers are already experimenting with an alternative approach. (In the New Zealand setting, the few, well-publicized cases have included Hubbard's Wholefoods, The Warehouse retail chain and a number of Japanese subsidiaries such as Nissan – at least until the Nissan assembly plant was closed in 1998 due to the removal of tariffs.) Here, business becomes more like a sporting club or family grouping, or a university from earlier decades: a place that is interesting, full of fun and opportunities to enjoy stimulating new experiences and develop new skills. It becomes a place which is not run under a regime of terror but where there are shared expectations of a decent days work for a decent days pay (cf. Hazledine, 1998, chapter 16, and Akerlof, 1984); a place where one works with enthusiasm, loyalty and a sense of being valued, that is not measured merely by the size of the pay packet.

6. The Economic Rationale of Universities: A Reconsideration

6.1 INTRODUCTION

The aim of this chapter is to explore whether universities as we nowadays take them for granted are necessarily the most appropriate institutions for delivering efficiently the kinds of products that their customers and/or society at large wish for them to provide. My focus here arises partly because of my reflections on the changes that have been taking place in the tertiary education sector over the past decade or so. These include:

- Well publicized central audits of research and audits of teaching performance by visiting panels of academics (for example, in the UK), with subsequent allocations of funds being made dependent on the results of these audits.
- Mergers of institutions and the emergence of autonomous 'new universities' from former university colleges and polytechnics;
- The growth of private universities.
- Articulation agreements between universities and other institutions and the advocacy, particularly in New Zealand, of 'seamless' education systems in which students might begin tertiary studies at school and subsequently take course credits with them as they moved on to and/or between polytechnics and universities without having to surmount bureaucratic hurdles.
- Increasingly open rights to tender for research funds, which have left university staff in some countries competing with private individuals and private research institutes or other government agencies;
- The rise of new information technologies such as email and CD-ROM storage systems.
- The erosion of academic tenure and increasing talk of privatization, corporatisation and user charges.
- Suggestions (for example by Ritzer, 2000) that higher education is undergoing a process of 'McDonaldization'.

My interest in the delivery of tertiary education is also due partly to an impression I believe I have in common with many academics, namely that universities are prone to be highly politicized, bureaucratic leviathans that are slow moving and difficult to change, where there are quite major differences in performance associated with any level of remuneration. Finally, my interest in this topic has grown out of much of the work in industrial economics on the so-called 'New Institutional Economics' that has belatedly grown out of Coase's (1937) article on the nature of the firm. Here, I apply Coase's thinking to the 'education industry'.

6.2 THE SIGNIFICANCE OF CONTRACTUAL INCOMPLETENESS

As we have seen in the previous two chapters, contractual incompleteness plays a crucial role in Coase's depiction of the nature of the firm. Market contracts involving goods and services are typically for something quite specific, such as an economy class seat on the 12.15 Air New Zealand flight from Christchurch to Wellington on 26 May 1994. Some contracts are very specific indeed, containing all sorts of contingent clauses (X will be undertaken if and only if Y happens) and very precise details concerning the quality of what will be supplied and penalty payments that will be due if it is not delivered as specified. By contrast, the contracts that bring employees and shareholders together in a firm are very loosely specified in comparison to the roles that they involve. Shareholders have some well-defined rights but these stop short of any right to a particular stream of dividends. Employees may be hired in particular roles within a management hierarchy and with some specification of the terms by which satisfactory performance may be judged and conditions under which the contract may be terminated, but their employment contracts will give them very little guidance about what they will be doing at any particular point of time during their association with the firm. They do what they themselves decide to do, in the light of their assessments of the work environment and directives issued by their bosses from time to time.

An academic's employment contract epitomizes the notion of an incompletely specified contract. For example, my contract as Professor of Economics at Lincoln University in New Zealand formally ran for eight pages plus a covering letter from the Personnel Registrar, but its essence reduced to just a few lines:

> The successful applicant will be expected to serve terms as Head of Department. The Professor of Economics will be responsible either directly or through the Head of Department to the Vice-Chancellor for teaching and supervision of

courses in Economics at graduate, undergraduate and diploma level. He/she will be expected to initiate and develop research in the field of economics and to participate in the University's extension and consulting activities.

This was very vague indeed, as far as saying when I would do which tasks, or in defining terms. Did my inaugural lecture come under the heading of 'extension' activities, for example, and would I have run into trouble with the University had I refused to accept the role of supervisor for the two Masters dissertations and one Ph.D. in Marketing that I supervised, or the Ph.D.s in Farm Management and in Tourism for which I was an associate supervisor, given that the contract referred only to Economics? A substantial part of many employment contracts is implicit: both parties have overlapping expectations about reasonable demands that are not written down (everyone knows that new professors do inaugural lectures, don't they?). If expectations are somewhat divergent the relationship between employer and employee nonetheless often lasts for considerable periods, not through formal contract renegotiation but instead on the basis of give and take, until either party decides they have had enough and can make superior alternative arrangements.

As was emphasized in the previous chapter, managerialists see vague contracts as potentially open to opportunistic behaviour. For example, a head of department cannot be monitoring all his/her staff simultaneously and hence staff may be able to get away with doing less for their employers than they would be prepared to do if their efforts could easily be monitored: a lecturer might *claim* to be at home marking assignments if not present at the university, but he or she might actually be spending time running a consulting operation or personal farm. Vague employment contracts also tend to be associated with expenditure on managers, who themselves will have vague contractual ties to their employers. They are needed not merely to extract a fair day's work for a fair day's pay but also because, without a team of managers to coordinate activities and give out directions, a group of employees could end up pulling in conflicting directions if they each tried independently to decide what to do when they encountered events that were not specified in their contracts.

Employers/entrepreneurs only incur the risk of opportunism in the face of contractual incompleteness and the costs of management in order to avoid, at the margin, even more significant costs associated with getting things done by more specific contracts. Attempts to design contracts to cover long periods of time are likely to result in many redundant clauses whilst still running the risk of failing to cover situations that actually arise. The beauty of Coasian employment contracts is that they involve relatively low set-up costs, since they lack fine print, and they can be in place for a long period. What Coase might have added was that, when employers leave output requirements rather vague, employees may actually do a lot more for a given remuneration than they would if they were only obliged to deliver a particular amount: for academics on probation it is never very clear what the minimum requirements for tenure are, so there will be hesitancy about saying 'No' if senior staff keep putting more tasks on their desks.

Once an entrepreneur has decided which sorts of product to be involved in making, the key strategic task then becomes deciding which activities should be internalized – brought within corporate boundaries to be undertaken by employees – and which should be commissioned from subcontractors. For example, should a university employ computing staff to deal with hardware and software problems, or should it call in outside firms that specialize in handling computing difficulties, as and when the need arises? Between internalization and subcontracting there lies the fuzzy world of relational contracting: developing goodwill relationships and implicit long-term contracts with outside contractors, even though the later are formally only hired on the spot (Richardson, 1972; Kay, 1993; Williamson, 1985). Such trading relationships encourage the subcontractors to make investments that help them deliver a better service for their customers: for example, part-time tutors hired on an hourly basis may tool up with course-specific knowledge if they are given reason to believe they will get called upon regularly, just as lecturers will make similar investments on an understanding, nowhere written down, that they will get to teach the course for several years in a row.

With the recognition of phenomena such as relational contracting, the boundaries and defining features of firms have become fuzzier to economists in recent years as Coase's ideas have been extended. But with this fuzziness has also come an increasing tendency to analyse economic organizations in terms of alternative contractual systems, to ask, 'Would it not make sense to arrange things differently?' Let us now go through just such a comparative institutional analysis of methods for delivering tertiary-level education.

6.3   A DECENTRALIZED, USER-PAYS, MARKET-BASED SCENARIO

The degree and diploma industry in many countries is largely the preserve of state-owned, budget-based institutions rather than privately owned profit seeking firms. It shows how much can be achieved on the basis of very vague contracts and relational contracting, rather than through legalistic specification of tasks in fine print. Academics carve out their niches not merely within the universities that employ them but also as members of professional networks where implicit contracts and a concern with goodwill are much in evidence: for example, much refereeing and journal management is done on an unpaid basis or for nominal fees that in no way reflect the opportunity costs of time foregone from activities such as consulting. However, it is quite easy to imagine tertiary-level teaching and research activities being arranged without any involvement of institutions like present-day universities.

In a fully decentralized, user-pays market-based delivery system, customers – students and research clients – would make contracts with self-employed academics just as some students hire private tutors and individuals or organizations purchase professional services from lawyers, dentists or management consultants. Firms whose primary business activities involved the delivery of related services might also provide educational services – for example, why not study accountancy with an accountancy firm? If self-employment arrangements are common with other 'professions', it is not obvious why academia is not built around them too, particularly given the common view that academics are people who tend to avoid working in the private sector or public service because they want to be their own bosses with control over how they spend their time. The net earnings of freelance academics would be derived in the manner set out in table 6.1.

The picture here is perhaps best understood via a parallel with how musicians assemble a living from teaching, performing with orchestral groups, session work and so on. Students might not emerge with degrees after studying with particular suppliers of educational services (though I will consider this possibility shortly), but they would be able to report to potential employers that they had, say, studied behavioural economics with Peter Earl, just as a freelance classical guitarist might be able to report studying with John Williams. A market-based delivery system by no means precludes continuation of professional work and activities that do not involve fees, such as less-prestigious journals continuing not to demand submission fees so long as they could find academics prepared to spend their time refereeing for no fee (possibly because these academics were interested in fostering non-mainstream work or the kind of research that would lead their own ideas to become more widely known).

The student fees that academics received under such a system could come from government vouchers given to tertiary students and/or from self-funded students: a user-pays delivery system is entirely compatible with a continuing government involvement in funding tertiary studies. Decisions about the level of funding per student would affect academic incomes somewhat indirectly, depending on the number of academics willing to contest the market for students in particular disciplinary areas. Students would have to decide for themselves how to budget their finances between different academics' offerings: they might opt for relatively poorly rated but cheap units in some areas of study in order to invest more to study other subjects with renowned scholars. Academics would thus have to compete with each other for business, as they do within present university systems.

Table 6.1: The A to Z of being a self-employed academic in a decentralized tertiary education system

---

Income

A	Fees from students taking one's own subject units
B	Earnings as a subcontractor to other academics' subject units
C	Fees as a student advisor or personal tutor
D	Earnings as an external examiner
E	Earnings as a referee
F	Earnings as a research consultant
G	Earnings as an educational consultant (e.g. as a mentor to peers or for services to an accreditation body)
H	Research grants received
I	Income from article photocopy/CD-ROM usage royalties and lending rights
J	Royalty income

Less

Expenses

K	Rental of lecture rooms, teaching laboratories and tutorial rooms
L	Rental of office space
M	Secretarial fees and computing assistance
N	Payments to subject subcontractors (e.g. tutors, demonstrators)
O	Payments to external examiners of one's subject units
P	Payments for educational consulting (e.g. mentoring services, advice on teaching and subject design)
Q	Accreditation fees and membership of professional bodies
R	Promotion expenses
S	Payments to research assistants
T	Rental of computing equipment and laboratory space and equipment
U	Purchase of data, books and journals
V	Library fees
W	Communication costs (fax, post, telephone, email)
X	Printing and stationery
Y	Depreciation and maintenance of own computing equipment; purchase of software
Z	Submission fees to journals
AA	Accountant's fee

However, the payoffs to competitive success would accrue directly to individual academics rather than, as at present, taking the form of greater staffing allocations to the departments of which they are members. It would be up to individual academics how to price the subjects that they offered and the terms under which they would accept students: those who were in high demand might opt to run large classes and subcontract tutorial work, or they might opt to limit admission to particular kinds of students. Decisions here would probably depend on the standards they wished to set with a view to the long-run generation of their reputations as teachers. Some of those who could command high fees as teachers might opt to teach fewer hours in order to spend time on developing teaching materials (texts, study guides and so on) based on their expertise and from which they might earn additional incomes; others might choose to spend more time on unfunded research or in chasing research funds.

There is no inherent need for a nesting together of tertiary teaching activities to be accommodated in a set of buildings owned by a single institution known as a university. Just as it would be possible for universities around the world to sell off their physical assets to property companies and then pay fees for using them, so it would be possible for freelance academics to rent the infrastructure facilities that they needed to run the subject units they were selling to student clients. The situation would be analogous with that of, say, a psychologist who opts to go into private practice and rents office space and secretarial services for normal consulting activities and who occasionally puts on seminars for fellow practitioners in hotel conference facilities rented out specially for the occasion. There might, of course, be marketing advantages from being located near to fellow academics offering both competitive and complementary subject units. If so, suppliers of office and lecture spaces in particularly sought after locations would be expected to ration their scarce resources by charging premium rentals. It is possible also that teams of academics, like private health professionals and lawyers, might actually form partnership arrangements and invest in their own work accommodation if they felt there were advantages compared with renting. However, difficulties in arranging for prompt exits from partnerships would tend to militate against joint ownership of academic premises by those academics that were not confident of being able to generate a steady stream of earnings to support their practices.

6.4   QUALITY ASSURANCE IN EDUCATIONAL MARKETS

Before we consider the pros and cons of a delivery system based around freelance academics it is necessary to devote careful attention to the nature of what is being delivered and alternative ways in which the educational services might be packaged for students. At the outset it should be noted that, under present arrangements, university students are buyers of a product whose nature is incompletely specified. This is not a simple, one-off impersonal transaction like the purchase of a taxi ride; rather, students have a contractual relationship with universities that has much in common with an employment contract. Education is a product that cannot be summed up in a fully specified contract, even though many modern textbooks try to delude students to the contrary with promises that, 'By the end of this chapter you will be able to...'. For one thing, there is the paradox noted by Arrow (1962): insofar as a contract concerns the supply of information, the actual delivery of information becomes unnecessary if it is detailed in the contract. Someone who had an unsigned copy of the contract would never need to sign it and pay for the information. Another area of difficulty is that what students get out of the educational process will depend very much on what they put into it. It will be very difficult to specify the intellectual capacities they will need to apply to make progress at a particular rate, and very difficult indeed to monitor the extent to which their progress is being hindered by their lack of effort rather than intellectual difficulties or poor quality teaching.

Now, if academic incomes depend on maintaining a throughput of fee-paying students, and if the achievements of students can be affected by the intensity of teaching, then academics face a conflict of interest that would not exist if educational services could be delivered via fully specified contracts. There is potential for them to succumb to the temptations to accept as students anyone who has the wherewithal to pay for tuition, and to award degrees to them after giving little by way of tuition services and expecting little in terms of effort and ability. Working against this temptation are, in addition to personal integrity, the difficulties they may expect to run into in the long run if people start to think that the degrees they award signify little about intellectual achievements. Buyers of tertiary-level education need to be able to signal to potential employers that their education has reached a particular standard. They also require a means of judging the quality of the tuition they are likely to receive from choosing a particular course of study. In short, students do not want to hand over money only to find that they get little by way of services in return and that even if they contribute a lot themselves their qualifications are not taken seriously.

Under present institutional arrangements, senior staff in universities can be seen as having a key role to play in guaranteeing standards of tuition and attainments. They select teaching staff with reference to their qualifications and professional standing. They oversee the introduction of new subjects. They are in a position to audit teaching and examination processes. They can attempt to demonstrate their students' levels of attainment by commissioning peer reviews of their processes, for example by appointing external examiners or by having their activities audited externally by teams whose members comprise senior staff from rival institutions. University management teams have expertise for judging the quality of academic staff and relative performance, which students cannot hope to possess. If universities vanished as legal entities and freelance academics began to deliver tertiary educational services, students would need new ways of judging the quality of tuition and of signalling the quality of their educational achievements.

Many different kinds of quality guaranteeing devices could appear if tertiary education were market-based. Indeed, Hodgson (1988, p. 174) goes so far as to suggest that a market can only really be said to exist as an *arena* for arranging transactions – as distinct from a set of bilateral exchanges – if institutions have developed to enable customers to make competent judgments about rival suppliers' offerings without investing inordinate amounts of time in examining suppliers' proposals and haggling with them. Some entrepreneurs might get into the business of providing directories of good academics, just as Egon Ronay prepares good food guides, or the Automobile Association rates hotels and garages. Even now, of course, students' associations offer their own ratings of staff within particular universities and directories of universities are published: universities are by no means functioning perfectly as agencies for guaranteeing and signalling academic quality. Students and employers may not have heard of a particular academic who teaches or examines a subject, but this might not matter if the person were listed on the transcript as rated by an academic rating agency as a four-star lecturer on a scale of one to five in the area in question, and that the person's subject was rated as a 100-level, 200-level or whatever-level unit. Indeed, such an agency might even offer a transcript preparation service for students whereby it collated and rated the results listed on certificates that freelance academics had awarded to them. These transcripts would take the place of traditional degree certificates and transcripts.

Given the wide range of subjects that students might wish to study, the whole business (note the word, business) of rating academics would probably be a multi-level operation. I might find myself wanting to pay, say, the Royal Economic Society or American Economic Association to consider my skills for accreditation at particular levels in particular areas and then pay, say, Moody's Directories to have my ratings entered into their publications. I might also receive some fees as a consultant writing references for fellow economists seeking accreditation. All this may seem rather odd to academics brought up under present institutional arrangements, but it is quite normal experience for, say, a clinical psychologist, who may find it difficult, even in the absence of legal restraints, to earn a living without being accepted as a member of a professional association or as an accredited counsellor of a particular kind. The same may be said for used-car dealers, plumbers, international removalists, and so on: as Hodgson stresses, professional bodies are a key means by which suppliers of particular services signal the quality of their work.

Franchise arrangements are an institutional device that we might see emerging as a half-way house between academic freelancing and traditional universities; indeed, they are already evident even in the present university system and Roger Douglas (1993, chapter 5) has argued a case for private schools using them as a device to expand their geographical coverage without using the boarding-school strategy. (See Dnes, 1992, for a study of franchising from the standpoint of the New Institutional Economics.) Under this system, the franchiser typically invests in pioneering the teaching system, trains staff in its delivery, undertakes nationwide marketing of the product and acts as a monitor of quality; franchisees pay a fee for the right to offer the teaching programme along quite heavily specified lines within a particular territory. A royalty per student would be paid to the franchiser to give an incentive to ensure that the educational product remained of a standard that kept attracting fee-paying students to study with the franchisee.

6.5   BUNDLED VERSUS MENU-BASED SERVICES?

When students enrol at a typical university, the tuition that they purchase comes as a package deal. The only additional study-related bills they expect to incur are for textbooks, stationery, a personal computer, photocopying and printing. Minor challenges to this philosophy have been going on for some time, with varying degrees of success. For example, in the face of escalating departmental photocopying bills, it is sometimes suggested that students might be expected to pay for extensive handouts of course materials. This sort of suggestion is prone not to be implemented, however, due to worries about administrative costs and fears that students may protest about paying on the ground that this is one of the sort of things that their up-front lump sum fees are supposed to cover. By contrast, universities have been willing to charge students to have their exam grades reconsidered – the charge is apparently there to discourage frivolous requests, but none of the revenue finds its way from registry offices to the hapless academics who find their research time eaten up by requests to reconsider most of the C or D grades that they dared to award. In this section I intend to consider the economics of a much more radical 'unbundling' of the degree package.

Modern information technology makes it possible for students to be billed on an itemized basis for the educational services that they consume. It is already common for attendance lists at tutorials to be collected and then recorded on subject spreadsheets. With on-line or full-text CD-ROM sourcing of journal articles being increasingly the path ahead, it is probably inevitable that libraries will start operating increasingly on a user-pays basis in order to ration their scarce supplies of information technology. But we could go much further than this by issuing each student with an ID card with a personal barcode and installing barcode readers linked to individual academics' computers and, if felt necessary, from there to an agency that specialized in billing students on behalf of the academics. Such equipment has been advertised in the *Times Higher Education Supplement*, for monitoring examination attendance and library usage. In technical terms it is but a short step to a world in which students are charged on a minute-by-minute basis for their use of the library and for the borrowings they make. There would no longer be a need for photocopy cards of the kind we presently have, merely for barcode readers integrated with photocopiers, printers and other library information systems. An extension of this technology would involve requiring students to have their barcodes scanned before lecture theatre turnstiles would let them in, and at the start and finish of each consultation in a lecturer's office.

In a market-based educational system, some academics might find that they could make their services appeal to some students by delivering them in this unbundled sort of way, giving the students greater freedom of choice to invest their scarce funds in ways that seemed best to suit their needs. Other students might prefer to forego opportunities to assemble their preferred mix of education services in favour of a cheaper product involving something akin to a set-menu meal in a restaurant, that involved little scope for paying more for customized service. Programmes might include particular sets of courses, with guaranteed admission to a particular number of lectures, tutorials and hours of office consultations, types of feedback on assignments and so on. Such programmes might be assembled and marketed by entrepreneurs who specialized as educational wholesalers offering branded products that were easier for employers to judge than would be the kinds of educational transcripts produced by rating agencies. Some wholesalers might organize activities in a franchise manner, whilst acting as a fee collection and student-forwarding agency for franchisees. Others might subcontract a range of quite specific tasks to various freelance academics, as well as arranging rental of facilities for the academics to perform in, just as a rock concert promoter may arrange ticket sales, hire a set of venues, PA systems and artists, and the artists have simply to present their acts for a flat fee without having to spend time making all the necessary prior arrangements.

The parallels between a wholesaler of tertiary-level study programmes and a promoter of concerts may be extended into the question of who bears the risks under alternative systems of organization. This is a major issue, for there is no guarantee that freelance academics will find enough demand for the services they wish to sell as a means towards earning a living. Under the present system, the universities' balance sheets bear the immediate brunt of unexpectedly low enrolments; staff incomes are not reduced, though staff on short-term contracts may find that their employment is not rolled over into a new contract. Unexpectedly high enrolments are often a gain for the university and a burden for the staff whose teaching loads rise until additional staff are eventually hired but whose incomes do not adjust in line with increases with their teaching productivity. University heads of departments allocate teaching duties to staff over a limited set of courses, so competition for numbers is between a few institutions who can keep an eye on each other's course offerings. Academics in a freelance system of teaching would be prone to offer too many courses, in order to guarantee their incomes: for example, if I don't have a local monopoly over offering second year microeconomics units, then I might also offer, say, a macroeconomics unit in case competitors offer microeconomics units, and likewise, a macroeconomics teacher, fearing competitive offerings, might hedge his or her bets by also offering a microeconomics unit. To the extent the academics can credibly teach in a range of areas there is potential for the Richardson Problem of poor coordination and unduly cut-throat competition (cf. Richardson, 1960, and chapters 1 and 3 of this book).

Uneconomic duplication of subject offerings could be reduced somewhat if academics moved from individual self-employment to cooperative ventures in which they offered a range of subjects but specialized in which ones they taught. Academic wholesale operations could provide another means by which coordination problems could be reduced to acceptable levels, a means which does not involve internalization. Wholesaler entrepreneurs could negotiate contracts with particular academics for block purchases of student places on their courses. They would then seek to fill these places via a retail network of student advisers who, like travel agents, would book places for students once they had worked out their goals and capabilities. The wholesalers would thus offer a guaranteed income for the self-employed academics but then take the initiative in pricing and marketing subject units and take any profits or losses as their rewards. Permutations involving sharing risks may also be envisaged and might appeal more to some academics and would-be intermediaries.

6.6 ADVANTAGES AND PROBLEMS OF A MARKET-BASED SYSTEM

The analysis so far presented may be easier to keep in mind with reference to figure 6.1. It is an analysis intended to show that, in principle, those who wish to receive a tertiary-level education do not have to deal with modern universities, typically large organizations employing hundreds or thousands of teaching staff with extensive investments in physical infrastructure. It is easy to envisage the delivery of education being arranged instead in ways similar to those employed in professional and leisure services. I now turn to consider some of the pros and cons of the kinds of contracting systems I have been outlining.

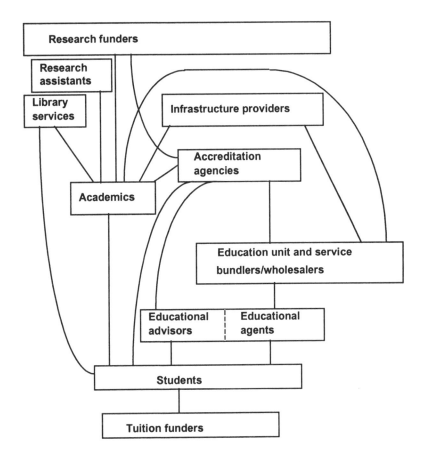

Figure 6.1: Decentralized funding, coordination and delivery

Advantage 1: improved utilization of physical resources
The combination of privatized physical assets and freelance academic providers of human assets sounds like a recipe for greatly reduced infrastructure costs. The typical university at present makes little use of the potential for internal pricing systems to ensure that its physical resources are

efficiently used. Many lecturers' offices are empty for major parts of the working week whilst their supposed occupants are elsewhere teaching, researching or working at home. If lecturers had to rent their own offices there would be a major incentive to devise space roster arrangements similar to those that private sector suppliers of other professional services are used to contracting from companies that sell serviced office space on an hourly or daily basis. Problems with safeguarding property such as academic libraries and files might tend to make academics keep these resources at home, and in some countries they would be able to claim tax relief against the parts of their homes devoted to work activities.

If academics had to pay for their own teaching facilities from their own teaching budgets, they would have an incentive to shop around in terms of both location and time of day for economical deals. No longer would prime timetable slots and sought-after modern lecture theatres be made available very much at the whim of timetable committees with no use made of prices to ration scarce space. Instead, suppliers and consumers of educational services would be encouraged to ask serious questions about what they were prepared to pay in order for subjects to be offered at particular times of day and in particular kinds of premises. In the event that owners of teaching and office spaces did not offer deals as appealing as those available elsewhere, freelance academics could signal this by *exiting* – in contrast to the situation at present in some universities where lecturers can *voice* their objections to the way that resources are being allocated but often feel powerless to do very much in the face of an unresponsive bureaucracy (cf. Hirschman, 1970). I predict that in a decentralized system of provision of tertiary education much more teaching would be conducted outside of normal office hours, using space rented from schools and firms and that purpose-built accommodation would also have higher rates of occupancy. Owners of school and business premises would be more inclined to have their facilities designed to capture the tertiary market, trading the costs of doing so against the cost of receiving no revenue during periods when they were not being used.

Advantage 2: a heightened concentration on servicing clients
In general there would be more scope for academics to experiment with innovative subjects and teaching styles. Academics with good reputations who wanted to pioneer subjects that threatened to steal numbers from colleagues' enrolments would no longer have to battle through departmental 'retreats' and subsequent endless layers of faculty and university committees before being given approval and being *allowed* to teach their subjects. Rather, they would pay to have their proposals rated for academic level by an accreditation body and entered in databases used by professional advisors of students; then they would be able *freely* take their chances over whether they achieved any sales. In order to stay in business, accreditation agencies

and academic database compilers would need to offer a service at least as good as potential suppliers of such services; as with international credit rating agencies such as Moody's Investors Services and Standard and Poor's, we might well expect there to be actual competition rather than monopolistic provision of accreditation services.

Libraries provide another area where services can be more entrepreneurial and responsive to client needs if privatized and run on a user-pays basis. Library firms could engage in cooperative inter-loan arrangements just as university libraries do at present, but one might also expect academics in some cases to deal direct (via email and courier services) with distant libraries that offered access to superior collections if this enabled them to obtain books and papers more rapidly or at less cost than they could if they used local libraries as intermediaries. One might also expect that, as email networks develop, a further source of supply would be direct from authors, in the event that enough libraries failed to stock their books or deterred their use via high lending charges. (One suspects that much of the supply by this means would involve breach of copyright agreements with journal publishers.) Under a user-pays system, private enterprise libraries would be under market pressure to develop their collections in ways that ministered to the preferences of their customers: it would be in their interests to ensure that ordering of stock were not the haphazard process it tends to be under the common present system of relying on recommendations from academic staff, many of whom are too busy to make orders or too inclined to presume that someone else will be ordering even if they are not. Either libraries would employ subject librarians who had considerable expertise in their subjects, or they would buy advice in from academic consultants or from agencies that specialized in keeping an eye on what was being published and how it was being received by reviewers .

Advantage 3: More efficient use of human resources
With coordination dealt with via individual responses to market conditions or, for a fee, by organizers of degree package deals and academic database services, there would be little need for academics to spend their time in meetings of the kind often satirized by novelists such as Malcolm Bradbury and David Lodge. Present systems of departmental and faculty board meetings are conducted in many universities with little regard for their cost in terms of academic time foregone from other uses, or with any consideration for resources eaten up in photocopying. Many staff are present at such meetings merely in order to ensure that the numbers will guarantee the fates of particular politically based proposals or simply to speak very briefly on particular issues; much of the time, they have little reason to be there. Under a market-based system, where academics charge for their time, interchanges between individual academics and/or between academics and

entrepreneurs specializing in providing coordination services will be avoided unless they concern specific inquiries; committees would be replaced by consultancy investigations.

The unbundling of teaching services seems likely to assist in bringing the marginal benefits that students derive from the services they consume more into line with the marginal cost of providing them. This is more likely to be a consequence with itemized billing for office consultations, since it is easy to monitor whom is receiving a private consultation and each consultation involves an additional demand on the lecturer's time. (With large lecture theatres, turnstile devices would be needed to monitor attendance and indivisibilities of size mean that empty seats could accommodate extra students at no cost to the lecturer.) Here, there are some parallels between the problems that arise in the bundled fees approach to charging students and those associated with a charge-free health care system, a small proportion of whose customers are hypochondriacs. Professionals in both systems end up spending a disproportionate amount of their time seeing a few of their clients again and again – clients who in most cases would have more fulfilling lives in the long run if they could be eased out of being dependent.

At present, the chief cost to the student of a consultation with a member of staff consists of time foregone from the next best alternative activity, including time spent queuing to get to see the member of staff. A further restraining factor may be the feelings of guilt that the student might feel from seeing the lecturer too frequently, insofar as this conflicts with expectations about what it is reasonable to get from the lecturer rather than from one's own work. However, students – particularly full-fee-paying overseas students – may start feeling less guilty about demanding more when increasingly high bundled fees are demanded by universities. To the extent that they seek and receive advice by email, their time costs may be greatly reduced, and likewise any feelings of loss of face insofar as their membership of a large lecture class means that they are not known by sight to the lecturer. If the returns to private study time in a library and/or private thinking about how to answer a question are seen as low, there will seem little reason not to call for advice from a lecturer, in the hope that the advice will short-cut the need to read or think. No wonder, then, that students may be prepared to sit and wait for the next vacant opportunity to seek advice from lecturers in universities that pride themselves in offering an 'open door' policy. Under a bundled fees system, the student is not encouraged to think of the lecturers' time as having any opportunity cost and is not given a great incentive to try to become more self-reliant and develop vital skills in studying and tackling problems. Such incentives only arise insofar as it proves difficult to get to see the lecturer because so many other students are queuing up to do so. Under such a system it seems likely that the bulk of office consultations will be with students with poorly developed study skills since those who can work effectively on their own will normally be unwilling to risk having to queue for a long while and forego productive study time.

In the absence of a formal system of charging for consultations, lecturers are likely to begin to find the open door policy becomes completely unworkable once the staff/student ratio deteriorates beyond a particular point. (With small class sizes the implicit contract over reasonable conduct may limit the number of times their students see them on average even though queuing is not a problem.) They will begin to incur so many interruptions to their other tasks that in order to avoid burnout they will start imposing prices on the students, whether in the form of limited office hour consulting times (to raise queuing costs), consultations by appointment only (to impose at least some kind of an upfront administrative hurdle and so that they can use long lead times to deter those who seem particularly lacking in self-reliance), or simply offering perfunctory rather than consummate assistance (in other words, they give advice but with 'frown costs' as part of the atmosphere of the transaction). This outcome is understandable in economic terms but is hardly a sign of efficient delivery of educational services, particularly if institutions promise more than their staff can deliver by way of personal advice.

Advantage 4: Greater choice of work lifestyle
Under a freelancing system academics would have greater scope for piecing together the sorts of working lives that most appealed to them. Academics could control their lives more by choosing where to sell their labour time to implement which particular tasks, instead of buying into a vague contract that might result in them finding more and more tasks put on their desks with vacation leave being foregone merely to enable them to keep abreast of the demands of the workplace. Academics who wished to specialize in teaching particular kinds of classes and who wish to avoid being involved in administrative matters could do so, by bidding for the kinds of subjects they preferred and by using the services of coordination agencies – signing up simply to teach with all the hiring of facilities and registration handled by the agencies – and by not selling their time on educational consultancies. Those who wanted to work part-time or teach less and spend more time as paid referees, or in chasing research funds, could likewise do so. So long as contracted tasks were done according to contract, recipients of a service would be in no position to ask questions about how academics choose to use their time when not engaged providing that service.

Possible disadvantage 1: Academics may spend a considerable amount of time negotiating contracts

This possibility is hard to ignore, given my opening discussion of Coase's analysis of the nature of the firm versus the market as a means of coordinating economic activities. However, as we think about it we should keep in mind the likely emergence of coordination services competing for good academic inputs just like holiday package tour firms that need the goodwill of their client suppliers of tourism services just as they need the tourist clients who wish to consume them. Like conventional academics who decide that their present university employers run an overly bureaucratic or chaotic system and therefore seek to move to better managed institutions, so freelance academics could experiment with alternative strategies and suppliers if they felt they were spending too much time fixing things up for themselves or dealing with poor quality suppliers of coordination and other services.

Possible disadvantage 2: It might be too difficult (or easy) for deviant academics to gain accreditation

If professional bodies took a narrow view of what constitutes acceptable or excellent academic performances in their disciplinary areas, those academics who failed to fit in with the party line could find it difficult to gain approval and hence to win places in academic directories vital for marketing themselves to students. The closed-shop tendencies of many professional bodies are well known and are of great concern to those who take a relativistic view of scientific knowledge (cf. Feyerabend, 1975). However, so long as there is a free market for accreditation services, then deviants might seek recognition elsewhere. In economics there are clear signs of how deviants do get organized into professional groups that run their own journals, for example, the Association for Evolutionary Economics and the Society for the Advancement of Socio-Economics. Probably the real disadvantage of a free market in tertiary education in respect of accreditation is not that some academics will experience difficulties in gaining recognition but the opposite – that, for a fee, *anyone* might gain accreditation, just as people can buy 'degrees' from unrecognized but plausibly named 'universities' and rusting hulks can gain certificates of seaworthiness from profit-making agencies associated with governments who let their insignia be used as flags of convenience. In the absence of public sector regulation, students might need to be educated at school in ways of judging between types of accreditation or might purchase advice from a higher level market or public agency that specialized in accrediting accreditation agencies.

Possible disadvantage 3: Short-term contracts may distort research

This possibility is related to familiar arguments in favour of university staff being hired on contracts that, following a successful probationary period, provide for lifetime employment. The 'tenure' argument is normally advanced with respect to a need to guarantee academic freedom. However, a further dimension is that those who are on short-term contracts may work out research programmes very much with a view to keeping themselves marketable, going for projects that will rapidly bear fruit in the form of articles and steering clear of major acts of scholarship that have very long gestation periods. Freelance academics might be able to reduce such pressures insofar as they could negotiate, say, five-year forward sales of block bookings for their services with educational package deal agencies. The costs of reviewing academics for accreditation might also mean that this procedure were undertaken somewhat infrequently – rather as in the present Research Assessment Exercise system in the UK – unless the academic were seeking to be elevated to a higher level of accreditation.

Possible disadvantage 4: Students may not see merit in spending more than the bare minimum on their studies
Students may be inexpert judges of what it is in their best long-term interests to do. Prior to their choices of educational programmes, and subsequently when they a undertaking them, they could pay for advice, but they might be suspicious that the advice could be coming from those who stood to gain from giving particular kinds of advice. It might be necessary for governments to introduce a regulatory framework similar to that used in to deal with analogous conflict of interest problems in the financial services industry. Something less than a free market might be needed to counter a further problem: unbundled, fee-for-service forms of delivery of tertiary education involve greater risks that students might try to get their degrees 'on the cheap' and actually end up paying more in the long run because they were too conscious of the costs of seeking advice and prone to underestimate the benefits of individual consultations. A possible strategy for dealing with this arises quite simply if students are only partially funding their tertiary studies and are required to purchase study vouchers from the government at a discount. These could student-specific, so that no secondary market emerged, and the government could oblige students to purchase a minimum number per year of full-time tertiary studies. It would then be up to the students to decide how to use their vouchers and, with their funds sunk into the vouchers at the outset, students would be inclined to use them up to the full.

Possible disadvantage 5: The range of options available to students may decline
This possibility is related to the one just considered. At present, subjects with low enrolments are subsidized by 'service' courses where one academic lectures to several hundred students. With a market-based system, more attention would be given to the costs and benefits of offering unpopular

subject units. Cost-conscious students might be inclined to take cheaper units where low prices were achieved on the basis of large enrolments. An apparent consequence would be increasing similarity among patterns of study in particular areas and a bias against new units because of their set-up costs. Two main forces could work against such an outcome. First, subjects with low enrolments could be based more around guided private reading, whilst localized small groups of students in particular subject areas could be concentrated together via the use of distance education methods. Secondly, if the kind of voucher-based system discussed in the previous paragraph were introduced, then, in order to make the most of their budgets, students might opt to use some of their vouchers to pay for studying relatively unpopular subjects, rather than to pay for, say, more intensive tuition as a means of achieving higher grades on popular subjects whose basic costs were lower.

Possible disadvantage 6: A loss of equity across the student population
A student with a great inclination and ability to invest in a programme of high quality tertiary education might opt to spend more than less affluent and less well-motivated students. For example, under a freelancing system one would expect tuition from academics involved in unfunded research to be more expensive: unless they were prepared to buy research time as a luxury by foregoing income below target levels, academics would only be able to engage in unfunded research if they could earn at a higher rate per hour when teaching, for time spent doing research is time not available for teaching. Students would not pay these higher teaching fees unless they were convinced that their education would be enhanced (or would appear to prospective employers to have benefited) by being bestowed by active researchers. In an unbundled system, slow-learning students who needed higher more consultations with their lecturers would, other things equal, be less able to afford an education with research-oriented academics, and similarly for less affluent students, unless scholarships were available.

Valid though these claims might be, we might note that prevailing systems whereby universities charge pretty much the same fees but choose whom to admit on the basis of academic records are hardly equitable themselves: if academic high-fliers wish to be taught by academics whose teaching loads are low enough to enable them to push back the frontiers of knowledge, they tend to find that such academics are very happy to admit them in preference to those with less promising records of academic achievement.

Possible disadvantage 7: Loss of 'atmosphere'
Following Williamson (1975), New Institutional economists have recognized that the productivity of systems of economic organization are affected by their 'atmosphere' and that attempts to contrive a particular kind of

atmosphere as part of a contractual arrangement may be very difficult to engineer. Even in present systems it is clear that the atmosphere of distance learning and commuter universities is different from that at residential universities, and this probably affects learning processes. It is doubtful that a decentralized tertiary education system in which students bought unbundled packages of educational services would have the kind of collegial atmosphere offered by a typical university where most students reside on campus. Consultations with staff, and between staff, would just not be the same if accompanied by the sound of a ticking clock against which consulting fees would be calculated. If students were piecing together their educations in all manner of different ways they would be less likely to intermingle and learn outside the classroom on a social basis. Having seen how few of my 'commuter students' realize what they may be missing in terms of social learning by not being resident on campus, I wonder how far educational entrepreneurs would be successful in selling the benefits of franchised package deals that sought to enhance the social side of the learning process. Freelance academics would face much the same problems as students with disparate learning programmes. However, they might be expected to attempt to overcome them by investing more in attending conferences and participating in local gatherings of professional societies.

6.7 CONCLUSION

From the standpoint of the New Institutional Economics a university is seen as a coordinating device that signals and upholds academic standards as well as allocating resources. But it is by no means the only conceivable way of achieving these ends. If a government with a 'New Right' persuasion closed existing universities, auctioned off their assets and opted out of any further involvement in arranging the delivery of higher education, it is by no means obvious the forces of free enterprise would select universities – albeit private ones – as the dominant delivery system for tertiary teaching and research. It is quite possible that several systems would prove viable in the long run, though it is likely that the transition process would be quite messy unless the change to the free market system were signalled well in advance of its implementation – in contrast to what has happened in countries such as the UK where almost overnight many new universities were created out of former polytechnics. In New Zealand, attempts by the government in the early 1990s to foster a 'seamless' education system fell a long way short of promoting the extreme free market system outlined in this paper. However, they did recognize that if a variety of institutions (schools, polytechnics and universities) have the capacity to offer similar services to students then students might benefit from being given more choice in how they put their educations together and when they make the move from one institution to another. If universities teach at the first-year level in ways that give students the justifiable impression that they are merely experiencing a re-run of their final year at high school, then the ability to count the latter towards a degree might help to concentrate the minds of university planners on whether they should be offering something rather different. At least universities themselves also appear to be opening their minds about possible ways of delivering educational services that increase student choices without compromising standards: they are making cross-creditation of subjects much easier; they are increasingly making use of specialist consultants or external teaching contractors rather than presuming that, wherever possible, tasks should be handled internally by long-term employees; and they are even getting involved in franchising activities.

It remains unclear how far the extension of the market should go in tertiary education. Signs of institutional failure are certainly not hard to uncover. Here I will mention just three examples. First, private sector personnel managers must be astonished by the way that some universities take years to fill vacancies, particularly at a professorial level, or hire manifestly under-qualified junior staff (particularly in the business area), because senior management are out of touch with the realities of the labour market. Considerable staff time can be eaten up in these processes. Secondly, in the UK and Australia in the late 1980s/early 1990s, the tendency of 'new universities' to award chairs to senior staff with research records nowhere near to those typical in established universities has caused much disquiet – for example, the *Times. Higher Education Supplement*, 18 March 1994, reported that Dr Phil O'Keefe of the new University of Northumbria resigned his chair in protest in his own inaugural lecture. Parallel but less dramatic grumbling was heard in Australia a few years earlier as the binary divide there came to an end. Thirdly, as someone originally trained in the UK, I have been horrified over almost two decades to observe a lack of double marking and external examining of undergraduates in Australasia. This means that lecturers who believe that degrees are being awarded in too slack a manner can appeal to no external reference point if trying to uphold their raw marks against empire-building heads of department who would prefer to cook the marks into something more palatable to those who allocate resources between departments and institutions.

On the other hand, universities can be portrayed as remarkably effective devices for economizing on the costs of using markets by offering flexible bundled products called degree or diploma programmes and hiring staff on exceedingly vague contracts. Academic professionalism and dedication have enabled many universities to function on the basis of much give and take with much smaller management structures than private firms with comparable numbers of employees. By not making many things the subject of fresh contracts they have sidestepped the problem that, if items have to be charged for on an individual basis, the number of things that can be purchased may be reduced by the consumption of resources in the contracting and billing process. It is conceivable that opportunistic behaviour may be far less in universities than in the world of business. Thus in many cases academic integrity may have been sufficient to stop standards from being compromised despite minimal formal monitoring and auditing of performance.

Insofar as the delivery of tertiary education is indeed based on professional expertise and largely intrinsically motivated non-opportunistic conduct, it may be unfortunate that education ministers are, via their demands for greater accountability, leading to growth in corporate-style management with expensive new senior appointments and demands that staff fill out audit forms in triplicate. Such costs of management could be a major drain on resources that might have been used for teaching and research, for little or no gain in operating efficiency. It is paradoxical that government demands for accountability are increasing at the same time as governments are trying to facilitate competition in the delivery of higher education. If competition between alternative delivery modes is intense, it will be in the long-run interests of those who provide educational services to take their own steps to ensure they are not squandering their resources and that they can convince potential customers of the quality of their products.

7. Principal-Agent Problems and Structural Change in the Advertising Industry

7.1 INTRODUCTION

This chapter explores opportunism in the advertising industry in a rather different context from that which normally provokes debate amongst economists. The common battleground has been that the welfare implications of expenditure on advertising are frequent. Debate here kindled particularly by the classic anti-advertising works of Galbraith (1958) and Packard (1957) (see Utton, 1982, chapter 4, for a useful discussion). In 1982, Stephen Littlechild made a pioneering attempt to bring some psychology to bear in this area, and recently Hanson and Kysar (1999a, 1999b) have published major articles on the scope for market manipulation that pave the way for a behavioural approach to law and economics. Here, however, I focus on the competitive process in the advertising industry itself, rather than on the question of whether advertisements subvert consumer sovereignty. Although my particular interest lies in whether the companies that spend money on advertising are likely to be getting a fair deal in their own terms, the analysis is indirectly relevant to the normal discussions about advertising's effects on consumer welfare. If advertisers could get their campaigns conducted more cheaply, they might offer consumers lower prices or, by ploughing higher current profits back into research and development, they might be able to supply better products in years to come.

At first sight, there seems to be little cause for concern about the operations of the industry. Marketing texts characteristically portray advertising agencies as competing keenly with one another. Casual reflection on the nature of the business and modern technology relevant to it initially lends strong support to such a view. Consider the following passage from Tom Friedman's best-selling book on globalization, *The Lexus and the Olive Tree*:

> [W]ith a single personal computer, credit car, phone line, modem, color printer, Internet link, Web site and Federal Express delivery account, anyone could sit in

their basement and start his or her own publishing house, retail outlet, catalogue business, global design or consulting firm, newspaper, advertising agency, distribution business, brokerage firm, gambling casino, video store, bank, bookstore, auto sales market or clothing showroom. And it could be done overnight at a very low cost, and the company could become a global competitor by the next morning (Friedman, 1999, p. 65).

To Friedman's list of inputs, we might add some creative artistic, cinematic and musical capabilities, a digital camcorder, MIDI keyboard and appropriate software if an upstart advertising agency were to be able to offer multi-media services, but his basic point nonetheless remains. In principle, this does not sound like a high-cost industry to enter. Even before the technological revolution advertising agencies were often small-scale operations: in 1982, there were 8,000 advertising agencies in the US employing in all only 82,000 employees (Bovee and Arens, 1982, p. 116). However, with the rise of mega-agencies and media conglomerates in the merger mania of the 1980s, questions arose about whether the advertising market was becoming less hotly contested than in the past, particularly if the emerging giants were tending to gobble up the smaller players. Whilst there are still small players around into today's world of electronic commerce, it is clear that the top-ranked companies handle a disproportionate amount of advertising work. The details of the top thirty UK agencies published in *Campaign* (23 February 2001) reveal declared billings of the top firms that are typically in the range £200–400 million, and the names of the agencies generally appear to be similar to the 'name' agencies of the past. The agencies themselves appear to be as keenly interested in their rankings as pop musicians are in their places in the charts for sales of recorded music. Indeed, one is left wondering to what extent the advertising industry is like the music business, where the market share achieved by superstars is out of all proportion to any advantage (if any) they possess in terms of creative talents (cf. Adler, 1985). If superstars achieve huge sales because they are well-known rather than because they are particularly outstanding, then it may be a long road to success for anyone setting out to undermine the brand equity of established advertising agencies – even if they are particularly gifted in terms of creativity.

7.2   THE IDIOSYNCRATIC NATURE OF ADVERTISING AND THE SCOPE FOR OPPORTUNISTIC BEHAVIOUR

There are two main risks that may act as deterrents to would-be opportunists. One is that the victim will discover what has been going on and in future turn elsewhere: the short-run gain may not seem worth the long-run loss of future business. The other may be present even with one-off transactions: it is that by one means or another the potential victim might be alerted to possible dangers and ways of avoiding them by dealing with alternative suppliers. Implicit or explicit collusion by suppliers may reduce the scope both for being found out and for the suspicious customer to turn elsewhere. But collusion by incumbents is likely to be of no avail if they are aware of potential entrants who would be able to contest the market without fear of having to exit at significant loss if the established players tried to 'teach them a lesson'. In other words, opportunism is unlikely to be as much of a problem in buyer–seller relations if the market is hotly contested in Baumol, Panzar and Willig's (1982) sense.

Despite the minimal capital requirements for setting up as an advertising agency, the way that the advertising business works in practice seems at first sight to offer considerable scope for opportunistic ploys. Though an intending advertiser may invite a number of agencies to pitch for the right to conduct its campaign, what actually gets supplied will vary according to which agency gets the contract; it is not something that will be pre-specified in a highly detailed contract. The situation is very unlike that in, say, the business of subcontracting to supply automotive components to a particular specification, where the incentive to deliver to the required standards and on time is considerable because a breach of contract can be easily identified. In addition to the product not being precisely specified, an advertising agency would potentially be in a position to hold up a client's marketing activities by suddenly trying to renegotiate its terms to its advantage on pain of otherwise not getting a campaign ready on time. On the other hand, the product-specific nature of an advertising campaign means that the advertiser often has scope for refusing to pay once the campaign design has been finished. There is, in short, much scope for bilateral bargaining. As Kay (1997, pp. 33–5) points out, these are precisely the kinds of conditions that would lead Williamson (1985) to predict the failure of the market mechanism in this context and a very widespread tendency of firms to arrange their own advertising. If worries about acrimonious market exchanges were extensive, it would appear that the main deterrent to do-it-yourself advertising is economies of scale, yet, as Kay notes, the mean size of an advertising agency in the US in the early 1980s was a mere ten employees (see the figures quoted earlier from Bovee and Arens, 1982). As further evidence that economies of scale are not strong in advertising Kay notes that advertising industry mergers tend to result in worsened overall performances of the agencies in question. Despite this, the services of advertising agencies are called upon by major businesses, rather than merely by the small fry that could not justify employing their own advertising staff fulltime.

During the construction of an advertising campaign representatives of the agency will normally keep the client informed of progress and seek approval for their plans. But prior to such meetings one may expect debates within the agency about the strategy to be selected. In both situations the scope for opportunistic behaviour is considerable. Consider, for example, the difficulties in assessing proposals by creative staff. Nowadays, many 60-second television advertisements involve production outlays many times greater than entire programmes between or within which they are sandwiched. It is possible that the business of making them gives great satisfaction to art-workers or video makers, even though something far less lavish could have had an equal or better effect. If the creators try to justify their works with reference to their supposed basis in semiotics or their psychological workings, it may be difficult for other members of the agency to refute these claims because they lack the specialist knowledge required to do so. Account management and media buying skills are very different from those involved on the creative side. Disputes may also arise over the wisdom of paying big bucks to get a famous movie star to appear in an advertisement. For example, in the late 1980s, Foster's advertising agency BMP DDB Needham paid actor Burt Lancaster £500,000 for ten days' filming in Scotland and director Bill Forsyth about £10,000 a day in order to recreate the mood of the film *Local Hero*. It is debatable how justified this was as a means of selling Australian beer. On the one hand, such kinds of expenditure may be argued to guarantee far more attention than a larger number of screenings of advertisements that were much cheaper to construct. On the other hand, more time spent on creative thinking might be able to produce attention-grabbing advertisements for a fraction of the cost. A classic example is the award-winning advertisement 'Ode to a Pea', starring a solitary Batchelor's tinned pea and made by Park Village Productions in less than half a day for a mere £2,000 (these examples come from Olins, 1990).

Differences in expertise may thus make it difficult for members of an agency to discover the extent of each other's self-serving behaviour. Likewise, differences between an agency and its clients in terms of know-how and access to information may enable the former to get away with conduct that would be precluded if clients had inside information. But sometimes this may work to the client's benefit. For instance, an agency's staff may have a genuine hunch about the creative potential of a particular campaign design and yet *need* to engage in downright deceit in order to get the go-ahead from a sceptical client. An example here concerns the well-known Silk Cut cigarette advertisements, whose deeper undertones satirical novelist David Lodge (1989, pp. 220–4) analyzed as part of a layman's illustration of the nature of semiotics.

According to Ferry (1990, p. 54), these advertisements were originally written in the late 1960s by one of the Saatchi brothers who was then working at Collett Dickenson Pearce. On that occasion the client rejected them. He then proposed the same advertisement years later when Saatchi and Saatchi won the account. This time, the sceptical client insisted that the agency should try the advertisements out on the public. The test results did not square with Saatchi's intuition:

> "It was awful. Most of our sample had no idea what the hell it was. The few that did said it was a split lung, a ripped coffin lining or something even more disgusting', recalls an ex-Saatchis man. To his colleague's horror, Saatchi straightfacedly told the client the research results were the best they'd ever had. (Ferry, 1990, p. 54)

Things might have been very different had the client engaged a third party to run the test.

Such considerations suggest that purchasers of advertising services might be wise to specify their contracts not in terms of what is to be supplied, but in terms of the results, with penalty clauses for failures to reach particular standards and bonuses for higher attainments. Such contracts are indeed starting to emerge and, as the *Economist* (1990a, pp. 15–16) has argued, econometric modelling and the information output from supermarket checkout scanners are helping to make advertising more accountable. Likewise, the use of 'people meters' to audit more accurately audiences of the electronic media are making it easier to assess the quality of media planning and buying services (Shoebridge, 1990, p. 89). However, it is by no means obvious how success might be measured, given the difficulties of isolating the impact of advertising from other factors that might be affecting sales, including slackness (for example, in terms of quality control) on the part of the advertiser or its distributors. Most easily measurable are recall rates and coupon responses. But there is a danger that the agency will concentrate its efforts on producing the outcomes that are agreed on because they are measurable even if members of the agency themselves harbour doubts as to their effects on sales. For example, an anti-Aids campaign might enjoy high recall rates and yet have little impact on sexual behaviour.

Results-based fees come into their own if a campaign is as conspicuous a flop as that which Hill Holliday ran for most of 1989 as a build-up to the launch of Nissan's Infiniti luxury car brand in the United States. The advertisements talked about the car but did not show it, or even parts of it, in an attempt to ensure that the product did not get in the way of the message about the brand's new philosophy of Japanese luxury (Hill Holliday's strategy is detailed in *Car Magazine*, 1989). But the results of a campaign that 'dwelt on rocks, streams and trees, but not cars' (*Economist*, 1990b) were dismal brand recognition and sales – at around a third of those achieved by Toyota's less cryptically advertised Lexus – that were barely half what the company had been expecting. However, outcomes are usually much more debatable and costs of measuring results may discourage advertisers from insisting on results-based fees. If the market research required for assessing the campaign is subcontracted, it would obviously be unwise to award the contract to a subsidiary of the agency whose work is being examined. The market research arm of a rival agency could barely be said to be preferable in terms of conflict of interest. A specialist research agency has attractions as a supplier of an independent audit.

Where a client does feel that the agency has delivered a defective campaign, the scope for obtaining redress is likely to be limited, even if the contract is so detailed as to specify things such as image recall rates. For example, it may well be possible for the agency to commission an audit which reveals much more favourable impacts of its campaign. Although the campaign may have turned out a flop due not to opportunism but to incompetence, poor judgment (probably the case with the Infiniti advertisements), or the relative creative ingenuity of rivals, one would well expect opportunistic behaviour in the face of complaints. (Of course, one could imagine the setting up of a judicial tribunal to resolve such disputes, whose own audit team's assessment would be definitive. However, the longer the dispute dragged on, the harder it would be to assess what the actual impact of the campaign had been.) In most cases a suspect agency will simply be fired.

Clients would not normally find it in their competitive interests to tell other firms about their experiences with advertising agencies that appeared to have indulged in slack behaviour and sharp practice. This is rather different from the consequences of the discovery of opportunistic behaviour in consumer markets, where, unless the embarrassment is too great, people tend to spread the word amongst their social networks; one act of opportunism thus results in the loss of many sales. However, in this industry an alternative restraining factor is the fact that major changes of advertising agency clienteles are usually given media coverage by trade journals such as *Marketing*. The fact that only about 10 per cent of accounts change hands each year (*Economist*, 1990a, p. 4) might be construed as implying that most of the time agencies are seen as striving vigorously and competently to do the best thing for their clients. But there is another way of viewing this situation.

7.3 REPUTATION AND THE CONTESTABILITY OF THE ADVERTISING BUSINESS

The idiosyncratic nature of advertising opens up a major role for reputation to determine whose services are contracted. The costs of failure and the difficulties of proving that one has been a victim of opportunism or incompetence may make it seem vital to choose a reputable, reliable agency in the first place. At first sight, this appears to open up scope for such agencies to command fees that generate supernormal profits. It seems that newly established agencies will experience difficulties in picking up customers even if they try to compete on price, because they will not be able to guarantee to match incumbent suppliers in non-price terms. Prospective advertisers may find it very difficult to discern opportunism on the part of a supposedly reputable agency whose pitch seems to involve greater expenditure than that suggested by an interloper who promises a different way of meeting the client's stated goals. Clients who lack experience of doing the job themselves may feel it is reasonable to judge the likely quality of a campaign by its estimated cost. A similar barrier may arise in respect of entry pitches that focus on the prospect of a wildly innovative campaign: decision-makers in the client organization may be poorly equipped for assessing the chances of success.

As an example here we can note that, for all his reputation as a creative hi-flier in the Australian advertising business in the 1980s, even Siimon Reynolds initially found it hard going when, at 23, having already had a couple of years' experience at as creative director at Grey Ltd, he co-founded the OMON agency.[1] In an interview, he lamented the cautiousness of many prospective clients, who seemed to adopt the maxim 'No one ever got fired for choosing IBM' to provide a basis for sticking with an established advertising agency (see *Australian Way*, 1990). No marketing manager will relish the prospect of a fiasco ensuing if a tried and trusted agency is dropped on his/her recommendation. Many may thus be in danger of ending up paying over the odds for a relatively ineffectual conservative campaign run by an agency with whom they have felt satisfied in the past. So long as they meet their aspirations, they are under no pressure to do something radical.

In fact, matters are less in favour of incumbent firms than they initially appear. As they decide on their pitching strategies, senior staff in incumbent agencies should be worrying about three main threats to their positions. First, major advertisers may be willing sign over small parts of their accounts to other agencies as an experiment. A new agency's growth can thus be based on the reputation it achieves following success at 'chipping' off bits of the blue chip accounts (see Browne, 1990, p. 56). Secondly, entry by staff that defect from established agencies in order to set up their own businesses is made easier insofar as they can take clients with them and then use these clients as a basis for attracting new business of their own. This is easier when the latter recognize the success of particular campaigns may have been due not to the fact that they were handled by particular supposedly reputable

---

[1]   This did not hold back OMON for long, however, and in two of the four years he was there, the firm won the Agency of the Year award twice and in 1989 opened an office in New York whose clients soon included Toyota, Philip Morris and the Trump Organization.

companies but due to the skills of the particular personnel that handled them. Thirdly, entry may come from established companies who lure well-known advertising hi-flyers (and with them, their established clients) into their organizations by paying appropriate 'golden hellos'. These firms may include rival agencies or major users of advertising that are choosing to *internalize* all or part of their advertising activities – the ultimate restraint on opportunism by subcontractors is to do it oneself, at the risk of being let down by members of one's organization. They may also include other established firms that are trying to set up agencies of their own, hoping to build on their existing skills in somewhat similar lines of business (say, travel services or video production). The 'internalizing' entrants may be adopting a taper integration strategy in which they internalize only part of their advertising activities. By splitting their supply of advertising services between internal and bought-in sources, they can build up expertise about the value for money likely to be associated with the pitches of external suppliers of advertising services.

These scenarios seem not to have been much on the minds of those who helped finance the takeovers that led to mega-agencies such as Saatchi and Saatchi or WPP in the 1980s. (The history of the Saatchi brothers' activities up to the end of 1988 is outlined in Kleinman, 1989.) In many cases, over-inflated sums were paid for agencies based on their past earnings even though their key assets were their personnel. Subsequently, some agency partners found that the fortunes they made from selling out to the likes of Saatchi and Saatchi did not compensate them for the feelings that came with being owned by someone else (Ferry, 1990, p. 56). If they, or their more junior staff, subsequently tried to restore their morale by quitting to set up on their own accounts, the mega-agencies would be left with a smaller market share. Hence, unless such agencies enjoy advantages of size that outweigh the costs of servicing the debt burdens incurred in order to stitch them together and any other disadvantages that go with larger size, their long-term positions look precarious.

The aftermath of the Saatchi brothers' 1980s merger mania makes particularly interesting reading in the light of the foregoing analysis. By the end of 1994, shares in their agency that had been worth £50 in 1987 were worth a mere £1.50 apiece. Consequently, Maurice Saatchi was forced to resign as Chairman on 16 December 1994 and his former company adopted a new name, Cordiant. The shareholders' revenge was short-lived. Aided by a French partner firm Publicis, Saatchi immediately set about building a new agency, M&C Saatchi. Cordiant's annual revenue soon fell by 6 per cent (£40m) when several major accounts, including British Airways and Mars withdrew their business. By February 1995, Cordiant's share price was barely over £0.80. Saatchi had been followed by three senior Cordiant staff and his new firm rapidly poached around 30 of Cordiant's creative staff

(*Economist*, 1994, 1995). A major legal dispute broke out between Cordiant and M&C Saatchi. In May 1995 a truce was reached whereby M&C Saatchi agreed not to poach any more clients from Cordiant for the rest of the year. Cordiant dropped its court action that had been intended to stop its former staff working for its new rival. When Cordiant cut their losses in terms of legal costs and severance pay, M&C Saatchi were left free to develop into a large-scale global rival, as the following newspaper report indicates:

> *Top campaigners to M&C Saatchi*
> Auckland advertising agency M&C Saatchi is claiming a major coup after signing one of the world's top creative teams.
> Fergus Fleming and Richard Grisdale, known worldwide for their award-winning campaigns for British Airways, Volkswagen, British Telecom, and Dunlop Tyres, start work in Auckland next month after handing in their notice at rival company Saatchi and Saatchi in Sydney. They joined the Sydney office 15 months ago, after 18 years at Saatchi and Saatchi in London.
> Their new employers hope the team will help the agency to win more high-profile accounts, particularly from the car industry.
> M&C Saatchi was set up by brothers Maurice and Charles Saatchi in early 1995, following a shareholder revolt at the agency they founded.
> The Auckland branch was set up in February last year and is one of eight international branches. (*The Press*, Christchurch, New Zealand, 12 April 1997)

The expansion process continued in this vein and by February 2001 the firm had eleven offices and was ranked fifth largest advertising agency in the world, having moved ahead of the 'old' Saatchi and Saatchi (for relevant articles from *Campaign*, see the 'news' section at www.mcsaatchi.com). The new firm emphasizes that 'All of our people work here because they want to, not because they have been bought' (Principle 5: 100 per cent Saatchi).

7.4   PROBLEMS WITH GLOBALIZATION

The mega-agencies that Charles and Maurice Saatchi and their emulators (most notably, the Saatchi's own former finance director, Martin Sorrell) put together in the 1980s were not intended to struggle under the weight of a crushing debt burden. Their aim was to reap the benefits of alleged trends towards the globalization of markets that Levitt (1983) had identified (Marks and Kleinman, 1987, p. 77). It was expected that a global advertising agency would be able to pitch more successfully for the lucrative accounts of companies that sought to market 'world' products via unified campaigns. A London-based manufacturer that, say, allowed the London office of Saatchi and Saatchi to handle its United Kingdom advertising might use the same campaign in Australia. If so, an Australian office of Saatchi and Saatchi could handle any extra work, such as media planning and buying, needed to implement that campaign in Australia.

This strategy did not come unstuck merely because global marketing proved in many cases to be a concept ahead of its time owing to a lack of uniformity in buyers' tastes and needs. Those companies that do embrace a global marketing philosophy will be reluctant to concentrate all their advertising business with a global agency if they are not convinced that the agency can deliver a uniformly excellent standard of service from each of its branches. As the *Economist* (1989c, p. 24) put it, 'A dot on the map is not enough.' The idiosyncratic, creative nature of advertising ensures that agencies cannot standardize their branch operations in the way that McDonald's manages with its hamburger franchises. (Even McDonald's experienced difficulties in gaining adherence to its philosophy when it sought to expand from its home base – see Love, 1986, chapter 17.) Given the difficulties of judging the performance of an agency at a distance, and the fact the global agencies were the product of rapid growth by takeovers of companies with often opposing corporate philosophies, it is easy to understand why most multinational firms remain happy to leave to their local executives the choice of suppliers of advertising-related services. (See Boreham *et al.*, 1989, p. 96, for a discussion of the philosophical problems that arose when Omincom tried to merge its local Needham operation with the Sydney agency Magnus Nankervis and Curl.) Creative staff have tended to adopt a 'Not Invented Here' attitude to campaigns designed by other branches and have been reluctant to refer their valued clients to unknown staff in overseas offices who happen to to be colleagues merely as a result of a recent merger (*Economist*, 1989d, p. 76). The Saatchi brothers remain convinced that globalization is a vital theme for their business but now they seek to get around the issue of a standardized philosophy by building their agencies from the ground up, as their website makes clear.

7.5   CONFLICT OF INTEREST DUE TO CLIENT RIVALRY

Globalization strategies have also run into a particularly acute version of a principal-agent problem that is inherent to any kind of agency growth in the advertising business. As an agency expands its market share it will eventually find itself faced with the prospect of acting on behalf of rival companies. Sensitive information about one client's product or plans could be used secretly to win a contract to implement a devastating campaign on behalf of a rival. So long as the opportunism were subtle enough not to raise the suspicions of the client, one could well imagine the agency using the success of the rival's campaign as a basis drumming up more business from the victim – this time at the expense of the rival, and so on. The recognition of this possibility led long ago to the convention that if an agency found itself handling competing clients it would drop the least profitable account. The ousted client then had to find another agency.

What initially sounds a reasonable convention starts looking more problematic once one considers what the ousted client may then do. Suppose the company judges that it has been placed in its predicament because the going rate for advertising services has increased. If so, it may conclude a more expensive deal with a different agency, a deal that is profitable enough to persuade the agency to accept even though it will have to drop its account with a rival to the firm it is taking on. In other words, we seem to have a recipe for an expensive game of musical chairs. An initial disturbance, or simply a mistakenly generous client, may spark off a very tortuous adjustment process in which advertising agency fees continue to rise until (a) a displaced player stumbles upon an agency that does not deal with any of its rivals; (b) new agencies enter the advertising services market; or (c) some erstwhile clients decide to internalize the increasingly expensive services that they formerly contracted out to the agencies.

This version of musical chairs is expensive in terms of management time spent on establishing new deals. It also reduces the efficacy of reports of agency switches as indicators of client dissatisfaction. Worse still, it reopens the way for opportunism. Having ditched a client in favour of one of its rivals, the agency can hardly be expected to unlearn all that it has discovered in the course of its dealings with the former. It will serve its new client most effectively if it exploits this information.

These conflicts of interest make the formation of giant agencies via takeovers a potential generator of negative synergy, for established clients may have to be shed. The business press has been replete with examples of this, amounting to hundreds of millions of dollars of lost billings: see *Economist* (1986), Magnet (1986), O'Reilly (1986) and Boreham *et al.* (1989). As the concentration ratio rises in the market, a brake upon the profitability of such takeovers comes into play: the musical chairs problem will drive quite major clients into the arms of smaller agencies, or towards internalization. This problem will become all the more acute the more the advertisers themselves are engaging in merger activity, including global takeover strategies. Some potential clients may have so many interests that their lucrative accounts are simply too expensive to accept. For example, O'Reilly (1986, p. 76) reported that after 34 years of handling Proctor and Gamble, Young and Rubican resigned from the account in 1983 because of the cost of having repeatedly to turn away new accounts. An agency may find itself having to give up business even if the firms that it services are not operating as rivals in the particular markets for which the agency handles their accounts. For example, Nestlé might be using a particular agency to promote its infant formula in Pakistan and might then discover that the same agency's UK office is handling a chocolate bar account for Mars in the UK. Though the agency may not handle Nestlé's chocolate products in the UK, or indeed anywhere in the world, Nestlé may still prefer to find an alternative agency.

Much the same kinds of conflicts of interest were recognized in the financial services industry in the 1980s following its spate of diversification-oriented mergers. For example, a merchant bank division of a banking conglomerate handling a share issue would face less of an underwriting prospect if the investment advice division gave a favourable picture of the issue. The regulatory response in some countries has been to insist on the creation of 'Chinese walls' between different divisions. If such directives were implemented in an honest manner, many of the imagined gains of such mergers would be threatened, so it is hard not to imagine grapevine growing over the Chinese walls (for an example of the latter involving the Westpac Banking Corporation and Westpac Life, see Boyd, 1991). In advertising, a similar solution is being tried, and clients may harbour similar suspicions. Most convincing would be an organizational situation in which, following mergers of rival agencies, an M-form structure is adopted, which operates under the rule that no profit centre can handle rival accounts. The internal capital market aspect of such a structure would discourage insider exchanges of information unless – and this may be a major qualification – pairs of profit centres found two-way trades mutually profitable as a means of raising their billings against other internal rivals with whom they did not deal.

Ultimately, what matters for agencies is not the actual degree of confidentiality they can deliver, but the expectations of clients about likely performances and the prices they are prepared to pay for the benefits of a global network or expertise in advertising a particular kind of product. Advertisers in some industries, in some countries, may adopt a more relaxed stance, possibly because they accept the agencies' claim that leaks are more likely to result from defections by the clients' own senior staff. Despite running three parallel networks (Saatchi and Saatchi Compton, DFS Dorland and Ted Bates), Saatchi and Saatchi lost all Ted Bates' Colgate-Palmolive business shortly after the Bates takeover because Saatchi and Saatchi Compton were handling Colgate's rival Proctor and Gamble (Magnet, 1986, p. 46). On the other hand, Saatchi and Saatchi still had the accounts of four carmakers. Likewise, in the UK all the clearing banks were once all handled by Charles Barker and even when inter-bank competition intensified one could still find both the Trustee Savings Bank and National Westminster being handled by J. Walter Thompson (O'Reilly, 1986, p. 77).

7.6   ADVERTISING AGENCY PRODUCT PORTFOLIOS

Advertising agencies seem for many years to have taken the view that it pays to offer a variety of services that are vertically or horizontally linked. It has been standard practice for an agency to provide expertise in creative thinking and copy production, and in media planning and media buying. Holding the operation together is the account manager (the 'suit') who liaises with clients and ensures that they pay their bills. Having accumulated such resources, many agencies are likely to be well equipped to become involved in activities employing related skills, such as direct marketing, telemarketing, market research, public relations, graphic art, design, typesetting and film production. It is perhaps no surprise, therefore, that agencies have been diversifying into such fields, or even beyond. Saatchi and Saatchi had been very successful as middlemen and financial managers – collecting money from their clients early, and paying it to media companies as late as possible. Perhaps this was why they made their ill-fated bids for merchant bankers Hill Samuel and for the Midland Bank, even though they claimed that the basis for their interest was that they could use their marketing skills to revive the bank's fortunes (*Economist*, 1989c, p. 22). However, they seemed to ignore both the fact that the Midland's troubles at the time were largely due to non-performing Latin American loans, and the possibility that they could simply have sought to convince the Midland to pay for their expertise. Given this, and the 'Ponzi financing' methods they used to build up their empire, it is no wonder that the Bank of England decided that they were not 'fit and proper to own a bank'. It was this verdict that caused their share price to tumble and brought their acquisitions programme to a halt (see Ferry, 1990, pp. 55–7). For a time, this firm even experimented with providing computing and management consultancy services, though the Saatchis' consultancy acquisitions were put up for sale once it was discovered how little synergy they had with advertising (*Economist*, 1989d, 1991).

The basis for getting involved in such areas is not simply that they are linked in terms of production and research synergies to the traditional core activities, there are two other considerations, both of which relate to matters of information and opportunism and which ultimately may be classified under the heading of marketing synergy. First, there is the matter of clients being concerned with the possibility that sensitive information about their new products and marketing strategies – and, indeed, about their operations generally – may get into the hands of rivals. To deal with a full-line advertising agency rather than a set of specialized contractors may seem to reduce the risk of such information seeping out. If a single firm is responsible for one's market research, one's public relations and for one's advertising in general, it may be easier to pin down the origins of any inconvenient leaks than if several firms are involved. The conglomerate agency's leadership should recognize both this and the size of business that they might lose if leaks are discovered. Hence they might be expected to take greater steps to ensure confidentiality. Here, then, is a plus-point for the advertising conglomerates, though, of course, they may be less vigilant if they expect to be able to get away with suggesting that blame for any leaks actually lies not with them but inside the client firm or with another of its suppliers.

Secondly, if the agencies can win a client for one of their activities and appear to perform well in that function, they can hope to have an edge when the client is looking for other services: better the devil you know, as they say. More generally, diversified agencies can claim to offer the advantages of 'one stop shopping' – in other words, lower transaction costs – to both potential and established clients. Since it is also costly for an agency to establish a relationship, one might expect that discounts would also be offered to clients that signed up for the agency's full menu of services, but so far this does not seem to be the practice (*Economist*, 1990a, p. 13).

There is again a parallel here with the strategies of players in the financial services industry in the UK in the late 1980s. By diversifying into real estate agencies, the banks, building societies and insurance companies hoped to pick up bigger slices of the mortgage market. Even if they could not sell people the houses they wanted, an estate agent might at least fix them up with finance from the parent institution which they could then use to buy the homes of their choice (see Earl, 1990, pp. 180–1). In either case, one-stop shopping may save the buyer valuable time that would otherwise have been spent on establishing fresh relationships with other potential suppliers, but it may also result in the buyer getting a poorer deal than would have been possible had she chosen to shop around more.

Consider a firm that has employed a particular agency's market research division to undertake a market survey on how its products are perceived. If that survey discovers that the firm's image falls far short of what it had intended, the firm may then find itself in the market for a fresh advertising campaign. Having already established a relationship with the client, the agency is in a prime position to discourage the firm from seeking alternative bids. Even if the firm seeks rival pitches, the first-mover may have an advantage due to its greater hands-on knowledge of the firm. To be sure, this may enable it to construct a proposal that is more suited to the client's needs; yet its package may cost the client more than would have to be paid if such knowledge were also available to the rival pitchers. The key point here is that the appeal of a proposal lies not just in its likely cost but also in its likely efficacy and the latter depends on how well tailored it is to the problem at hand.

When an advertising agency has a range of linked services to offer, a strong incentive may exist for top management to manipulate information acquired by one division to generate business in another. A market research finding that implies a need for advertising is obviously much more attractive to the agency than one which stresses the need for modifications to the product. If the agency is also in the media buying business as well as in media planning, a campaign that involves major media expenditure is also better for the agency. This conflict of interest has long been present in the industry, owing to the nature of the traditional billing system. When the typical agency offered creative inputs, media planning and media buying services as a package, its income came from fees that were based on the value of media expenditure commissioned – service fees from their clients and commissions from media companies – rather than from itemized accounts.

The incentive for agencies to skimp with creativity and advertising production inputs and to try to produce an impact by sheer volume of media spending was acute with such a method of billing. But itemized billings do not remove these conflicts of interest from the multi-service agency, for the key thing is still the bottom line of the account. For example, under itemized billing, a large agency that has its own television studios is more likely to want to recommend a television campaign than one involving a similar amount of spending on space in the print media. If the client is worried by the bottom line, the managers of such an agency may be tempted to make a case for cutting the bill by spending less on air-time and taking more time in the studio to make more memorable advertisements that would not require screening so often. The increased studio charges would be aimed to offset the agency's loss of commission as a media buyer.

The main deterrent to opportunistic intra-agency generation of business lies in the self-serving tendencies (or, better, the integrity) of managers of an agency's specialist divisions. This is also a problem for a synergy-seeking, full-service agency whose cross-referrals have no opportunistic intent: as the *Economist* (1990a, p. 13) notes, 'despite the helpful prodding of their bosses, many of the boutiques remain bolshy about cross-referring clients. For a good reason. They often have little idea how good their sister company is and are unwilling to lose a client in the process.' A particular division's own work will have greater credibility if it does not end with a recommendation that the client then commissions further work from another arm of the parent agency. Lack of knowledge of the standards of other arms of the business will be more acute the more distant and different these are from the operations of a specialist division. The incentive to make cross-referrals is also reduced by the effort required if the personnel that one would need to convince to take up the service (for example, those involved with public relations or quality management) are not the same as those with whom one has so far been dealing (for example, a local marketing manager). It is thus not surprising that even Saatchi and Saatchi could only win about a fifth of its new projects via cross-referrals (*Economist*, 1989c, p 24).

Unbundling is a phenomenon that we must explore in detail, but before we move on to do so it should be stressed that internalization is not a prerequisite for obtaining rewards at the expense of clients through exploiting linkages between various advertising-related activities. Separate firms may conceivably engage in cooperative behaviour, exchanging information with one another about clients or buying and selling information for a fee if the flow is prone to go one way. Of course, there may be legal restaints on such abuses of these kinds of inside information. Alternatively, firms specializing in different niches in the advertising industry may habitually recommend each other's services, just as with international airlines and their preferred domestic carriers and rental car firms. Strategies involving mutual recommendations without commissions are unlikely to prove viable if the parties distrust each others' claims about the efforts they make to cross-refer business and if the distribution of gains is felt to be lopsided.

7.7   UNBUNDLING AND THE RISE OF PROVIDERS OF SPECIALIZED ADVERTISING SERVICES

Service unbundling and itemized billing based on 'head hours' spent performing particular services are options that full-service advertising agencies might have offered their clients at an earlier date had they been forced to do so by competitors who offered such choices. But a state of implicit collusion appears to have prevailed until the rise of 'boutique' operators specializing in providing particular advertising services. Prior to 'Advertising's Big Bang', the industry was dominated by the convention that an advertiser bought a bundle comprising creative inputs, and media planning and buying, with billings amounting to 15 per cent of spending on media space (*Economist*, 1989a). Now, advertisers can, if they wish, put together for themselves a full line of advertising-related services from a variety of agencies and specialists, and then compare the cost of doing so with the cost of buying the whole bundle from a single supplier. Their task is made easier by the entry of specialist consultants who advise on which agencies should be selected to undertake each service, and how much they should be paid (*Economist*, 1990a, p. 17).

In addition to encouraging shopping around and making it easier to reduce risks of falling prey to opportunistic agencies, unbundling and the itemization of accounts may also encourage advertisers to start internalizing some advertising-related activities, for their opportunity costs become clearer. In particular, large account, regular users of media time and space are now likely to be far less inclined to use agencies as media buyers, even if they still chose to use their account planning and creative services. For example, consider an advertiser that lacks resources for engaging in the creative side of advertising and would not be able to use them on a full-time basis even if it cultivated them. Whether or not it opted to do its own media planning and buying could hinge on its ability to subcontract creative inputs, artwork, jingle and video production. (Of course, the firm might indeed consider cultivating such resources and then subcontracting out their surplus capacity, but it might fear that potential clients might be deterred by overlaps in their areas of interest.) These services may become increasingly easy to purchase if creative workers in middle-ranking agencies feel they cannot work at their best in giant organizations and therefore opt to branch out on their own as their employers are gobbled up by takeover-hungry giant agencies. If the giants are not to lose market share in these areas they will need to demonstrate they can match the deals offered by the specialists.

Advertisers may be attracted to use specialist providers of particular advertising services if they believe that a focus on a particular activity may enable them to do a better job, offsetting the greater search and other transaction costs that are the downside of not dealing with a conglomerate agency. The services of specialists may also seem attractive as a result of the latter staunchly pursuing the strategy of being independent, aloof from conflicts of interest with other levels of production in the industry. An excellent example here is that of Australia's largest independent media buying company, Mitchell and Partners, the only non-agency-owned operation in the top five media buying companies in 1990 (see Shoebridge, 1990). With around 500 clients on its books, Mitchell handled $800 million in spending on media advertisements. Until 1990 Michell's closest independent rival had been Merchant and Partners, who, in 1987, had won the media planning and buying business both of both Ogilvy & Mather and J. Walter Thompson when these two agencies closed their media departments. One wonders what these companies made of the purchase of Merchant by Interpublic, then the fourth largest advertising agency holding company in the world. To Harold Mitchell, the move could only be good news for operations like his own. Shoebridge (1990, p. 86) quotes him as saying that 'In a service industry like media buying, which relies on advertising agencies as its client base, a media buying firm cannot be owned by an agency. The conflicts are too great. I predict an uneasy period ahead for Merchant.' A decade later, the long list of member companies at the interpublic.com web-site displays no sign of separate media buying subsidiaries, but Mitchell Media Partners Pty. Ltd. still operates in Sydney.

British Telecom provides a good example of the kind of mixed strategy that may become commonplace in a world of partial internalization and of increasingly respected specialists. As the *Economist* (1989a, p. 62) notes,

> British Telecom spends around £250 million each year on what it terms 'call stimulation' – split between four agencies, all chosen *à la carte* and paid

performance-based fees. BT looked at the idea of running its own media-buying shop. Instead, all its television buying is handled through a new independent firm IDK Media and all its press buying is directed through a sister company of IDK. BT handles media planning itself, talking to 2,000 people each month and anonymously measuring how much 80,000 families around Britain use their phones.

We should not jump to a conclusion that the appeal of the specialists will necessarily deter the conglomerates from behaving with opportunism. Not all advertisers will be aware of the conflicts of interest that face conglomerate agencies. Of those that are aware of such hazards, not all need judge that the costs of shopping around represent a sufficiently low premium to pay to ensure that they receive appropriate standards of service, given the possibility that confidentiality may be lost as a result of more agents having access to their secrets. For a full-service agency that seeks to convince its potential clients that it is at least as trustworthy as independent specialists, the wisest strategy may be to structure itself so that it appears to clients as a several specialized companies as well as a full-service firm. Clients who prefer to make banquet-style purchases from a single company can continue to do so. Those who do not may also continue to do so, without realizing it, as they purchase various services from seemingly separate organizations. Whether or not such an organizational/ownership structure leads to the attenuation of opportunism then becomes a matter of the nature of internal incentives. If the seemingly separate divisions are competing with each other for corporate resources, as in an M-form structure, then the clients may come out on top unless opportunistic negative cross-referrals are made. However, unless a mega-agency is actually organized as a set of smaller full-service agencies (each of whom is prepared to provide unbundled deals), rather than as one full-service agency plus a variety of specialists, managerial difficulties would be expected due to lopsidedness biasing top management's attention.

7.8   ADVERTISING AGENCIES VERSUS THE MEDIA BARONS

In October 1988 Saatchi and Saachi attracted much attention when they announced that they were forming the Zenith media buying house by merging the media buying arms of their three British agencies (Saatchi and Saatchi Advertising, BSB Dorland and KHBB) with their newly acquired media buyer, Ray Morgan and Partners. Henceforth their agencies would concentrate on creative and media planning work. The creation of Zenith would be to the advantage of customers, it was suggested, since Zenith would be better placed to counteract the selling power of media barons such as Rupert Murdoch and Robert Maxwell.

One specific ploy of media conglomerates which a company such as Zenith claimed it would counter is block-booking (*Economist*, 1989a, p. 62), a practice whereby a firm finds it can only purchase, say, television time if it also purchases space in the same media conglomerate's newspapers. We can illustrate how this works by adapting Stigler's (1968, p. 165) classic example of how movie producers used to profit from a block booking policy at the expense of movie exhibitors (see also subsequent work on product bundling by Adams and Yellen, 1976, and Cready, 1991). Consider two advertisers who are trying to reach somewhat different audiences and therefore value differently the media outlets of a particular company. Assume, for simplicity, that buyers can only purchase one unit of each service. Given their assessments of the payoffs to placing their advertising dollars with rival media organizations, the two advertisers rate as follows the maximum worth to them of the media company's products:

A would pay at most $8,000 for a television advertising slot *and* $2,500 for a full page in a newspaper;
B would pay at most $7,000 for a television advertising slot *and* $3,000 for a full page in a newspaper.

Now, if the media company is to sell its television and newspaper spaces separately, and if it cannot charge the buyers different prices for the same services, it must price TV slots at $7,000 and newspaper pages at $2,500. Higher prices would entail failure to sell newspaper space to A and failure to sell TV time to B. Its total revenue from these two clients would be $19,000. If it block-booked these clients, insisting that they could only buy TV and newspaper space as a bundle, for a cost of $10,000 each, it would make an extra $1,000.

The firms dealing with such a media conglomerate could be either advertisers that were buying space on their own behalf, or their agents. Naturally, they would been keen to understate their willingness to pay for particular advertising slots, leaving it to the media owner to try to infer their upper limits by seeing what price would make them carry out a threat to go elsewhere. Learning is difficult in this situation, not merely because the population of advertisers and their campaign strategies will change through time but also because a switch-inducing price only applies given the particular set of offers made by rival media companies on the occasion in question. The rivals may be pleasantly surprised to win business on this occasion and then experiment with a more demanding offer on a future occasion, just as the company that had earlier overstepped the mark starts making rather more humble bids for business. It is also possible that some buyers could be deliberately switching at prices *below* the maximum they are prepared to pay, as an opportunistic means towards getting better terms in future – sometimes it may pay to 'cut off one's nose to spite one's face'.

The Saatchis' justification for Zenith seemed to be that it carries enough buying clout to produce softer quotations by media conglomerates. However, it is not particularly clear that threats to deal with other suppliers might be more troublesome if made by a large agency acting on behalf of a group of advertisers than if made separately by advertisers or small agencies, each acting on their own initiative. The situation is rather analogous to that which exists in the market for new cars: why do fleet purchasers get a better deal than individuals? Certainly, if a major buyer does switch to a rival supplier, the firm that loses the business will have a major chunk of capacity to fill by other means. Defections of customers to rivals are by no means guaranteed to crowd out the latter's regular customers and cause them to fill the space vacated by the defectors, for the rival firms may normally maintain spare capacity to take advantage of opportunities to expand their goodwill (see chapter 10). (Capacity constraints would probably be less significant in the print media than in the electronic media where advertisement/content ratios are regulated, though obviously newspaper and magazine buyers may become annoyed if they judge that too much space is being devoted to advertisements.) But it is altogether too simplistic to suggest that the supplier, whether a media company or a car manufacturer, may give better deals to large buyers simply because of the possibility of having spare capacity to fill. A multitude of alternative clients might switch in the firm's favour if *they* were offered low prices instead. Moreover, although a company the size of Zenith clearly could cause havoc if it, say, implemented a threat to withdraw its business from News Ltd, so, too, could a set of smaller buyers that simultaneously withdrew from News Ltd a similar total value of advertising business.

Economists might normally make sense of price discrimination in terms of differences in price elasticity of demand between the various customer groups. It might cost a car manufacturer less in terms of the expected value of lost revenue to have a satisfactory chance of winning a contract with a fleet buyer, than it would cost if prices were subsequently cut to increase sales to individuals to offset the loss of the fleet order. This analysis is less obviously applicable to the context of media buying, when the parties negotiating with the media owners are merely agents for the ultimate customers. The latter can switch between media buyers to get better deals with a given media owner, whereas individual car buyers may find it difficult to pass themselves off as fleet buyers.

An alternative way of looking at the issue is in terms of transaction costs. Consider once again the car market analogy. The costs associated with fixing up a single fleet deal involving several thousand vehicles may be much less than those involved in selling the same number of vehicles to individual buyers. More finely targeted advertising media can be used, and fewer hours of staff time are likely to be involved with a fleet deal, even if greater effort is lavished on wooing an individual fleet buyer. (With this type of product we should not ignore the possibility that fleet sales may actually serve as a marketing device in respect of sales to individual customers: for example, people who learn to drive in a particular car may then purchase one of their own. This marketing role may be worth paying for via lower prices, if this is necessary to clinch the contract.) Inventory costs may also be lower, not merely because fewer demonstrators will be needed but also as a result of the fleet buyer making a forward purchase of a standardized product, rather than expecting on-the-spot choices of a range of specifications. By forming a buying collective, a group of individuals could in principle set about trying to reduce many of these costs for the manufacturer, but to do this would obviously involve *them* in other kinds of transaction costs.

It is easy to extend this line of thinking to the case of media buyers if we envisage two kinds of firms in this role. Some may operate as intermediaries who earn commission by bringing media owners and users of media space together. Others may act as 'time brokers' that make forward bulk *purchases* of vacant blocks of media space which they then partition and resell to advertisers. (The former are analogous to stockbrokers in Britain prior to the 'Big Bang', the latter are like jobbers.) Carat Espace pioneered the latter strategy and by 1990 was handling about a third of media buying in France (*Economist*, 1990a, p. 14). Clearly, a media conglomerate would find it far more convenient to make large, infrequent deals with a giant time broker than to make a stream of smaller deals via a number of traditional media buyers. In addition to lower costs of dealing with media buyers, it might feel it enjoyed a stronger base of future revenue against which it could make its programming commitments. However, we should also recognize that time brokers that push their luck too far may find themselves in a very vulnerable position compared with traditional media buyers. Suppose a time broker carries out a threat to withdraw its business and make a giant advance block booking of space with a rival media conglomerate. The ditched media supplier can try to pull the rug from under the time broker's feet by incurring the transactions costs of negotiating directly with the firms that want the advertising space (or with other media buyers to whom they might turn for alternative quotations). The time broker could end up having to resell its media slots at a discount.

Comparing differently sized media buyers that do not act as time brokers, we can note that larger operators will probably have more occasions to arrange deals with any particular media owner. There will thus be more scope for bundling together transactions that smaller operators would have had to process separately. If there are economies of scale in gathering information about prices at which alternative media slots can be obtained, one would expect larger media buyers to make more forceful claims to media owners about the possibility of buying equally effective media slots more cheaply from rival media firms. In particular, larger media buyers may enjoy economies in respect of the use of advanced computer systems for keeping track of the availability of particular kinds of media space and matching them with clients' needs.

These advantages of size do not mean that the future necessarily lies with companies such as Zenith that are subsidiaries of giant advertising conglomerates. Major independent operators, able to attract business partly because of their perceived freedom from conflicts of interest, may also exert considerable buying clout. For example, Shoebridge (1990, p. 86) reports that in 1987 the independent Australian media buyers Mitchell and Partners pulled all of their clients' television spending out of the Ten Network because the network's then owner Frank Lowy was demanding an increase in advertising rates of about 50 per cent. This amounted to a loss of sales of about 15 per cent of the station's advertising time and Lowy relented as the Mitchell ploy helped push the network into the red. From this it would appear that Lowy found it easier to retreat than to set about trying to sell the network's time directly to advertisers or through other media buyers. Interestingly, enough, Mitchell and Partners' independence from advertising agencies might not have been be sufficient to make all their clients feel happy that they were *completely* free of conflicts of interest. At that time, the company owned 21.4 per cent of Sonace, which in turn owned 15 per cent of Brisbane radio station 4BH and 32 per cent of Sydney's 2GB (Shoebridge, 1990, p. 89).

The possibility that larger media buyers can extract better terms from media companies does not necessarily mean that advertisers will end up paying less for space in the electronic and print media. For a start, there is the question of what the media companies may do in order to make good the losses they incur by giving in to media buying giants such as Zenith. If previously they were keeping their advertising rates down to a level which kept their earnings low enough to discourage entry, one might now expect them to raise the rates they charge to those who have rather less bargaining power. According to Simpson (1989, p. 35), a number of major advertising spenders, including Nestlé, were so worried by this possibility that they actually considered getting together and setting up their own media buying group.

Secondly, if a giant media buyer can obtain media slots on better terms than its smaller rivals, it may then stand to capture some or all of the difference. How much it passes on in terms of reduced billings may depend on how far it believes it is safe to push its luck before it will lose future business due to clients switching to other media buyers (including other giant operators) or internalizing the activity. These risks will vary among advertisers, so price discrimination is likely to be attractive to media buyers.

In Australia, different advertisers do indeed pay different prices for similar media slots (see Hearne, 1987, pp. 10–11). In the United States, by contrast, media owners are prevented by the Robinson-Packman Act from offering special deals to one advertiser over another (*Economist*, 1990a, p. 14). In economies where price discrimination is a possibility, advertisers could try to guard against it by seeking quotations from several media buyers and then choosing the cheapest quotation, but, clearly, this involves higher transaction costs.

Thirdly, we should recognize that if, in future, non-independent media buyers start seeking to get better deals by acting as time brokers, they will face a conflict of interest. Suppose the media-buying arm of an agency has committed itself to more space than clients appear to want, and that it is experiencing difficulties in attracting extra clients (for example, due to the difficulties of finding potential clients who are not rivals of existing clients). If so, the agency is under strong pressure to avoid embarrassment by ensuring that its media-planning arm inflates its estimates of the need for space by its clients. Once again, though, advertisers may be able to avoid this conflict of interest if they use an independent media buyer, as part of an unbundling strategy.

Finally, in respect of the implications of changes in relative sizes of media companies, advertising agencies and advertisers, we may consider what happens to the distribution of trade credit. Bigger agencies may be better able to delay payments to media companies and speed up payments by their clients. This would enable them to generate positive cash-flows and hence fund expansionary activities or reap the benefits associated with placing large blocks of funds on the money markets.

7.9   CONCLUSION

This is an industry replete with potential conflicts of interest but one that also has a number of checks and balances to deter opportunistic tendencies. The question is whether the latter are sufficient to overcome temptations to succumb in respect of the former. Moves towards unbundling of advertising services by full-service agencies rather suggest that the advertising industry is becoming more competitive, with less of a tendency towards implicit collusion. So, too, do moves towards internalization by larger clients and the emergence of specialist providers of services. However, there may be informational advantages associated with dealing with integrated agencies that make the risk of agency opportunism seem worth taking, especially if a full-service agency has a good reputation. Pressures for larger agencies to trim their costs will be lessened to the extent that they are able to exert bargaining power with media suppliers and to the extent that they recognize that it does not pay compete amongst themselves on the basis of price. Growth by merger may enhance bargaining power but also bring problems of lost goodwill due to client perceptions of conflicts of interest arising from a single agency handling accounts of rival clients. The advertising industry probably could set potential clients' minds at ease if it established an open access computer register of agency/client relationships and agency/subsidiary relationships. Such a facility would make it easy for clients to check up on potential conflicts of interest. But it is rather hard to imagine this service becoming available on such a scale as to contend with the complexity of globally organized markets.

8.   Marketing as Information Economics

8.1   INTRODUCTION

Economists typically have little time for marketing as a discipline and are prone to label it as a Mickey Mouse[1] subject that lacks the rigour and elegant unity of general equilibrium analysis. With much of mainstream economics teaching and research conducted on the basis of the assumption that there are no information problems, there is no occasion to discuss marketing anyway, regardless of whether the intellectual content of marketing is as facile as most economists seem to believe. As Neil Kay (1984, p. 36) points out,

> The marketing function is based on the existence of information imperfections on the part of the consumer. If the consumer is poorly informed then sales promotions, whether of the persuasive type or the informative type, may succeed in changing his consumption pattern. ... In assuming the absence of information imperfections we also eliminate the justification for the existence of the marketing function in the first place.

Students meanwhile are increasingly voting with their feet in favour of marketing and business studies, which they see as having some practical use, and against economics, which they see as difficult, arcane, and abstract, and less likely to lead directly to employment (see, for example, Lewis and Norris, 1997). If economics departments are not to wither away while those focusing on marketing and business studies grow, there may be a need to reengineer what university economists do and reposition the discipline in the minds of potential customers. In this chapter I wish to contribute to this re-engineering and repositioning process by arguing that if economists follow Don Lamberton's suggestions about the need to look at economics with a focus on matters of information and knowledge, then they can offer theoretical foundations for marketing. If students can be shown that to become good marketers they need to have a good grasp of information

---

[1]   Marketing theorists themselves actually take the Mickey Mouse phenomenon rather seriously in its broader social terms: see Holbrook (2001).

economics, then economists who develop capabilities with a view to providing this should find themselves with a receptive and growing clientele.

The chapter is structured as follows. In section 8.2 the relationship between marketing theory and economics is discussed in the light of Lamberton's information-centred interpretation of the theory of monopolistic competition. Section 8.3 examines the role of consumer strategies for gathering and processing information in shaping patterns of brand preference, while Section 8.4 extends these themes into the area of conspicuous consumption, an activity that would make little sense in a world of complete information. Section 8.5 considers the institutional nature of markets as information structures to reduce transaction costs, and portrays marketing as a manifestation of the limited capacity of market institutions to facilitate transactions. Though such a view of marketing might sound somewhat tautological at first sight, it actually serves to link marketing to the post-Coase industrial organization literature on markets and hierarchies that has already drawn economics and management together; it also provides a view of the idea of an imperfect market that is sharply at variance with traditional economic perspectives. Before the conclusion, there are two sections essentially concerned with database-driven marketing and which relate to the social impact of information technology: Section 8.6 focuses on the role of both formal and informal customer knowledge in the emerging relationship marketing paradigm, while section 8.7 considers links between marketing and information technologies such as electronic means of payment and the Internet, and their significance for consumer welfare.

8.2 MARKETING AND THE THEORY OF MONOPOLISTIC COMPETITION

According to the working definition adopted by the American Marketing Association in 1985, Marketing is the process of planning and executing the conception, pricing, promotion, and distribution of ideas, goods, and services to create exchanges that satisfy individual and organizational objectives (*Marketing News*, 1985). This definition is consistent with the focus in marketing management on the 4 Ps of marketing: price, product, promotion and placement. It hints at the discipline's underpinnings in Chamberlin's (1933) *The Theory of Monopolistic Competition*, which paved the way for a focus on the no-price aspects of competition and cast the firms optimization problem not merely in terms of finding the most profitable price/output combination but the best combination of price, product design, promotional strategy and distribution system.

Academic marketing as a discipline had earlier grown out of Mid-West agricultural economics (Cochoy, 1998). Given this, and Chamberlin's demonstration that management's economizing problem entails a far richer set of tradeoffs than in the world of perfect competition, it might have seemed natural for economists – normally eager social science imperialists – to trumpet the idea that marketing is merely economizing carried out in a particular context. Indeed, within each area of marketing, problems could have been set out in terms of optimal tradeoffs: in promotion, for example, a bit less radio advertising versus more print advertising, or fewer prime-time television advertisements and a lot more off-peak ones, or less on advertising and more on commissions or training for sales personnel, or less lavish advertising video production and more air time, and so on. The trouble is that marketing is really too rich an arena for economizing activities: the task does not collapse to two dimensions and entails coping with cost and revenue functions that are interdependent. In principle, choices of marketing strategies involve choices between rival multidimensional plans that do not lend themselves to encapsulation within the economist's normal diagrammatic frameworks. The task of choosing the ideal strategy is not only complex, the links between the many variables and market outcomes may be weakly understood and context specific.

In practice, of course, marketing decisions are not handled in a reductionist manner where any decision variable might be adjusted against any other. Rather, they involve a top–down process of budgeting and functional specialization: the problem is decomposed in a 'top–down' manner akin to Kay's (1979) portrayal of the allocation of resources to research and development, where details are inked in as one proceeds to lower levels, just as Chamberlin himself considered selling costs and product differentiation in separate chapters of his treatise. The ideal strategy is something that might be discovered by trial and error insofar as the market environment will stay still long enough to allow experimentation, so long as experiments are not irreversible. The latter two conditions are central to the mainstream economist's way of thinking but at odds with competitive marketing that entails launching new products – a process of Schumpeterian creative destruction during which producers and consumers both learn. Practical marketing and the *ceteris paribus* world of static optimization do not go together. The marketer may successfully stumble across a particularly effective promotion campaign or develop a product which has, as modern marketers say, a USP (a unique selling proposition), but competitors will adjust their strategies in response and rents may normally only be captured temporarily and need to be ploughed back into new policies for long-run survival.

This non-equilibrium view of monopolistic competition and its relationship to marketing is very much in keeping with that expressed by Don Lamberton (1971) in his introduction to *Economics of Information and Knowledge*:

The undermining of perfect competition does not stop with the introduction of Selling outlays. It must continue until effective competition embraces product competition, perhaps the most important form of competition that exists. (Lamberton, 1971, p. 9)

In the real world, fraught with uncertainty, firms attempt to increase profits by searching for those things which satisfy the want which is just emerging, the least important want. For when wants are known and either stable or controllable, uncertainty disappears and monopoly power is possible. This is what Chamberlin ... was trying to uncover. Competition then only exists in a world of incomplete information. (Lamberton, 1971, p. 10)

Lamberton's view was published almost simultaneously with Romney Robinson's (1971) monograph reappraising Chamberlin's work. Robinson reached a similar conclusion, which was forcefully endorsed by Loasby in a way which highlights the fact that marketing involves grappling with knowledge problems on the supply side as well as removing ignorance and doubt on the part of potential customers:

Certainly Chamberlin's view of the firm employing the three variables of price, product and selling cost conforms much more easily with the idea of a firm searching for customers whose preferences, whose whereabouts, even whose existence are suspected rather than known, than do the traditional sorts of model, in which product differentiation appears as a trick, and all selling expenditures are by definition wasteful, if not actually pernicious. (Loasby, 1976, p. 195)

Research in marketing and the AMA definition of the subject are consistent with foundations that, like Lamberton and Loasby, see monopolistic competition as a process of search and experimentation. But marketers have got to this position mainly via immersion in case studies and with very little help from economics texts encountered during their studies, since these invariably have neither presented Chamberlin in this way nor introduced them to heterodox economists who focus on problems of information and knowledge.[2] However, unless economists make a commitment soon to exploring the relationship between economics and marketing, they may later find that marketers have achieved a competitive lead in doing this in top-ranking scholarly journals. Already, the leading marketing journals display evidence that marketers are picking up ideas from information-oriented approaches to economics and using them as a basis for reconstructing

---

[2] Elsewhere, I have provided an innovative text which includes an extensive coverage of the both heterodox economics and case study methods to assist both academic economists and marketing students in this process (see Earl, 1995).

marketing theory (see, particularly, Dickson, 1992; Hunt and Morgan, 1995). Some leading marketing scholars even publishing in economics journals – see, for example, Hunt (1997a, 1997b).

8.3   INFORMATION AND CHOICE

In the area of consumer behaviour the flow of ideas between marketing and economics ideally should be more in the opposite direction, as it is mostly the marketers who have picked up information-centred themes as a basis for research. For example, when Lancaster's (1966) model of consumer demand in terms of preferences for product characteristics began to be widely discussed, it was soon noted that it had much in common with multi-attribute models of brand preference that dominate empirical consumer research in marketing (Ratchford, 1975). However, whereas Lancaster chose to write as if there was an objective technology of consumption in which commodities produced intrinsic and in principle quantifiable outputs of characteristics when consumed, the marketers preferred to accept that consumers form personal constructs of the set of attributes a product might have and how it might perform in respect of them. This opened up scope for market positioning strategies to influence how consumers construe products (cf. Ries and Trout, 1981). Different images might be cultivated in different markets for the same physical product: hence, for example, a Peugeot 405 could be positioned in European markets as, in effect, a mass market car for sales representatives who really enjoy driving, but in Australia, where it had to be priced further up-market because of import duties, its positioning was more as a chic vehicle for the individualist professional.

Marketers have been far more willing than economists to recognize that individual preferences might be shaped by social interaction involving demonstrations of products, exchanges of information and peer pressure. Their most popular multi-attribute decision model, the Fishbein theory of behavioural intentions, not only assumes subjective assessment of outcomes but also predicts choices to be a function of a combination of beliefs of reference group members about alternative courses of action, along with motivations to comply with these beliefs (Fishbein and Ajzen, 1975). In seeking to understand the diffusion of new products, Marris (1964, chapter 4) and Prais (1973) were for many years almost alone among economists in proposing that the process should be analysed in terms of information networks and in terms of analogies drawn from the study of medical epidemics. In marketing, by contrast, this sort of thinking has been developed formally in recent years into a theory of fashion (see Miller, McIntyre and Mantrala 1995), from which contemporary evolutionary economists would appear to have much to learn. Fulbrook's (2002) recent edited volume

Intersubjectivity in Economics is a sign that within heterodox circles matters are beginning to change.

Marketers and economists (or at least, behavioural/institutional economists) have perhaps their strongest affinity in work which assumes that buyers' choices are essentially based on the implementation of simplifying procedures for processing information (the seminal marketing contribution is Bettman, 1979, which cites the work of Herbert Simon extensively). These decision rules are employed because they seem to work adequately, without their users having any particular basis for knowing how far they fall short of optimality, for in a complex world it is problematic to specify what would be ideal, let alone find it. In allowing choosers to economize on the amount of information they process, decision rules may deny a fair hearing to products that conflict with them, as with the simple rule 'if it works, don't mess with it' (see Hoch, 1984), which is conducive to brand loyalty, not experimentation. Marketing can thus be seen as an activity focused on lending weight to rules consistent with the purchase of the brands one manages, providing buyers with a case for mentally repositioning one's brands more in congruity with their decision rules, or providing consumers with a case for adopting alternative rules that favour one's brands. For interlopers, the trouble is that established brands have status as institutions: people who choose them as solutions to particular kinds of problems are unlikely to be asked to justify their choices, even if they were made without much attention being given to alternatives and in the absence of any specific sets of decision criteria. The rule is, if in doubt, conform and remember the saying, 'Nobody ever got fired for choosing IBM'. Deviants need to be well armed with supporting information unless they are recluses.

Brand loyalty and brand equity are alien to a world of complete information. A brand is essentially a shorthand summary of a set of product characteristics or of the capacity of a manufacturer to judge what mixes of features will be valued *ex post* by consumers who, *ex ante*, may have little idea what they will value in a product they have not hitherto experienced. Brand connotations provide a basis for corporate strategy in terms of economies of scope. If I am fully informed about what is available in terms of mixes of product characteristics, and if I know what I want, then the good reputation of TDK audio cassettes will not influence my choice of video cassettes, nor will my years of trouble-free use of Canon cameras affect my choice of brand of fax machine, printer or copier. In the real world of uncertainty, my decisions will be influenced by proxies and my lay-person's hunches about product technology and hence I am likely to be favourably disposed towards TDK video cassettes and Canon office products if I already have information that favours seemingly related products that carry the TDK and Canon logos. Meanwhile, I may be utterly intolerant of unfamiliar brands whose consumable products might damage my expensive consumer durables: if I cannot buy TDK, or if TDK are significantly more expensive than Sony video tapes, I may buy Sony, but not a much cheaper, unknown, non-Japanese brand. In typically being willing to purchase any one of several brands (Ehrenberg, 1988), brand loyal customers are not acting in a one-eyed manner in the face of quality uncertainty but, even so, they are presenting unknown suppliers with a formidable marketing problem. The latter may end up trying to solve thiss problem via a strategic alliance with an established brand (as with Chinon's supply of pocket cameras for sale under the Kodak brand name: see Assael, 1990, p. 51) or via endorsements from an agent (a relevant celebrity user, for example: see McCracken, 1989) likely to be construed as knowledgeable and trustworthy.

The notion of brand equity and its basis in consumer perceptions rather than objective information is spectacularly illustrated by the ability of the Toyota Corolla greatly to outsell the significantly cheaper Geo Metro car in the US despite the fact that the latter is simply a badge engineered version of the former (see also section 2.6). Since both come from the GM/Toyota joint venture factory in Fremont, California, there should be no underlying basis for preferences of this kind in terms of measurable differences in product quality, while, aside from warranty claims, there is nothing to stop Geo buyers from having their vehicles serviced at Toyota dealerships, if the latter are perceived as superior. Such purchasing behaviour would be impossible to understand in a world of complete information and is evidently problematic for Lancaster's model of choice. More subtle illustrations come from the world of designer brand clothing and conspicuous consumption goods.

8.4   CONSPICUOUS CONSUMPTION AND THE VALUE OF BRANDS AS SYMBOLS

Conspicuous consumption is an activity that would make little sense in a world free of information problems. In the real world, status symbols have been significant constituents of demand for centuries, though the precise mode of status display and degree of ostentation seems to exhibit cyclical patterns as the decades pass (see Mason, 1981). Those seeking to demonstrate their wealth as a means to joining particular social circles do not attempt to do so by pinning to their chests statements by accountants certifying their net worth. Even if such statements could be taken on trust with reference to the reputations of the accounting firms that had prepared them, they would not be sufficient to signify that people of a certain standing in terms of wealth possessed the necessary know-how to be able to behave in a manner consistent with the expectations of the target group in terms of good taste. Acceptance by a social group will not be granted unless a person can demonstrate, via actual behaviour of the accepted kind, that s/he has cracked the group's code of conduct. The nouveau riche, such as lottery winners, successful sports people or self-made business people, may thus demonstrate by their crass displays of wealth that they are not ready for membership of the established upper orders. Indeed, as Rolls-Royce found in the late 1960s, when their cars became popular with high-earning pop musicians and footballers, nouveau riche customers can be a liability. In part this is because their often conspicuously casual attitudes towards preserving their investments harm residual values by increasing the risk of encountering a 'lemon' in the secondhand market. They also lower the social tone of the customer group, leading some traditional buyers to opt for alternative marques that serve as more subtle means for defining their positions in society. (For example, the Range Rover provided a means by which old money could literally look down upon the lesser orders whilst hinting at the extent of their country estates.) However, those who understand the code in question may be able to gain membership by carefully misrepresenting their wealth, as with one of novelist Kingsley Amis's characters, whose Porsche and designer brand luggage and clothing enabled him to fit in so well at weekends in country houses and parties in fashionable parts of London that he rarely had to spend his evenings in his shabby bedsit.

The market for and marketing of expensive cars illustrates particularly well the powerful links between information and brand status. In a world of ignorance and incomplete information, manufacturers of socially accepted brands can enjoy high returns without a great need to keep updating the external appearance of their products in ways that proclaim 'this year's model'. Subtle evolution maintains both the classic images and residual values of prestige brands, whereas fancier variants of mainstream brands depreciate particularly rapidly. Someone who drives a BMW with a personalized number plate may thus be able to leave their audience guessing just how much the car has cost: it might be close to a decade old and recently purchased for relatively little; it might be brand new; or it might be something that they bought new some years ago. By contrast, those who drive what is obviously the latest model Ford may be driving something that cost far more than the BMW cost its owner but could have cost far less than the BMW would have done if the latter is new. Worse still, Ford's brilliant price discrimination strategy, developed in the early 1970s and since copied by other mass marketers of cars, marks the Ford driver out as a person of particular standing in the corporate car pool: the Ford driver with a Mondeo GLX is one step up the ladder from the colleague with the Mondeo LX but not successful enough to warrant a Mondeo Ghia. The value of the LX, GLX or Ghia badges as symbols is such that price differences of the various models may be far greater than the marginal costs of adding additional product features and better-quality trimmings. BMW stands aloof from such status badging of specification levels, enabling owners of spartan entry-level models, that sell for less than ritzy similar sized Fords, to benefit from the fact that everybody knows that, by the time it has been laden with optional extras, the average BMW is a much more expensive car. Entry-level BMWs also benefit from trickle-down of the quality aura of elite models in a higher league from the top-range offerings of mass-market producers. The cachet of badges such as BMW in a world of bounded rationality makes possible the otherwise nonsensical used-car dealer's slogan 'budget priced prestige' (cf. Leibenstein, 1950, p. 203). However, even though mass-market brands may have poorer residual values, they may pay off as the basis for company fleets, not just in terms of low running costs but because of their motivational value in processes of internal competition (cf. Andrews, 1993) – their badges and trim levels enable them to symbolize the status of a particular worker in an organization.

The informational status of prestige brands poses a formidable barrier to manufacturers seeking to capture market share from them, and it is by no means clear that the problem can simply be solved by throwing money at advertising – though this will at least enable the product to stand a bigger chance of being recognized if observed or mentioned in conversation. To match existing prestige brands in quality and price is to provide no reason at all for deviating from the norm, particularly if interlopers are less easily recognized and decoded as symbols. A strategy of matching quality and undercutting price may be unsuccessful if the brand has no status connotation, for more rapid depreciation may overwhelm any initial advantage a lower initial price might give. The third route is to offer a product that sells for a similar price to the target prestige model but offers conspicuously more performance or other features for the money – this ploy was typified in the market for expensive sports cars in the 1990s by the Mitsubishi 3000GT which, for BMW and Mercedes-Benz prices, offered a twin turbo engine, six speed gearbox, four wheel drive, four wheel steering, active aerodynamics and active suspension damping. There is then the risk that, even if the product lives up to is promised performance, it will be seen as a desperate display of technological overkill that gives away its humble heritage in matters of styling details or choice of trim materials. Lack of subtlety, and uncertainty about long-run maintenance costs associated with such complexity, may also disadvantage residual values and help maintain the status of existing prestige brands that appeal on a less is more basis.

Given these diffiulties, it is no wonder that mainstream car makers have been buying up firms whose brands enable them to command premium prices but whose small scale has made it hard for them to generate adequate investment funding. By developing new premium brand models that, under their skins, have much in common with mass-market models, firms such as Ford can reap the advantages of economies of scope and brand equity – so long as their customers and those to whom their customers are seeking to make displays of status remain essentially ignorant of the degree of overlap between the premium and mainstream products.

8.5   MARKETING AND MARKET EFFICIENCY

With much of the discussion in the previous two sections serving to highlight informational barriers that face firms seeking to capture market share at the expense of suppliers of existing successful brands, it is appropriate for us to turn our attention to a broader perspective on the social role of marketing in a world of information problems. This entails an analysis of the relationship between markets and marketing.

The mainstream economist's view of the nature of a market is essentially of some kind of an arena in which a set of potential suppliers and a set of potential buyers mingle, gather information, make comparisons and do deals. This vision was much inspired by the mental images of the stock exchange and primary commodity markets that were once physically centralized trading pits but are now increasingly virtual phenomena based on computerized trading. It has led to the structure–conduct–performance paradigm and a general lack of interest by economists in marketing. Wonder at how prices emerge from the bustle of these organized markets has led economists to construe the concept of an imperfect market with a focus on the possibility that, if there is a limited number of producers, consumers may face prices in excess of marginal costs or, in cases where production is carried out under conditions of falling costs, prices in excess of long-run average costs of production. To a lesser extent, imperfect markets are discussed with reference to the possibility that, due to search costs, price dispersions may exist with some consumers paying more than they need to do in order to obtain a particular item. Either way, the focus is on the question of whether or not the consumer is, to put it colloquially, 'ripped off' by firms extracting excessive profit margins. By and large, the traditional perspective on imperfect markets leads to a focus on barriers to entry in relation to production costs and advertising, concern over possible threats to consumer welfare posed by vertical integration, and a hostility towards collusive behaviour. Even phenomena such as periodic 'sales' are prone to be viewed with cynicism from this standpoint, as devices to perpetuate price dispersions by introducing noise into consumers data on price information (see Phlips, 1988, p. 14).

It is clear that buyers potentially are indeed at risk of making suboptimal choices, for they often need to choose in contexts characterized by incomplete and dispersed information, contexts that are starkly different from the world of the stock exchange and commodity dealers. In a world of durable goods and technological progress, buyers typically may participate infrequently in a particular market and each time have to deal with a changed array of products. Similarly acute information problems face tourists, choosing in unfamiliar geographical settings with limited timeframes, or those who unexpectedly find themselves for the first time urgently needing the services of a plumber, lawyer or undertaker. Once the ignorance and inexperience of buyers is highlighted, it is but a short step to conflate marketing with selling and see it, as it is often seen, as an activity designed to seduce and exploit the buyer. Yet it can also be seen as an activity which can enhance the quality of choices, reducing buyers' needs to search around, providing them with potentially useful appraisal criteria and relevant information, and exposing weaknesses in claims that other firms have made with guileful intent.

The extent to which firms find it worthwhile to engage in marketing activity will depend on the extent to which markets fail to eliminate transaction costs, for, according to Hodgson (1988), markets develop and evolve as partial solutions to the information problems that inhibit the formation of mutually beneficial bilateral exchanges. In Hodgsons analysis, a market is a collection of institutions that help to reduce transaction costs, just as, in Coase's (1937) analysis, a firm is a device whose rationale is to add value by superseding market contracting as a coordination mechanism, instead internalizing activities and substituting the costs of management for the costs of using the market. The institutions that make up a market comprise both legally constituted bodies such as firms and trade associations, and informal but enduring features of the trading environment such as reputations and codes of behaviour. The impact of the trade press should not be understated in this context. For example, glowing product reviews helped Toyota launch its Lexus brand as a cheaper alternative to a Mercedes-Benz – these expert appraisals implied that those who continued to purchase the latter had more money than sense, or were tastelessly breaking social codes by *overtly* engaging in wealth display since the extra expenditure was hard to justify in terms of extra quality and connoisseurship. Such reviews did not merely provide customers with information about product quality and value for money, they also provided a means of justifying the purchase of a Lexus. Toyota was thereby able to surmount the problem facing would-be interlopers into the market for prestige goods: it is not enough to be able to match or surpass the quality and value for money of established brands on the basis of lower production costs, one must be recognized as having done this without the costs of achieving credibility outweighing production cost or quality advantages.

More generally, it may be said that the process of forming judgments is often based on a complex network of reputations. These reputations may become tarnished if they become associated with poor quality or opportunistic suppliers. Friends, if they are to remain friends, have to be careful about whom they recommend. Celebrities stand to lose future endorsement opportunities if they are casual about which products they endorse, while a professional or trade association that seems unwilling to police its members' activities properly or to set standards in areas where customers require them may find its membership defecting to a new association that promises to get tough and clean up the industry. Likewise, As John Kay (1993) has pointed out, firms that offer long-term, no-quibble warranties are, in effect, offering hostages to their customers in order to signal that they believe in their products, since returns or warranty claims by dissatisfied customers could be very costly if they eventuated.

Technological standards and interface systems of the kind recently drawn to our attention by Langlois and Robertson (1995) are institutional features, too: they help buyers and sellers make connections in both transactional and physical senses and, by enhancing the ability of buyers to shop around for substitutable modules, they reduce the risk that buyers will become locked into a particular supply chain, vulnerable to monopolistic pricing.

A market may have a physical presence as a Marshallian business district – an agglomeration of rival and complementary businesses whose proximity to each other reduces supply costs by permitting external economies of scale (for example, specialized car valeting firms develop where there is a concentration of firms engaged in selling used cars), whilst reducing buyers search costs. A market may also have more of a virtual presence, as with classified advertisements and, increasingly, the Internet. Either way, the concentration of offers to sell provides easier monitoring of actions of rivals and a more hotly contested selling environment but it brings in a greater volume of potential buyers and thereby enables suppliers to prosper despite reduced opportunities to charge high margins and exploit buyer ignorance.

The institutions that comprise a market help consumers to make judgments about the likely quality of a particular suppliers output, for market institutions enable suppliers to send signals to prospective customers. For example, if I need a plumber in a hurry I can check in the Yellow Pages to see what the rival firms are trying to tell me about their longevity, their membership of the Guild of Master Plumbers, and their policies for ensuring customer satisfaction. Outlay on a Yellow Pages advertisement and Guild membership may obviate the need for other promotional investments if potential customers do indeed 'let their fingers do the walking' and understand the significance of the messages in the Yellow Pages entry. But even the Yellow Pages investment would be unnecessary if the firm could rely upon re-buys and word-of-mouth recommendations to generate enough sales.

From this standpoint, the efficiency of a market depends more on the quality of the institutions of which it is comprised than on the number of suppliers jostling for business. If there are many suppliers of a particular class of goods and buyers nonetheless have a great deal of trouble locating good deals because there are substantial dispersions in terms of price and quality, then we would not claim to have an efficient market. By contrast, a market in which the price/quality/location of outputs of new entrants can readily be transmitted between would-be suppliers and potential customers may have much to commend it in welfare terms, even if the set of suppliers is presently quite limited. Contestability depends not just on an absence of sunk costs on the production side, but on an absence of marketing costs, which are much more intrinsically sunk costs: a machine or building may be sold to another producer, but if market exit entails liquidating a business (and hence its goodwill cannot be captured by its sale as a going concern), there is no secondhand market for advertisements that have been broadcast or for the elapsed time of a sales person.

The work of Hodgson, on markets as sets of transaction cost-reducing institutions, and Coase, on firms as devices for economizing on the costs of market-based coordination, leads, in short, to a rather different way of conceptualizing imperfect markets from that of the mainstream structure–conduct–performance paradigm. A market may be said to be imperfect to the extent that, owing to a limited capacity of its institutions to reduce transaction costs, marketing expenditures and/or the internalization of value-adding activities are necessary to facilitate interactions that increase consumer surplus. This view sees marketing as an activity which involves the internalization of transaction costs by suppliers to reduce the need of buyers to incur transaction costs themselves in order to overcome the limitations of the market in question as a device for economizing on transaction costs. When transactions costs are internalized, the supplier's hope is that buyers will be prepared to pay a price that covers both production costs and marketing costs rather than incur their own search costs and buy from rivals whose lower prices are possible because less of an investment has been made in marketing.[3] If transactions costs are concentrated on the supply side, considerable communication economies may be achieved in the system as a whole. Moreover, there should be no presumption that customers are being exploited in cases where marketing costs form a major part of the price

---

[3]   For example, in New Zealand during 1997, in the face of growing public concern that the Imported Motor Vehicle Dealers Institute had failed to develop systems to prevent its members from duping customers by selling vehicles with illegally wound back odometers, Toyota advertised that its dealers were now selling 'Signature Class' imports of used Toyotas with guaranteed ex-Japan mileages and comprehensive warranties; at something of a premium price. These vehicles provide risk-averse buyers with a ready opportunity to eliminate costs of search and appraisal.

consumers are paying: it is possible that investment in marketing is necessary if economies of large scale production are to be achieved.

This perspective lacks the anti-business connotations of the conventional view of an imperfect market, and is much more consistent with the 1985 AMA definition of marketing. It has much in common with the work of Scitovsky (1985, 1990) on non-price competition, which he portrayed as 'making shopping frictionless and even enjoyable'. Yet it is likely to make some readers ask whether it can accommodate the selling side of marketing, such as advertisements that focus on persuasion via reference to the customer's image. Neil Kay (1984, p. 194) has an answer that allows a less manipulative view of advertising:

> [T]he distinctiveness of image advertising is illusory. If we push our perfect knowledge assumption far enough it becomes apparent that the sports car fan would know in advance of the advertising whether or not purchase of the sport car would change his image – the actual advertisement is redundant in this respect. Similarly the purchaser of the washing powder does not need the TV advert to inform them that the powder is associated with a happier home life – the truth or otherwise of this message would be known in advance of this advertisement.

Though any marketing strategy may employ rhetoric much as a lawyer does in attempting to persuade a jury, the quality of the rhetoric may be judged in terms of how well it succeeds in demonstrating the intended ways of looking at the world and means for coping with it. In the real world, unlike the world of *homo economicus* in which buyers have complete preference orderings, decision-making can be seen as a meta-level activity: the buyer *chooses a basis for choice* from amongst those supplied by producers and their distribution chains, or gathered personally with the aid of market institutions and social networks.

Finally, note that the view of marketing as transaction cost internalization ties it to the economics of vertical integration. Where markets are inefficient, would-be buyers may in some cases internalize production rather than go without. For example, in the household context, note that the market for do-it-yourself products owes much to transactional difficulties in the market for skilled tradespeople.[4] Despite all the credentials that would-be suppliers list in the Yellow Pages, it often remains difficult to avoid the suspicion that one could easily end up being ripped off unless one incurs a lot

---

[4]   Economists who do not habitually look for an information perspective on resource allocation would most likely explain such failures to exploit comparative advantage in terms of relative price distortions associated with taxes and lack of opportunities for paid over-time working.

of time-costs in getting competitive quotations arranged. There is also the problem of providing access during working hours and the prospect of security problems and a need to monitor what is being done to ensure the required output is actually delivered. Unless the costs and risks of making a mess of the job oneself seem substantial, it often makes sense to do it oneself, albeit rather slowly, aided by advice, materials and tools from one's local DIY store.

8.6   RELATIONSHIP MARKETING

The Chamberlinian approach to marketing management in terms of a focus on discovering the best combination of product, price, promotion and placement strategy is currently being challenged by the emerging paradigm of relationship marketing (see, for example, Dwyer, Schurr and Oh, 1987; Christopher, Payne and Ballantyne, 1991). The focus is no longer on the individual transaction but on the development of long-term customer loyalty. In terms of economic theory this paradigm shift is equivalent to replacing traditional theories of competition, in which producers and consumers have been treated very much as ships that pass in the night, with non-equilibrium perspectives from Marshall (1890), Andrews (1949, 1993) and Richardson (1972), who analysed the determination of market share with reference to the notion of customer goodwill. In neoclassical theories of competition, buyers are seen as indifferent between rival suppliers of identical combinations of product characteristics, so market shares are difficult to explain without reference to a U-shaped average cost curve to ensure that a firm which randomly finds itself facing more than the optimal number of would-be customers will be under pressure to get rid of the excess by raising its prices. By contrast, in the Marshall/Andrews analysis, firms are typically holding some spare capacity and new buyers arrive less via random processes than through word-of-mouth recommendations from contented past customers who continue to purchase from the same supplier so long as its performance at least matches what is imagined to be obtainable on similar terms elsewhere.

   To some extent one can understand the change in perspective within marketing as a belated recognition of the fact that it may be far cheaper to devote marketing expenditures to keeping past customers with experience of the product, than winning new replacements who need to be persuaded to experiment with it. For example, a firm might use loyalty discounts, special attention to regular customers, or promotional campaigns that aim to get the customer to feel more like part of a club or extended family. By this means, customers are discouraged from getting up-to-date quotations from alternative potential suppliers. Such ploys may be costly but less so than winning buyers from rivals because of the difficulties of demonstrating conclusively the case for making a switch, particularly if the potential new customers are already in relationships with rival suppliers and are not particularly open to considering alternative suppliers. However, there is a further basis for concentrating on retaining existing customers, based on the set-up costs of getting to know one's customers rather than on the cost of getting customers to know one's business.

Marketing costs may be considerably reduced if investments are made in building up knowledge of potential customers. In an ideal world, customers would be able to know instantly where was the best place to turn to obtain something that was a perfect match for their goals and circumstances, and they would be greeted by the supplier in question all geared up and ready to serve them. Life would essentially be a seamless experience rather than something punctuated by a need to define problems, find solutions to them and implement those solutions. Market research of the questionnaire and clipboard variety is evidently a rather limited means for generating customer satisfaction by making life approximate the seamless ideal. What is really required is telepathy; in its absence, there will be lost opportunities for making the most of specialized capabilities.

The telepathy problem can be used to make sense of the division of labour in an organizational context, as with the tendency for university professors to do much of their own typing and photocopying: it is often quicker to do it oneself immediately than explain to office staff what needs to be done and wait for them to do it. The problem is basically the same as that which gives rise to many do-it-yourself products. However, further reflection on the professor/secretary scenario results in the thought that, if professors made more use of their secretarial staff, the latter would get a better idea of the former's needs and be able to anticipate tasks rather than having to be instructed to carry them out. If interactions are based on a set of patterns that can be memorized and recognized, then there is a basis for an effective working relationship enabling task specialization on a far greater scale than would be possible before any investment has been made in giving the service provider knowledge that will enable reliable inferences to be made.

Now, just as relationships can reduce management costs pertaining to activities internalized in an organization, so they have a basis as a means for reducing marketing costs. As with building personal relationships, relationship marketing involves getting to know the other party and building up a memory that can be used as a basis for performing repeat transactions in a more routine manner and for anticipating mutually beneficial transactions. Customers who seem particularly contented with repeated dealings with a supplier might seem vulnerable to opportunistic ploys due to their reluctance to investigate and/or sample alternative suppliers. However, the signals they send about their loyalty and how much they are willing to spend imply that a considerable stream of future earnings will be lost if they do indeed exit after discovering they have been ripped off, particularly if they warn off potential customers to whom they might otherwise have given recommendations. Would-be opportunists, and those whose standards of supply are prone simply to lapse in respect of customers they start taking for granted, thus have an incentive to concentrate on serving their loyal customers particularly well.

The informational basis of the relationship marketing paradigm is particularly easy to appreciate in the context of services. For example, if I use the same team of plumbers each time tree roots block my drains, they will already know about the layout of pipes and access points and hence be able to get the job done more rapidly. Moreover, I will already have an account and credit record to facilitate the billing process. If I get my car serviced by the same firm each time, then, just as when I visit my regular doctor or dentist for treatment, records of past services and ailments will enable more rapid diagnosis of what needs to be done. If I use the same bank, car rental firm, financial adviser or lawyer time and again, then I will not need to spend time each visit filling in a detailed picture of my circumstances. If I stay in the same hotel or drink in the same bar time and again, the staff sooner or later will be able to serve me 'the usual' (for example, breakfast, newspaper, wake-up call at a particular time, or type of drink) without me having to specify anything in detail.

Though there is a tendency to think of rebuys in terms of a particular type and brand of product, repeated interactions with customers have a particular significance for the supplier who offers a *range* of complementary goods from stock or whose ability to get goods rapidly depends on their having invested in building up relationships with wholesalers. The information content of a sequence of individual purchases by customers who are never seen again is far less useful as the basis for planning inventory orders and delivering a superior standard of service than is an identical volume of expenditure made up as a sequence of related purchases by one client. For example, suppose I am an enthusiastic amateur musician willing to spend a great amount of money on equipment for a high-quality home studio. If I divide my purchases among the rival local music stores, none of them may form a clear picture of the equipment I have accumulated. Hence there is a smaller chance that anyone will realize that gaps in it will be likely to cause problems for which a solution can be supplied (for example a MIDI-mixer to enable a mass of synthesisers, sequencers and effects units to be hooked together in a manner that both facilitates their flexible use and prevents synchronization problems that can arise if items are merely interfaced in a lengthening daisy-chain), or realize that by spending a bit more in one area to meet a particular need I may be able also to meet another need more cheaply, because I can use the new device in conjunction with equipment that I already have. If I find an acceptable store and give it my loyalty, it may grow in status in my mind as it seems increasingly to anticipate exactly what I need. Overall I might spend less on equipment because the store enables me to save money by making the most of consumption synergies, but it gets all my business in that area. Alternatively, I might end up spending even more in total, despite the consistently cost-effective service, because the store's staff increasingly know which newly released items will pleasantly surprise and delight me, even though I enter the store with other needs in mind.

The complexities of modern musical equipment retailing are themselves very much bound up with the increasingly information technology-based nature of music and illustrate particularly well the importance of cultivating customer relationships when lessons can be derived from studying patterns of sequential purchases. However, the general point is relevant in more everyday contexts with far less expensive items that make up consumption lifestyles. Consumers who switch readily between supermarket chains, or airlines (which tend to networked with hotel and car rental providers) in response to special offers reveal far less about their lifestyles than those who deal essentially with the same organization and enable it to build up a record of their consumption patterns. In terms of oligopolistic competition, the proliferation of supermarket loyalty reward schemes, discount cards and frequent flier schemes can appear as signs that strategists have failed to anticipate the likelihood of retaliation by rivals, producing a situation in which all suppliers are worse off with both reduced revenues and considerable administration costs. In terms of information economics, however, we may take a more sanguine view of the situation insofar as the firms can increasingly benefit from building up detailed profiles of regular customers' purchasing habits, from checkout scanner data or reservations records and which assist in selecting products to promote and in targeting their promotions.

For relationship marketing to bear its full fruit, the supplying organization must be able to maintain continuity of staffing wherever the marketing environment involves the tacit knowledge problem identified by Polanyi (1958): in other words, the customer's situation may be so complicated that it cannot simply be recorded on a computer database to be immediately called up on screen and understood by an employee newly assigned to the task of managing the relationship. This opens up scope for employees to capture from their employers the rental earnings that arise from cultivating such relationships with customers. A threat to quit may be sufficient to achieve this, for when an employee defects to another organization or sets up on his/her own account, customers may defect too, because in some important senses the relationship is with the former employee, not the company. We have already seen this in chapter 7, in the case of the advertising industry. At the level of the consumer, a good example is provided by the market for hairdressing services (as is evident in advertisements placed to notify clients of new affiliations): even if a replacement hairdresser at the original salon can provide a continuing standard of service in terms of styling and cutting hair, the lack of familiarity with past clients will affect the quality of the social interaction during the hairdressing process. Financial services provide a more subtle case. Because of the impossibility/cost of documenting everything that particular bank managers know about their long-standing customers, there is a risk that promotions of staff and/or organizational restructuring will have adverse impacts on customer goodwill owing to customers feeling that the person newly assigned to them does not understand their situations as well as the predecessor did.

To end this section, I think it appropriate to note the significance of relationships with customers as a means of assisting suppliers to allocate their time when providing customer service in respect of complex products such as consumer durables and holidays. In the absence of consumer track records, it is difficult for suppliers to judge how seriously any individual should be taken as a prospective purchaser relative to anyone else who might be an alternative recipient of attention. Where full-service retailers are competing with discounters who achieve lower prices by economizing on service (for example, by using cheaper but less knowledgeable staff), it is possible that some potential customers are visiting the former purely with the intention of gathering information that will enable them to make a well-judged purchase from the latter. With some products, such as used sports cars, which may be sampled before purchase, rather than merely being discussed in the abstract, dealers may find themselves having to contend with those who actually have no purchase intention at all and are merely using the sampling process as a form of consumption, testing out theories about products they could otherwise afford to enjoy only in their imaginations. There will always be something of a lottery in making judgments about how seriously to take prospective customers, particularly when the latter may be trying to give misleading signals in this respect, for example dressing up to indicate more wealth than they have, or dressing down to indicate that their budget constraint really is as tight as they intend to claim when haggling over the final price.

The larger the market, the more opportunities there will be for sales personnel to fall victim to timewasters. It is hard to operate for long as a 'tyrekicker' in a town small enough only to have one or two sports car dealers, for they will remember previous cases of timewasting just as they will recognize former clients (and their cars, which helps in judging quality: cf. Akerlof, 1970) who are returning to trade in and upgrade. Indeed, in a small community, retailers may know quite a lot about even those with whom they have not yet had any dealings, and vice versa, so all will have reason to cultivate their reputations with care.

8.7   INFORMATION TECHNOLOGY AND THE FUTURE OF MARKETING

In the previous section, I noted the scope for supermarkets to develop quite complex profiles of their customers by integration data from their checkout scanners and shopper loyalty membership listings. This is the marketing equivalent of the way that modern detective work is done via profiling on computer databases. Just as police increasingly can pin down potential suspects from computer records instead of via informants and door-to-door inquiries, so a synthesis of information technology and marketing strategy reduces the need to use traditional market research methods to gain intelligence that manufacturers of goods stocked in supermarkets would be hard pressed to obtain for themselves. Supermarkets are therefore increasingly in a position to dictate even to giant food processing companies and other suppliers of household goods precisely what they should make. Information technology is providing the retailers with a counterweight against the leverage that manufacturers might hitherto have enjoyed (for example, by making ready supplies of their strong-selling brands contingent on the supermarkets being willing to stock their weaker brands). However, this is only the tip of the iceberg of potential the impact of information technology on consumer welfare via its impact on market processes..

Consumer power is also being enhanced by the emergence of the Internet. Shopping may become in large part a virtual experience when consumers can visit the websites of manufacturers and enjoy an interactive guide to firms offerings, greatly reducing the amount of time they will need to spend in a store and the expertise that sales personnel will need to possess. Alternative perspectives may be gleaned from the websites of consumer protection groups and product magazines. Insofar as virtual reality demonstrations can be provided, the need for retailer demonstrations of experience goods will be eliminated and consumers may feel comfortable about purchasing directly from manufacturers via the Internet, for home delivery. Tariffs and transport costs aside, consumers connected to the Internet will increasingly pay an identical global price rather than being asked to pay different prices due to manufacturers making the most of differing regional price elasticities of demand or of consumers paying the cost of regional marketing. Increasingly, in thinly populated markets, retailers will no longer hold items in stock for long periods. Rather, items will be sent direct from manufacturers. What the consumer is able to order in this manner may well be a customized product, one of a vast array of variants programmed into flexible production systems (see *Economist*, 1989b).

There is a tension between the two trends towards the power of retailers as brokers and the growing ability of consumers to deal directly with manufacturers. Unless the manufacturers offer comprehensive and highly diversified product ranges, they will be less well placed to engage in customer profiling than megastores with comprehensive scanner data. To be sure, some inferences may be drawn from the ways that potential customers navigate manufacturers' websites, and websites can be designed to force them to reveal market research data as the price of using the website. But websites that are onerous to use are hardly going to be effective tools for encouraging potential customers to get to know about the products they describe. The sort of customer profiling that manufacturers might dearly like to access is perhaps something that will eventually be provided by third parties unless privacy legislation is introduced to prevent it. For firms that manufacture consumer durables or provide travel and leisure services, finely detailed supermarket scanner data are likely to be of less interest than the information contained in a person's credit card and electronic funds transfer at point of sale (EFTPOS) records. Over time, such data could provide a very revealing picture of a person's evolving lifestyle.

This was noted at an early stage by Newstead (1986, p. 401) in a review of an Australian government publication on the implication of EFTPOS systems. After quoting a hypothetical case in which the computer analysis of a man's latest spending noted, 'Subject purchased third bottle of bourbon this month... Bought expensive lingerie; not his wife's size', Newstead commented that, 'It would be dangerous to dismiss this as light-hearted banter. Even on the least harmful level, it could generate a whole new regime of aggressive, personalized marketing.' In principle, information technology may make it possible to develop such an intimate knowledge of individual customers that they can, in effect, each be treated as unique market segments. Database-driven direct marketing initiatives could easily entail not merely the timely anticipation of customer needs and susceptibilities but also attempts at covert price discrimination on a large scale: already some charities personalize the suggested donation figures on their mailed appeals on the basis of their addressees' past donation records, thereby seeking to infer donors' decision rules and eventually steer their donations up to the maximum they are prepared to give (cf. Desmet and Feinberg, 2003).

8.8   CONCLUDING COMMENTS

A world of growing affluence, complexity and rapid technological change is a world apart from that of the days of Adam Smith when the average consumer was buying mainly local produce and a limited array of items offered by passing tinkers. The coordination task now faced by market institutions is immense, though information technology can clearly make a major contribution towards reducing transaction costs. Busy consumers may be reluctant to engage extensively in search and appraisal on many occasions, even if their homes are wired to the Internet. Yet for life not to be unduly stressful in the midst of novelty and success in reaching new spending leagues, consumers need to have access to easy ways to make up their minds about choices of complex products and then learn how to make the most of them. Here lies much of the origin of the significance of marketing and branding in today's world, as devices to help consumers solve the problems of coping with the pressures of affluence. The success of global fast food brands such as McDonalds, KFC and Pizza Hut should not, from this standpoint, be understood primarily in terms of the speed and cheapness with which they can deliver food and externalize activities that it would take longer to perform in one's own kitchen. Rather, their significance can be seen in terms of information: they provide fast food in the sense of enabling instantaneous location of food of a known standard. This is the crucial outcome of the investments made in marketing these brands and programming the production and service process. Without modern marketing to shift transaction costs from buyers into the cost structures underlying the prices that buyers are asked to pay, the modern consumer would increasingly be needing to study purchasing as an activity, just as purchasing and supply chain management are fast becoming core ingredients of industrial marketing education.

9. Latent Demand and the Browsing Shopper

Co-authored with Jason Potts

9.1 INTRODUCTION

Theories of consumer behaviour in both economics and marketing have been largely devoted to situations in which shopping activity entails the solution of well-defined problems. In economics, the problem often simply is to purchase the set of goods that maximizes utility in terms of a given preference ordering and subject to a well-defined budget constraint. Sometimes, the consumer is portrayed as having to engage in search activity to find the best price/quality options but the general presumption is that consumers have a clear idea of what they want, seen in terms of the trade-offs they are prepared to make. It is rare to find a mainstream economist trying to grapple with the idea that much of what we do as consumers may be unplanned. One instance is Becker's (1962) demonstration that a system of downward-sloping demand curves can be accounted for on the basis of random behaviour within a budget constraint, without any need for choice to be driven by a preference ordering. Veering to such an opposite extreme seems, however, to miss the potentially rich middle ground of behaviour that is somewhat haphazard and yet has some kind of systematic foundations.

Within marketing, the consumer is not portrayed as initially well informed and performing complex trade-offs in terms of all the goods that are available. Even so, consumers in marketing theory are often seen as highly purposive shoppers, setting out to solve particular problems by gathering information about possible solutions, evaluating it, making choices and then implementing the preferred purchases. Challenges to this perspective in the past two decades or so have come mainly in terms of suggestions (beginning with Olshavsky and Granbois, 1979) that in many situations search is very limited and choice is prone to be based on simple rules or social norms. There is also a small literature on impulse buying (summarized by Rook, 1999), which casts it along a spectrum that ranges from pathological consumer behaviour (compulsive buying), through some notion of contingent purchasing, to the perfectly planned acts of the fully rational shopper.

Economists would do well to follow the lead of writers such as Rook, Olshavsky and Granbois in marketing. The picture of consumers as purposive shoppers may not be a poor approximation in some cases, but the statistics show that a surprisingly large proportion of purchases are unplanned (over 50% fall into this category, according to Hoch, Bradlow and Wansink, 1999, p. 528). In this chapter we therefore present an analysis of unplanned purchasing behaviour that is focused on the middle of Rook's spectrum. That is to say, we examine the case where the consumer is not driven by uncontrollable urges to purchase, and yet ends up returning from a shopping expedition with items other than those whose purchase provided the initial rationale for the expedition. We attempt to analyse behaviour in malls and other shopping environments on the basis that consumers are prone to engage browsing because they are, for a variety of reasons, open to spending opportunities that grab their attention. Although trips to a shopping mall may (though need not) begin as a means of engaging in purposive search, consumers frequently end up being diverted into exploring other possibilities.

The 'middle ground' stance of this chapter includes an attempt to deal with the possibility that during the browsing process the allocation of attention is in part determined by needs to purchase that are not yet urgent but which consumers have at the backs of their minds. In other words, we shall be thinking of consumers as if they have latent demands for some kinds of products, rather than seeing them as completely open or completely purposive in their shopping activities. This perspective, and many other themes in the chapter, comes from introspection regarding our own behaviour as shoppers and from encouraging friends and colleagues to reflect aloud, sometimes in a group setting, on their shopping experiences. (Indooroopilly Shoppingtown in Brisbane, which provided a focus for many of these discussions, has figured in previous introspective writing on shopping, by cultural studies researcher Meaghan Morris, 1993.) The overt use of an introspective approach will probably seem unusual to economists but it has become recognized within marketing as a potentially valuable element in a pluralistic toolkit, following pioneering work by Gould (1991, 1995) and Holbrook (1995a) (see also Earl, 2001b). We hope to show that behavioural research into the economics of consumption can be usefully informed by self-reflection on actual behaviour as well as by using perspectives from cognitive psychology (following the lead of Simon, 1982) – which we also employ – and the radical behaviourism of Foxall (1997).

The chapter is structured as follows. Section 9.2 examines a variety of forms that browsing-based shopping may take, while section 9.3 identifies different kinds of latent demand that may become manifest when consumers encounter unplanned buying opportunities. The focus of section 9.4 is on the question of how a consumer's attention may be captured by items that were not the subject of the shopping expedition, while section 9.5 explores the theory of shopping mall design as it relates differently to browsing and searching. In section 9.6, which is followed by a concluding discussion, we explore a variety of factors, other than the normal notion of a financial budget constraint, that limit the extent of unplanned purchases and bring shopping expeditions to a close.

9.2 PURE BROWSING VERSUS CONTINGENT BROWSING

For much of this chapter we shall be considering how unplanned purchases arise as a consequence of consumers having their attention diverted from the search missions that provided the basis for their shopping expeditions. Such purchases are the end result of browsing that is contingent on particular promotional displays that cause the consumer to examine a class of goods other than that which they had expressly come out to purchase. It is perfectly possible, however, to think of shopping activity purely in terms of browsing behaviour, where people go shopping without any plans to search for particular items or any intention to purchase particular items from particular stores, without even engaging in search activity. We could simply imagine consumers as having 'money to burn' (or credit cards whose balances are inside their allowed credit limits), and as simply having a perceived need to get out and go shopping. The basis for this need to shop might have a variety of social-psychological foundations that have little direct connection with the goods purchased as a consequence of browsing. The goods that are purchased in such cases could even be seen as justificatory 'evidence' of purpose that serves as a cover for the real purpose of the expedition.

These socio-psychological factors appear to evolve through time as the retail environment and social conditions change, as is evident in two recent books. One, by feminist historian Erika Rappaport (1999), examines female shoppers in Victorian times in London's West End, an area that hitherto had been frequented almost exclusively by men. Shopping in the West End came to be seen as play and amusement instead of a duty and large stores such as Selfridges cast themselves somewhat in the role of a club in which lonely women could mingle. They offered many features redolent of male clubs (such as a library, reading, writing and 'silence' rooms) as well as restaurants, to keep the customers in the store as long as possible. Extensive in-store research spanning the past two decades is reported in the other work, by urban geographer/anthropologist/consultant Paco Underhill (1999). Extended shopping expeditions may now be much more natural for women than they were a century ago, but the motivations of female shoppers seem to have little to do with particular consumption ends. According to Underhill, we should see them in terms of 'reward, bribe, pastime, an excuse to get out of the house, a way to trawl for potential loved ones, an entertainment, a form of education or even worship...'. Some people may thus shop because their social lives are largely empty: a visit to a mall opens up opportunities for social encounters, at least including interactions with store personnel if not with other shoppers. We note also the emergence of 'retail therapy' as an everyday expression. This seems to suggest that consumers may be looking at spending time shopping, and then unpacking the purchased items, essentially as a means of diverting their attention from their personal problems, rather than as a means of returning their consumption activities to some kind of equilibrium. Here, the crucial thing for the consumers' states of well-being is the shopping process itself, rather than the use made of anything that they purchase. Of course, if they discover some great bargains, they may feel more capable people and more in command in their lives.

A good deal of browsing shopping arises because consumers are locked into particular locations with 'time to kill'. Airport duty free areas are full of captive shoppers with surplus attention capacities, for whom poor-quality sleep is the main opportunity cost of traipsing along the shop fronts and wandering inside particular stores. But these are by no means the only such cases; other examples include consumers who are between appointments or who have appointments that integrate poorly with the timing of transportation services.

Browsing behaviour clearly need not result in any unplanned purchases. Some visits to retail outlets may be purposively aimed at browsing in the sense of gathering information about what is available, and where, to keep in the memory for future expeditions when particular products are the subjects of search activity. For the purposes of this chapter, however, the significant point is that browsing is likely often to result in purchases because of the discovery of goods congruent with underlying latent demands that were not the original basis of the shopping activities.

9.3   LATENT DEMAND

When mainstream economists use the term 'latent demand' it is often in the context of econometric work on consumption, to represent the demand underlying a discrete choice. It is clear that browsing behaviour can result in discrete choices being made, as when a consumer makes an unplanned and tentative foray into a telephone company's retail outlet and emerges from it as a new recruit to the ranks of cellular phone users. Another example would be when the consumer judges that there is now enough choice in software available to justify the purchase of a DVD player and, in switching away from purchasing videocassettes, makes particular brand choices from the DVDs that are available. In this section we offer a broader view of latent demand to help explain browsing-based choices that do not have the discrete dimension, as well as some that do.

The latent demands that help explain how browsing leads to purchases come in two varieties that need to be differentiated from a kind of latent demand that is better seen as associated with search-based shopping. Within mainstream economics, consumers are either in the market for a particular good at a particular price, or they are not. From this perspective, to speak of a latent demand seems to entail some notion of market failure on the supply side. In other words, if only manufacturers would supply a particular type of product, they would discover that there is indeed a market out there that previously was going unsatisfied. From the standpoint of the Austrian approach to entrepreneurship (Kirzner, 1973), one might say that this kind of latency persists due to lack of alertness on the part of entrepreneurs, leaving some alert consumers frustrated because they have well-defined preferences for products that are not yet offered and which they are unable produce themselves. Such latent demand poses no problem in terms of the standard assumption of complete preferences in the goods space. However, this is a case where the alert, frustrated consumer is a searcher, not a browser.

A second kind of latent demand is problematic in terms of goods-space preferences but consistent with well-defined preferences in the characteristics space, as modelled by Lancaster (1966). For example, not many years ago consumers were unable to buy a combined fax machine/printer/photocopier/ scanner with a PC interface, but now such products are in the shops. Some consumers may not have envisaged this combination of product characteristics before it was offered but, on eventually coming across such a product, they may be receptive to it as a highly efficient technology. Despite never having set out to find such a bundle of characteristics before, consumers with this kind of latent demand would be readily able to rank the bundle relative to other bundles if asked to do so by a market researcher who described the product to them. If consumers could not express rankings in a way that fitted in with Lancaster's trade-off-based view of preferences, they might nonetheless be able to articulate their latent demand for the hypothetical product in terms of its fit with check-list-based decision rules of the kind discussed in Earl (1986).

Consumers who recognize their limitations in creative thinking about *potential* characteristics combinations, even though they know what they like *when they see it*, will have a motivation to scan consumer magazines for news of new developments and for engaging in browsing activity at retail outlets. These consumers are likely to flip from browsing to search mode in the course of shopping if they discover an instance of an unforeseen technology genre that is evidently a worthwhile purchase (a 'must-have'). Even if a consumer is prone to think in terms of checklists and engage in satisficing behaviour (Simon, 1959, 1982), such a pleasing discovery may result in a shift from browsing into search mode. The new product might comprise a highly desirable set of features but a consumer aware of the possibility of oversight will not automatically use it as a basis for specifying a set of performance standards for such a product. It might be inferior to other offerings in the newly discovered genre, if any can be found. Search may give the consumer a better idea of what might reasonably be expected from this type of product, providing a basis for defining what is 'satisfactory'.

A third kind of latent demand is much more problematic to relate to mainstream models of choice. This type arises due the running down of the consumer's stock of goods. Two kinds of depletion are relevant here. One is the physical decay of products (such as the wearing out of a pair of jeans). The other is the looming exhaustion of stocks of a product (such as a packet of dental floss). The key point to notice here is that the timing of the replenishment of the consumer's stock is highly discretionary, particularly where goods are compact relative to available storage space.

With this third kind of latent demand, two kinds of threshold effects define the boundaries of browsing activities as products suffer from entropy and turn into rubbish. The product gets on to the consumer's agenda of potential items for purchase attention when it is first seen to display a significant sign that it is no longer 'as new'. For example, the consumer of jeans first notices an emerging hole, or the dental floss user first notices the tell-tale sound of the emptying floss spool starting to rattle around inside its container. At this stage, there is something of a localized paradigm shift: a problem that will eventually require attention has become apparent where previously it was not recognized. The consumer is now receptive to opportunities to purchase replacements for the goods in question. We are presuming here that the consumer is not an obsessive person for whom the product must be just perfect or else is in urgent need of replacement: most of us are prepared to carry on consuming products that have something of a character-rich, battle-scarred, lived-in look to them.[1] Consumers only move

---

[1]   Some kinds of physical decay, such as the fading of denim clothing, may even be welcomed rather than being a trigger to keep an eye out for potential replacements. Furthermore, some consumers, such as those engaged in property gentrification, are always keeping an eye out for certain things that are prone to be discarded as rubbish by those engaged in modernization (Thompson, 1979). House-clearance sales and 'swap-meet' fairs provide fertile browsing environments for consumers on the look out for items that might eventually fit into their restoration plans, whether or not they are trying to find particular items.

into search mode once the scale of the problem has gone beyond a particular level: for example, the jeans develop a hole that is unacceptably large, or the container of floss is discovered to be completely empty.

This third kind of latent demand is related to Katona's (1960) critique of standard macroeconomic models of the consumption function and of Galbraith's (1958) claims about the power of advertising. Our perspective on discretionary spending is, however, closer to Galbraith in being more willing to accept scope for manipulation of consumer behaviour. Katona tried to draw attention to short-run instability in the consumption function despite extensive advertising by large corporations. He sought to explain this by noting that in affluent societies goods are often replaced long before they are completely worn out or beyond economic repair. Thus in Katona's analysis, aggregate consumption depends not only on the ability to spend but on the willingness of the consumer to do so, which may wax and wane with changing confidence. Consumers who become optimistic will dispose of old durables that, in a more pessimistic frame of mind they were inclined to keep using (see further, chapter 12 below). Whereas Katona sees spending as contingent on the 'feel-good factor', our suggestion is that the browsing consumer's *attention* may be drawn to opportunities for bringing forward the purchase of items that have not yet 'gone critical' in terms of a need for replacements. (Shopping malls could additionally be seen as devices for promoting consumer confidence in so far as they convey an atmosphere of prosperity and the impression that *other* shoppers are indeed feeling good enough to spend.)

Strategies that consumers use for managing the inventories of particular goods may be designed to prevent themselves from getting into search mode precisely because it is difficult to find replacements. For a consumer whose teeth are packed close together, getting the right brand of dental floss may be vital: most brands may be prone to fray and get caught between the teeth. If the preferred brand of dental floss is not consistently available from particular pharmacies and supermarkets, the consumer may operate with a rule of thumb that entails 'ideally' trying to have at least one unopened packet in stock. This is a somewhat fuzzy form of rule, which results in the consumer normally maintaining a stock of two packets. A failure to purchase a replacement packet before the reserve packet has to be opened does not trigger urgent search as the expectation is that browsing will result in discovery of a couple of replacement packets well before the reserve is completely exhausted.

9.4   CATCHING AND KEEPING THE SHOPPER'S ATTENTION

Economists so far have given little thought to the question of how decision-makers end up giving their attention to one thing rather than another at any moment. We deliberately use the messy phrase 'end up giving' here instead of the economist's key-word 'allocate' because, as Berger (1989, p. 219) argues at some length, 'The historical movement of attention is not to be explained by recourse to calculations of trade-offs with respect to given objects in the economic environment'. Attention is not allocated; but it does shift, and we require some framework for thinking about the way in which this process occurs.

We may arrange this as a nested problem. An important finding from cognitive-psychology is that the phenomenon of attention is most fluid at the interface of conscious and unconscious processing (for example, Treisman and Gelade, 1980; Treisman, 1988). In an oft-cited experiment, subjects are shown a stream of letters of varied colours with the task to halt the run when a particular letter of a particular colour is found. (We note that this is abstractly equivalent to the searching shopper.) The remarkable feature of this experiment is that when subjects are asked to recall the specific form of the other data, they can generally reproduce both the letters and the colours but not which went with which. This indicates that, when engaging in a directed search, the set of scanned characteristics and features remain effectively unglued and float about in the mind's eye. This presents a somewhat different view of cognitive processing from that of, say, Miller (1956) or Simon (1959), who see agents as having strict limitations on their abilities to process streams of data. Instead, we take such findings to indicate that highly paralleled search is, by the evolutionary adaptations of the mind,[2] a phenomenon that occurs largely below the threshold of consciousness. We identify this as the essence of the phenomenon of browsing.

A decision is of course – at least to economists – a conscious activity, and therefore we must ask how attention comes to be held and focused within the realm of consciousness. As long ago as 1758, Dr Johnson (quoted in Williams, 1993, p. 323) recognized the problem and hinted at its resolution:

---

[2]   We do not therefore regard browsing as something emergent to a wealthy leisured class in a consumer society. Rather, complex problem solving has been a persistent feature of human evolution, and our minds have been shaped by such requirements (see, for instance, Barkow, Cosmides and Tooby, 1992).

> Advertisements are now so numerous that they are very negligently perused, and it is therefore become necessary to gain attention by magnificence of promises and by eloquence sometimes sublime and sometimes pathetick. Promise, large promise, is the soul of advertisement.

Dr Johnson's emphasis on the ability of magnificent promises to attract attention is somewhat similar to the perspective offered by George Shackle (1961, 1979), one of very few economists to make attention central to the analysis of choice. Shackle portrays decision-makers as choosing in the face of uncertainty via a process that involves focusing, for each rival scheme of action, on a particularly attention arresting pair of gains and losses. The focusing process is driven by an 'ascendancy function': imagined outcomes are better at arresting attention the further they are from the 'neutral outcome' that the chooser uses as a reference point when reaching a decision. But very large prospective gains and losses will not hold the attention if the consumer can see all manner of reasons why they may not eventuate: it is a combination of plausibility and distance from the norm that determines ascendancy. We suggest that another way of seeing distance from a norm is in terms of deviance: incongruous as well as unusually large promises of performance (or worrying images that can be held at bay by a product) may be especially effective at attracting attention.

Shackle's theory collapses the choice problem to a single dimension, but the idea that things are better able to arrest attention the further they are from some normal reference point is compatible with a multi-characteristic analysis. A product may have many dimensions, but some can be made, via promotional strategies, to stand out and hook the attention particularly effectively.

Examples abound. In a world of PCs that embody boxy grey functionality, the colourful *très chic* styling of an Apple iMac in a shop window display is a clear instance of this. Nokia have also generated many purchases in much the same way with their eye-catching cellular telephones. Supermodels would not have such lucrative roles in the promotion process if women generally had their forms. In contrast to the cluttered shop windows of the 1870s (see Rappaport, 1999), the spacious designs of the present day make it easier for the eye to find something on to which to fasten its gaze. What is a shop window display for if not to arouse the consumer imagination? If purchase is sex then we might see window displays as acts of courtship.

In linking the Johnson/Shackle/deviance themes to the findings of evolutionary psychologists, our point is that the mind of the browsing agent floating in characteristic space does not solidify into a crystal of fully conscious choice in all dimensions at once. Rather, thoughts materialize along one axis at a time, although coalescence may proceed very rapidly once initial axes are in place. Sexiness may grab the attention well ahead of any aspects of product functionality about which the decision-maker eventually comes to ponder. In most cases, it is the initial arousal – the attention-arresting jolt into consciousness – that is the most challenging aspect for the merchant. All manner of devices are put to this service, such as mid-range car sales yards carrying a few exotic display vehicles, the ubiquitous use of improbably beautiful models, or, in some malls, ghastly acts of what, in Australia, has become common enough to earn the name 'spruiking'. The last device entails the use of vocal exhortation, with or without a microphone and PA system, to come and examine/take advantage of special offers inside the store and it may be seen as a kind of live substitute for the static theatre of window displays.[3] Viewed in this way, the role of sales people is not necessarily to sell, but rather to act as attention managers, and to minister to needs for reassurance during the decompression phase that is choice. Indeed, one might like to reflect on the easy substitutability of a partner or friends qua sales assistants when shopping.

Secondly, attention follows pathways as signs and symbols unfold in meaning and significance. For example, when you first buy a particular model of car, the roads will suddenly seem to be full of them and you will notice aspects that were previously invisible. (You might even assemble a profile of the other drivers, asking 'Am I that person?'.) In a similar manner, advertising works within a web of implicit meaning. For example, a poster featuring celebrity endorsement of a particular item may mean nothing to us if we are not familiar with the celebrity as the player of particular kinds of roles and symbolizing a particular set of values (see McCracken, 1989). For these sorts of reasons, we prefer to think of consumer attention as having a definite textual character, or, in modelling terms, as a partially stochastic path across a surface with multiple attractor basins. Browsing then acts as a mapping procedure and therefore as a precursor to 'consumption annealing', that is, as a way of leaping from one basin to another.

Thirdly, attention might be lost in one of two ways: under- and over-stimulation. Under-stimulation occurs as a failure of the imagination to build upon the initial attention stimulus. Over-stimulation is not a surfeit of possibilities in itself. Rather it is the inability to break a problem down into a format that is heuristically soluble, not because the decision-maker arrives in a state of multiple indifference, but because the decision-maker has no way of effectively programming the very structure of indifference in the first place. (Computer scientists call a problem like this 'NP-hard'; we wish there were an analogous term in consumer theory.) Again, the role of the sales assistant or shopping expedition partners may be crucial to this task of navigation between these points.

---

[3] Spruiking services may be subcontracted to specialist performers: see, for example, http://www.atspromotions.com/spruiking.htm.

The theory of attention that we are suggesting here is not a to be seen as a solution to a problem of the conscious allocation of attention, and neither is it something that might be modelled as an 'optimal stopping problem'. Instead, we view attention in the first instance as a shift between states of unconsciousness and consciousness. Secondly, we see it as a carnival of semiotic ministration, and, thirdly, as something that benefits from support-services.

9.5 SHOPPING CENTRES AS BROWSING ENVIRONMENTS

The physical form of the shopping environments has the potential to affect whether or not a consumer encounters particular promotional messages and flips from searching into browsing, or from browsing for one kind of good to browsing for something else. In this section we consider the design of shopping malls in terms of their abilities to prolong the consumer's overall attention on shopping and, by increasing the time spent in the mall environment, to increase the probabilities that the consumer will spend particular sums before leaving.

If shoppers were only engaging in planned, search- or knowledge-based activity then it would be harder to make sense of shopping centres with great varieties of retail outlets, or of shops such as department stores and supermarkets that stock many different kinds of goods. To group diverse types of goods in close proximity certainly provides the convenience of one-stop shopping. However, such groupings interfere with the advantages in terms of information gathering and competitive comparisons that are to be obtained – as Marshall (1890) recognized – from having similar kinds of establishments (such as car yards, musical instrument stores or bathroom supplies stores) grouped together.

From the standpoint of the searching shopper, the ideal layout of a shopping centre would be a circular, hub and spoke design. The hub would be the entry/exit platform around which were located entry portals to shops that specialized in selling each kind of good offered at that location. Ideally, retailers selling similar products would be located next door to each other, with shops selling complementary products also located close at hand. If they were not, the circular nature of the shopping centre design would mean that to get from one shop to another would require only one 'step' back to the central platform and one 'step' off into the target portal. Such a design would minimize scope for being diverted by attention-grabbing ploys of retailers selling products other than those that were the subjects of the shopping expedition, since it would not be necessary to go past their stores. On the other hand, it would also enhance opportunities for shoppers to spot their friends en route between shops. The shops in such a mall would all have pie-slice-shaped floor-plans with the entrance/exit doors at the pie-slice tip and scope for having delivery doors in the perimeter ('pie-crust') wall.

In practice, of course, shopping malls are typically not laid out in this way, even though it would be perfectly possible to funnel all shoppers from an underground or on-roof car park on to a single entry platform. One practical difficulty is that a finite amount of space is required for doors of a particular capacity. The more stores and customers that the mall is designed to accommodate, the larger the circumference of the central platform has to be in order to fit all the doors in and have enough room for the volume of shoppers to cross between doors. (The problem is similar to that of accommodating more and more people around a circular coffee table: it is only possible to fit more chairs in at the cost of having people sit further and further from the table.) We doubt that this difficulty would be particularly acute, even for a large mall, in terms of the distances it would require shoppers to walk. Shoppers can be required to walk considerable distances in real-world malls. These typically involve linked corridors or, if they entail loops on multiple levels, an atrium-style design with few opportunities for crossing from one side to another to obviate the need to circumnavigate much of a particular level.

A more serious limitation of our hypothetical optimal-search mall is that restricting shop-fronts to the width required for doors of adequate capacity precludes the shops from using window displays to show customers the kinds of things that the shop stocks or for promoting deals on particular items. This would require that purposive shoppers were familiar with shop brand names as shorthand symbols of the nature of each shop's business. It would also limit browsing to two main forms. Either it would become an in-store activity that happened when consumers went into a shop for a purpose and had their attention arrested by something else, or it would occur when consumers were knowingly browsing and randomly entered shops rather as if the mall were like a giant roulette wheel.

To judge from the designs of modern shopping malls, where similar kinds of shops are often dotted around at different ends or on different floors, the layouts are not intended to reduce the amount of legwork that consumers have to do in order to make any particular purchase. Rather, it is as though the layout is intended to maximize the probability that consumers engaged in purposive shopping will have their attention diverted by displays of other items as they pass en route between rival suppliers of the goods they have come to see. Consumers who have come shopping in search of, say, a particular CD and a new carving knife will tend not to find the record stores or cutlery stores adjacent to each other. In the process of walking between the stores that they have planned to visit, they end up being diverted into pharmacies, book-stores, shoe shops, and so on. They may return to the mall's car park with few if any of the items they had been looking for, but loaded up with things they had not planned to buy.

It is possible that modern shopping centres are simply badly planned, with store tenancies that are the result of historical accidents and asset specificity that makes it costly to regroup locations into miniature Marshallian business districts. Given the pressures of competition between malls, both for shoppers and tenants, it seem more likely, however, that they are very cunningly set out not to make search easier but to extract dollars by promoting browsing in the midst of purposive shopping expeditions. Given that brand-new malls appear to fail to group shops as much as would be possible by product type in a Marshallian manner, suspicion that the mall-management companies are trying to maximize floor traffic and browsing-based purchases would appear to be justified. That way, they can charge higher rents and yet consumers return home satisfied with the opportunities of which they took advantage, not realizing the extent to which they have been 'taken in' by the design of the mall (for extensive surveys of the wider scope for manipulation of consumer choices, see Hanson and Kysar, 1999a, 1999b).

Such rivalry between stores of a particular kind as is observed in malls might be dysfunctional from the consumer's standpoint, owing to the stores being insufficiently large to stock a wide enough range to cater for those with specialized preferences, and which compete for the mainstream buyers. For example, a single large record store stocking a huge range of albums would probably serve the public better than a couple of smaller stores at either end of a mall and which had a high probability of failing to stock anything that was not a mass seller. However, if mall-management companies limit the size of shop units in a mall, several small record stores catering to higher turnover parts of the market may be viable. Floor traffic may also be increased because the smallness of the stores reduces the probability of the record buyer finding a particular non-chart album in any of the stores. Limiting the sizes of stores enables more than one chain to be represented. In turn, the stores are pushed into using competitive promotional ploys (such as sale-price CDs on tables in the mall walkways outside the stores themselves) that may attract the attention of shoppers who were searching for other items and walking between stores.

The absence of Marshallian structure in shopping malls, and the kinds of behaviour we have described so far, leads to a view of the shopping process that is rather akin to the 'garbage can' model of organizational decision-making proposed by March and Olsen (1976) and in March (1988, chapter 14). In their model, an organization is a place where problems and courses of action may be kicking around for quite a time before happening to match up as satisfactory pairings. Some people have problems that they will sooner or later need to solve and other people have in mind favoured courses of action which would be consistent with their sub-goals but which have not been developed as solutions to particular problems that exist elsewhere in the organization. In the garbage can model, the process of matching up items on the agendas of problem solvers and those with particular strategies to peddle in no way involves optimization and is highly contingent on chance encounters within the organization. Even so, it may result in satisfactory outcomes for the parties involved. Our analysis suggests that shopping malls are, in effect, designed to function as decision-making garbage cans: they are designed to promote browsing behaviour that will result in more spending, rather than in consumers efficiently purchasing precisely what they came to purchase.

9.6 THE BROWSING CONSUMER'S SPENDING CONSTRAINTS

Despite succumbing to cunning mall designs and attention gathering ploys of retailers, consumers do sooner or later bring their shopping activities to a close. In a typical economic analysis, spending is limited by a well-defined budget constraint being exhausted and search is limited by a weighing up of expected marginal costs and benefits of spending time gathering information. In the real world of the shopping mall, the browsing shopper's stopping rules appear to be somewhat different in nature. Budget constraints are very fuzzy. On the one hand, consumers may often be operating well within the spending limits set by their existing credit cards or electronically accessible bank balances. On the other hand, if the consumer's attention is grabbed by the display for an expensive durable that meets a latent demand, in-store credit may be offered to facilitate its purchase. The consumer's income does not provide a hard constraint in terms of ability to service debt since repayment rates on credit cards (if not hire purchase) are highly discretionary. In any case, a spending splurge today might be offset by reduced spending at some unspecified point in the future, or by overtime at work, again at some unspecified point. When life is not a based around a once-and-for-all Walrasian auction, complete spending and income-generation plans do not have to be worked out. This leaves much scope for consumers to engage in wishful thinking to reduce cognitive dissonance and tell themselves that they will cross the financial bridge when they come to it (cf. Maital, 1982; Earl, 1992, and Earl and Wicklund, 1999). The following perspectives seem helpful for understanding limits to browsing-related spending activity on a single shopping expedition.

First, shopping may stop simply because the original mission has been accomplished or it has become clear that the planned purchases cannot be made. If we regard the consumer's planned search behaviour as the acting out of a programme, it comes to an end when the programme has run its course; here, the budget constraint issue simply does not arise. Put simply, an end to the shopping expedition will arise once the consumer finishes searching for the last item on the shopping list so long as it is possible to escape successfully to the car park or public transport without being diverted again into browsing activity.

Secondly, we note that Marshall's (1890) analysis of demand with reference to the marginal utility of money might be rather more realistic than the subsequent Hicksian approach to utility, as Hicks (1976) himself recognized. The process of shopping in a mall is clearly a sequential one in many cases: consumers do not typically do all their intelligence gathering, weigh up their options, work out the set of goods they will buy and then walk round and purchase them. Sequential shopping does not appear to entail comparing relative prices and marginal rates of substitution of diverse goods. But it appears quite well approximated by Marshall's notion that the marginal utility of a prospective purchase item is compared with the marginal utility of money that will have to be given up to buy it. Marshall's story has a speculative dimension to it, just as speculation figures in much of what we have said about unplanned purchases arising as the consumer seizes opportunities that may not be available (at least not without greater shopping effort) in future.[4] Unspent money (or unused credit lines) might be better used at a later stage when the choice set is different. From a Marshallian perspective, then, shoppers will eventually resolve not to buy items that have grabbed their attention if they judge that the gains from purchasing them today are less than the gains they might make on a future shopping expedition by having left their options open.

A third brake on purchasing may arise due to consumers recognizing that, whilst they may have the finances for purchasing items that have attracted their attention, the actual consumption of the goods will take up scarce time. This argument is taken from Linder (1970) and seems particularly likely to come to mind in respect of books, music, videos and clothing. For example, consider the plight of a consumer whose attention is grabbed for several minutes in a record store by a five CD boxed set of re-mastered albums and some hitherto unreleased material by 1970s rock band 'Free'. The band may be one of the consumer's favourites from this era but purchase may not occur if reflection leads to recognition that it has not even

---

[4] Note the overlap between Marshall's thinking and that of Katona, considered in section 2. It could also be seen as a kind of liquidity preference approach to demand, anticipating the analysis of portfolio choice that Keynes (1936) offers in chapter 17 of his *General Theory*. For further discussion of the speculative dimension of consumer choice, see Earl (1990, chapter 2) and chapter 11 of this book.

been possible to make time to listen recently to old tapes and vinyl LPs by the band. It is time scarcity, rather than a $A135 price sticker that that stops the purchase. (In Marshallian terms, one might say that the consumer simply judges that the five CDs in question are unlikely to get played enough to justify the expenditure.) If the consumer recognizes that listening to the CDs would get in the way of listening to ones previously purchased, or other goods, s/he might also notice that time spent shopping is getting in the way of making the most of his or her existing inventory. The shopping expedition could come to an end any time the problem of time scarcity is recognized, so long as the consumer has finished searching for the items that s/he had planned to purchase. Doubtless some shoppers who reflect on their time pressures will instead continue shopping; their minds now focus on time-saving devices that grab their attention: for example, the colourful iMac that stands out in a shop window may now symbolize the potential for saving time by shopping on the internet.

Institutional aspects can also bring shopping activity to a close. Under this heading we may include not merely the opening hours of the stores and the limitations of bus timetables, but also the broader fabric of the shopper's lifestyle, such as a need to take children to their Saturday afternoon sports fixtures, music lessons, and so on.

Finally, consider the role of physical exhaustion, as embodied in the modern maxim, 'Shop till you drop'. (In the 1870s, as Rappaport (1999) notes, female shoppers faced a further physical constraint: the absence of any public lavatories.) Consumers may not merely want to unload their weighty shopping baskets and sit down but may also perceive that the quality of their decision-making could be compromised by tiredness. Bigger malls are more likely to produce exhaustion, but they can ease it by providing places for consumers to take a break. Consumers may not have planned to spend so long in the mall, or to purchase what they have so far purchased, but the exhaustion of it all leads to further unplanned purchases: coffee and lunch.

9.7   CONCLUSION

Neither random behaviour nor some kind of psychological dysfunction needs to be invoked to explain unplanned purchasing by shoppers. When Earl enters a mall to buy a dietary supplement and leaves instead clutching a couple of new pairs of shoes, or when Potts goes out to buy fish and instead purchases a pair of hi-fi loudspeakers, there is method in their apparent madness. In this chapter we have put forward some factors that appear to shed light on how this sort of thing happens. We have also recognized that the things that make consumers seize particular purchasing opportunities may be themselves quite specific and rooted in their historical experience. The contingent nature of browsing-based shopping is going to make its formal modelling a challenge.

Mainstream consumer theorists in economics might wish to suggest that browsing activity does not change consumers' demands in the long term. For example, if latent demand is associated with inventory replenishment, it will simply affect the timing of purchases, with negligible consequences in terms of stock-carrying costs due to spare room in cupboards and wardrobes. At the level of the product category, this might well be true in some cases. Even so, there could still be an impact on the brands that the consumer selects, even in cases where the consumer has a strong brand preference. All that is required is for brands to differ in the ease with which they can be found by purposive search. For example, suppose a consumer of dental floss failed to grab at an opportunity to buy her preferred Reach floss that s/he happened to notice whilst in a pharmacy on another mission. She might then have no further encounters with the preferred brand until stocks at home completely ran out. With the relatively limited availability of Reach floss, the consumer might then have to get by purchasing the more widely stocked 'Oral-B' floss and be subject to its tendency to get stuck between his/her teeth. To avoid using the less reliable Oral-B product, the consumer would either have to search intensively – and possibly get diverted into browsing other kinds of goods – or go without floss altogether for a time.

Even if browsing does not affect brand selections, there remains the possibility that it will have path-dependence consequences for the consumer's overall purchasing activities. The important consideration here is the finite time taken up on a shopping expedition and the temporal gaps between expeditions. In the meantime, the set of goods offered and their associated promotional strategies may change, as may the circumstances of the consumer. An unplanned engagement in, say, a clothing sale may change neither the number of pairs of trousers a person consumes in the long-term nor the mix of brands of jeans or of types of trousers. But the fact that a particular chunk of scarce time is absorbed in purchasing trousers may result in other things not being purchased on that day. If the consumer had not had a latent demand for trousers, s/he might have been more susceptible to having his/her attention grabbed by a totally different type of product promotion.

The path-dependence aspect of browsing behaviour will be particularly significant wherever goods are interconnected, for example as technical complements or elements of product ranges of a particular brand (for a detailed discussion of the significance of connections in economic systems, see Potts, 2000). Suppose an amateur guitar player goes into a newsagent to purchase the Saturday newspaper. There, he happens also to buy a guitar magazine which includes a CD containing, in addition to the cover-items that had attracted his attention, awe-inspiring playing by a musician – say,

Swedish virtuoso Yngwie Malmsteen – whom he had not previously heard. Major consequences could follow. The consumer may end up spending a large sum collecting all of this artist's recordings, music transcription albums, instructional videos, concert tickets, and an expensive signature-series guitar designed to the artist's specification. In the course of tracking down these items, he may make yet more discoveries and purchases, as well as having his enthusiasm for doing music so revitalized that he spends more on other items of equipment and makes major changes in how he uses his leisure time. Had he not tried to buy the paper that week, he might have missed the magazine and not made the discovery, and so on. Such degrees of contingency (which will be readily appreciated by those who have seen the German movie 'Run, Lola, Run') are things that mainstream economists, with their focus on market-level aggregates, might expect 'all to come out in the wash'. To evolutionary economists, however, they seem likely to have amplifying effects when consumers not only weave themselves complex fabrics of interconnected purchases but also live within a social world and mingle with others who have similar latent demands. It is time that economists started exploring just how important these effects are.

ACKNOWLEDGEMENTS

We are grateful for the comments of an anonymous referee and to David Fisher for some pertinent references.

10. Normal Cost versus Marginalist Models of Pricing: A Behavioural Perspective

10.1 INTRODUCTION

The rekindling of the marginalist pricing controversy by Catherine Langlois (1989a, 1989b) occurred at a time when I was reconsidering my views of the classic works on both sides of the debate. An involvement in teaching marketing via case studies that often include pricing decisions led me increasingly to recognize the dangers that may arise from trying to view all pricing in the manufacturing and service sectors in dualistic terms (cf. Earl, 1995, chapters 1, 8 and 9). Rather than seeing pricing in black or white terms, as being exclusively based on *either* 'full-costs' *or* the weighing up of marginal costs and revenues associated with rival pricing strategies, a behavioural perspective fosters the recognition that *both* approaches warrant serious attention, and leads to the view that pricing is a context-specific activity. The latter position is similar to the one adopted long ago by Joan Robinson (1953, p. 590) when she commented that

> [I]t seems clearly impossible to replace the old text-book slogans with any simple generalizations. A debate which consists in defending or attacking 'principles', such as the 'full-cost principle', 'the marginal principle' or the normal-cost principle', and trying to fit all types of situation into one system is obviously foredoomed to futility.

The notion of a pluralistic approach to pricing clearly did not appeal to Catherine Langlois, for her work aimed, via a reinterpretation of mark-up observations, to absorb evidence consistent with full-cost pricing into the orthodox research programme. In this chapter I concentrate on showing how behavioural perspectives lead one away from an absorptionist stance. Information problems provide my unifying theme: competitive conditions between markets differ due to differences in informational conditions; these differences, and the information problems faced by corporate decision-makers, affect the use that is made of price as a competitive weapon. I do not attempt a point-by-point critique of the methodology that Langlois adopted but many of the examples that I use to illustrate problems of practical pricing choices concern the automotive industry upon which Langlois focused her empirical work.

10.2 BEHAVIOURAL THEORY AND THE DEBATE OVER MARGINALISM

Two kinds of analyses of pricing appear in the literature habitually used by behavioural economists. The first, most obviously associated with the work of Cyert and March (1963, chapters 7 and 8), sees pricing decisions as involving the reactive application of simple rules of thumb in response to cost increases, sales figures that fall short of target levels, and so on. The firm is portrayed as if it is myopic and fails to sort out the spillover effects of decisions that it takes sequentially. The second approach may be called a strategic approach to pricing and involves careful appraisals of the impact of pricing decisions for individual products in a firm's portfolio on the overall competitive position of the firm in the long run (for example Taylor and Wills, eds, 1969; Gabor, 1977). Decision-makers who have spent time studying marketing and in business schools should be well versed in elements of strategic pricing, but the extent to which in practice they can and do try to keep all of its subtleties in mind is an empirical question that has not really figured in the debate about marginalist versus full-cost/normal-cost approaches to pricing.

To date, this debate seems to have focused on three main issues that overlap with behavioural work. The first concerns the admissibility of, and interpretations to be placed on, case study evidence and material gathered from field questionnaires. In this respect, behaviouralists naturally find themselves on the side of the normal cost theorists, particularly members of the Oxford Economists' Research Group. The second concerns whether or not a full-cost approach to pricing is consistent with profit maximization. Chamberlin himself may have been the first to give the impression that it was not, when he suggested that in some monopolistically competitive industries 'business men may set their prices with reference to costs rather than to demand, aiming at ordinary rather than at maximum profits' (Chamberlin, 1933, p. 105).

Here, one might expect that the anti-marginalists would have warmly welcomed the behavioural contributions. Behaviouralists see the setting of multiple goals (for example, not only for profit but also for market standing, innovation, productivity, worker attitudes, and so on) and the use of rules of thumb as rational ways of dealing with complexity and uncertainty – environmental and cognitive facts of life which make optimization a logically problematic activity. By setting multiple targets members of a management team give themselves benchmarks for motivational and judgmental purposes. They are less likely to jeopardize the long-run survival of their firms by pushing products that are easy to sell today, whilst short-changing research and investment in equipment that will enable better products to be delivered in the future (see Loasby, 1976, chapter 7).

However, such a welcome was not extended to the behavioural theory of the firm: Andrews and Brunner (1975, p. 1) actually accused it of being a way of 'evading economic analysis'. The problem seems to have been that satisficing behaviour was seen as something that would only arise if the business environment were sufficiently slack as to permit a quiet life for incumbent firms (see Andrews and Brunner, 1962; Eichner, 1976, p. 50). It was not seen as something that is unavoidable, due to problems of knowledge, even in hotly contested competitive environments.

The third area of debate concerns whether firms actually enjoy demand curves that give them discretion in their pricing policies, or whether they feel bound by oligopolistic considerations – in particular, competition from actual and/or potential producers of duplicate or similar products. The early 'reactive' pricing work by Cyert and March certainly could be portrayed as devoting little attention to competitive factors that decision-makers ought to bear in mind in setting prices; indeed, it is this omission that seems to have led to claims that behavioural models presume slack market conditions. From the strategic standpoint, however, matters are more complicated.

10.3 COMPLEXITY AND THE MARKETING MIX

The earliest papers on the behavioural theory of the firm concentrated on the effects of organizational complexity on pricing. First, attention was given to the question of how organizational size might affect the responsiveness of firms to changes in sales rates (Cyert and March, 1955). The more layers there were to a corporate hierarchy, the longer it would take for information about market conditions to reach senior decision levels and for decisions to filter back down to sales personnel. Such lags could help explain how inventory levels (or waiting lists) build up, particularly if lower-level personnel had reasons of their own for keeping superiors poorly informed about the firm's success in the market. One would expect that this issue will become less important as firms install computerized information systems. It is harder to ignore a difficulty at the centre of the second Cyert and March paper (1956): when top executives eventually do come to discuss sales figures, they may express very different views about what has been going on and what should be done – either because they are bringing their different expert perspectives to bear on the problem or because they have personal interests in the verdict that is reached and actions that are chosen. For example, a decline in sales could reflect a loss of motivation on the part of the sales force rather than more competitive pricing and advertising by rivals. Alternatively, it might be due to the production department letting quality control slip with the result that re-buy orders are not materializing. Executives will be unlikely to admit that their departments' are where the difficulties lie, unless the outcome is likely to be that they will be allocated a larger budget.

Such a perspective on decision-making draws to our attention something that Chamberlin (1933) recognized very clearly but which has been lost sight of in the literature on the marginalist controversy: firms have to decide not merely how much to try to sell, and at what price, but also, what to sell and how to go about selling it (see further, section 8.2 of this book). The issue of 'which product' is best left until section 10.5 of this chapter, after we have considered the informational hurdles that need to be overcome for products to achieve market acceptance. First, though, we must note that once marketing costs are introduced into the analysis of pricing the independence of costs and revenues is lost and marginalist principles have to be looked at afresh.

If inventories are rising due to disappointing sales, measures such as an increase in expenditure on marketing, or a switch to a new advertising agency, may be much more appropriate than price cuts. In marginalist terms the task is to find the point at which the marginal dollar spent on marketing ceases to produce at least an extra dollar of revenue by moving the position of the demand curve.

Unfortunately, the pay-offs to increases in marketing expenditure or changes in the style of promotion are inherently uncertain -- as they say in the advertising world, 'Half the money spent on advertising is wasted, but we don't know which half.' Optimization seems out of the question here, and to the extent that rule-of-thumb responses are made to changing sales rates, any increase in marketing expenditure is normally added to fixed costs unless there is a well-defined linkage between sales and selling costs (such as commissions paid to sales personnel). As scholars such as Romney Robinson (1971) and Skinner (1983) have emphasized, Chamberlin in his original work not only gave selling costs the attention they deserve, he also did so largely in terms of their impact on average rather than marginal costs. This is in sharp contrast to Langlois (1989a): nowhere does her inventories-oriented optimal mark-up model for automobile prices consider the choice between price reductions and non-price methods of promotion. Yet it is impossible to read business history works on the automotive industry (for example, Moritz and Seaman, 1981) without being struck by the impact on sales that can come from factory-provided incentives to dealers or from innovative advertising campaigns. (In the case of Nissan Australia in the mid-1980s, for example, it was discovered that buyers were not resisting the firm's products due to uncompetitive pricing but rather as a result of a lack of brand awareness due to the company having kept a rather low media profile after changing its brand name from Datsun to Nissan; the firm promptly increased its media spending.) Given this, it is important that readers also examine her earlier paper (Langlois, 1989a), in which effects of advertising expenditure on sales rates for the Big Three automobile manufacturers are investigated and found to be significant if lagged for one quarter, but not if lagged for two quarters. However, in that paper the compatibility between an optimizing framework and advertising variables is ignored.

10.4 INFORMATION AND PRODUCT DIFFERENTIATION

The prices that firms would be wise to consider setting are not independent of responses of buyers to their own problems of ignorance and complexity. If buyers are fully informed about firms' offerings then a manufacturer of a product cannot expect to command a price in excess of the opportunity costs of potential producers of identical items. In this context neoclassical theorists (of the contestable markets school) would agree with Post Keynesian normal cost theorists, whatever their broader differences about how one should try to model the firm (see Davies and Lee, 1988). However, if one takes account of the work of Williamson (1975), it appears that both camps need to pay careful attention to the complications that problems of knowledge and legal costs cause for buyers and sellers. Such attention is conducive to a greater awareness of the role of barriers to entry in the competitive process.

Consider first the case of a standardized product or an item such as a component that is to be produced to a particular specification by whichever supplier wins a tendering battle. One may be tempted to say that, in such circumstances, the firms that submit tenders have no discretion over the prices they quote, for failure to quote the lowest price will result in them losing the deal. There is no downward-sloping marginal revenue curve to intersect the firms' marginal cost curves. Firms that fail to win such sales must be the ones whose normal costs are higher than those that do, or who have made erroneous assessments of the opportunity costs of their rivals.

Once contract enforcement costs are brought into the picture, it becomes apparent that buyers will not necessarily accept the lowest quotation, for that may be offered by a firm which is under great pressure to get orders to avoid bankruptcy or which is battling against a reputation for not delivering goods, either on time or to specification. It could be expensive to award a sale to such a firm and then have to take it to court to obtain redress. In this case, firms with reputations for reliability may a quote premium prices. Whether or not buyers will opt to pay a premium price seems likely to depend on whether they see the premium as an excessive amount to pay to insure themselves against being let down. Some may find it acceptable; others may prefer to take a chance and buy more cheaply.

Superficially, this appears consistent with marginalist analysis. Physically similar products offered by suppliers with different reputations are selling at different prices to buyers with different attitudes towards risk; suppliers therefore have a decision at the margin concerning the pay-offs from stepping up their spending to improve their reputations. However, it appears to be in order for normal cost theorists to point out that if firms with identical reputations do not quote identical prices for physically identical products, those which ask more will fail to pick up any sales so long as buyers are well informed about which prices are being quoted.

The marginalist approach looks on rather stronger ground in two cases. First, if buyers limit the amount of search that they undertake and do not generally put their requirements out to tender, a firm which quotes a premium price may still win some sales despite not offering a premium product or reduced risk of disappointment. Whether such a price strategy will pay clearly depends on the percentage of the market population that engages in little or no search, and on the extent to which buyers are likely to use social interaction as a source of information.

One might have expected professional buyers of machine tools, for example, to shop around carefully, but the empirical work of Cunningham and White (1974) revealed otherwise. A quarter century of personal experience in the market for motor vehicle insurance in the United Kingdom, New Zealand and Australia has also revealed quite marked price dispersions in quotations even after policies were standardized. This latter case is easy enough to understand from the position of the insurance companies, given the number of firms in the market and the difficulties many buyers have in finding social contacts with similar vehicles and circumstances to use as guides as to the value being offered by the best of a handful of quotations. Insofar as the search process is random and incomplete, the stopping rules used by consumers may permit the coexistence of firms that quote a very wide range of prices. If a quotation seems affordable and search costs are non-trivial, a consumer may accept it without bothering to find out whether or not it is the best on offer. If a sizable part of the buying population tends to engage in limited search, it may be perfectly rational for some firms to choose a 'rip-off' pricing policy rather than setting their prices according to normal costs (contrast this argument with Andrews, 1964, pp. 101–2). The situation is further complicated by scope for insurers to offer deceptively low quotations for the first year and then gradually ratchet up premiums in subsequent years on the basis of their assessments of how long it will take before customer goodwill is stretched too far and customers are then driven back into search mode – possibly ending up attaching themselves to another firm that is pursuing a similar policy. These policies may be particularly appealing to insurance firms in higher-inflation environments in which consumers find it hard to disentangle relative price movements from the general upward drift of prices.

Scope for price discretion also appears to be considerable in respect of idiosyncratic products whose specifications can neither be easily copied nor written down in contracts. Standards of service in high-class restaurants and hairdressers would come into this category (note that the franchise manual even for the highly standardized product offered by a McDonald's restaurant runs to 600 pages: see Love, 1986). So, too, would up-market consumer durables such as automobiles. It might be possible to pin down the 'build quality' and 'reliability' dimensions in terms of manufacturing tolerances and the rate at which parts worked loose or disintegrated over the life of the car, but these features are difficult to demonstrate to potential customers *ex ante* and have proved difficult – in some cases impossible – for interlopers to imitate.

If consumers both recognize the costs of erroneous choices and experience difficulties in identifying in advance what the offerings of interlopers will be like in practice, incumbent producers may justifiably feel that their reputations give them some discretion in the prices they charge. In other words, a belief that 'better the devil you know' may enable incumbent suppliers to continue to command premium prices that more than compensate for any volume they lose to interlopers. In so far as the products in question are intended for conspicuous consumption, incumbent producers may have little to fear from cheaper imitations if well-informed purchasers expect to experience difficulties in demonstrating to their less-knowledgeable reference groups that there is no need to spend so much to get products of a particular quality (see also section 8.4). Considerable marketing investments may be needed before interlopers can convince potential customers that their products have made the grade, and these marketing costs will work against any manufacturing cost advantage that might otherwise give the interlopers the chance to use price as a competitive weapon.

As far as competition between established producers is concerned, incumbent manufacturers of idiosyncratic products may feel under little pressure to match the prices charged by rivals whose offerings differ in their physical characteristics and images. Breaks in the chain of substitution give them some discretion in their short-run pricing: for example, one would not expect rival manufacturers of prestige automobiles to have to be constantly on the look out for small percentage discrepancies between their prices. Much more important for relative sales are the improvements that they are each making to their respective products.

None of this is intended to suggest that strategic pricing by incumbents should not take account of the possibility that, in the long run, reputations can be built up by hitherto unknown suppliers in particular market niches. However, it is by no means obvious that the appropriate pricing strategy should be one that sacrifices short-run profits in order to discourage competitive warfare from corporations with the resources and inclination to fight a long war of attrition. It is doubtful that incumbents in the prestige automobile market (BMW, Cadillac, Jaguar and Mercedes-Benz) did not, by the mid/late 1980s, take seriously the possibility that Japanese producers (such as Honda/Acura, Toyota/Lexus and Nissan/Infiniti) were both likely to be able to match their current standards in the long run and were being driven to do so by the threat from Korean producers at the lower end of the market. In so far as the incumbents did not appear to be holding back their prices as this possibility became apparent, their actions could be interpreted in a variety of ways.

One approach would be to say that they had chosen a pricing strategy that placed a premium on profits in the near future over those further down the track. This could reflect a long-run application of marginalist thinking, the view being taken that an entry-deterring approach to pricing would be expensive in terms of foregone profits and not in any case guaranteed to succeed. Alternatively, the thinking could be that if the profits from 'making hay while the sun shines' are ploughed back into research and development in respect of both products and production processes, it may be possible to stay ahead of the interlopers in the long run. If profit margins are being set according to such thinking, then what we really have is much more in keeping with the thrust of the Eichner's (1976) version of normal cost analysis of competitive oligopoly: the firm is not acting as a 'snatcher' even though it might superficially appear to be doing so; rather, it is setting its prices to help it preserve its long-run market position, the fat profits being necessary to pioneer new standards. If such a pricing strategy succeeds, the interlopers may end up matching the standards that the incumbents once set, but not succeed in stealing their customers en masse, owing to buyers in general moving up-market with increasing affluence. But a behavioural theorist, seeing pricing as an experimental activity undertaken in the face of uncertainty, makes no presumption that firms will always avoid strategic pricing errors.

10.5 'BUILT TO A PRICE'

In a rather neglected contribution to the debate about marginalism, Smyth (1967) suggested that empirical work purporting to identify cost-plus pricing might sometimes be better seen as evidence of a 'price-minus theory of costs'. In this section Smyth's idea is extended in strategic terms in a way that may help provide a bridge between the two sides in the debate. To do so, it is useful to imagine the case of an automobile firm whose executives see their major goal as re-establishing themselves as market leader by introducing a new model in a key market segment.

The executives' choice of what their product might entail is constrained by a number of factors. The price range within which it must be sold will be narrowed down by the prices charged by the current market leader and other producers of substitutes, and by the firm's desire not to lose profits due to sales of the new model cannibalizing the sales of its other models in higher and lower price bands. Within this range, the firm's strategists must grapple with the signals that their price will convey concerning the quality of the product. To price below the leader may suggest a failure to match its quality, but to offer a better product above the leader's price may also be unwise in so far as buyers are sceptical of promotional claims and may not be dissatisfied with the dominant product.

Having recognized this dilemma, the executives might then debate the best product packages that could be offered convincingly to the market at the prices that they had not eliminated, subject to the constraint that costs must not be incompatible with target profit rates being achieved if sales projections are within normal margins of accuracy.[1] If the market leader has been using the advantages of large-scale production to permit prices that are

---

[1] This discussion was originally inspired by various reports in the Australian motoring press concerning the development and pricing of the 1988 Holden Commodore, the product with which General Motors–Holden was able to topple Ford's Falcon model from its long-held position at the top of the sales league. Journalists frequently commented on how costs for the new models were being contained in the low-volume Australian market by leaving out modern features, such as independent rear suspension, that were fitted in the parent firms' European-market products. A decade and a half later, exactly the same logic seems to apply, even though the current Commodore and Falcon models both are much better built, better equipped and more expensive. As budgets have risen with economic growth, the two manufacturers have progressively upgraded their products, but normally with Holden taking the lead and Ford seeming to be the penny-pinching follower. Their list prices are remarkably similar but different non-price strategies are employed to entice customers. For 2000–1, for example, market leader Holden offered independent rear suspension and antilock brakes as standard on its base model, whereas Ford offered standard air-conditioning – a feature that most Australians would consider essential – at the cost of leaving it to customers to opt for safety features. Comparably-specified cars from the two firms still cost much the same, but one can see different strategies implied in the different areas of choice offered to potential customers: Ford appealed more to the traditional Australian buyer, whilst Holden was successfully positioning itself as more driver- and safety-conscious and hence more like a prestigious European import.

low enough to inconvenience its rivals' rates of return (but not so low as to lead to suggestions that it is engaging in predatory pricing), then the executives in the company in question may face quite a struggle to find any price/product combination that seems likely to give them sales leadership without compromising the kind of rate of return that will be necessary if they are to have a chance of maintaining such a position in the long run. Such limitations of development finance are likely to result in the 'bean counters' persuading their fellow executives to omit some features that they would ideally like the product to include. The end result is either a compromise product that seems likely to enable corporate goals to be met, or a decision to search for a new strategy, such as a joint venture arrangement with another firm.

These debates can certainly be framed in marginalist terms. One can model them as if they involve the optimal choice of a price/product configuration in the light of estimates of likely sales and costs associated with each element in the set of rival schemes being considered. One can also portray the optimization exercise as if it is carried out subject to the constraint that the price/product choice is not at odds with the firm's long-run objectives, and then see whether the solution set is empty. In this way one can have products being sold at prices that appear to be based on full-costs, even though the decision about which product/price combination to choose involves a concern with marginal revenues that may be gained from marginal outlays. As one envisages executives debating this type of decision, it is difficult not to have a basic sympathy with marginalism, if not in respect of decisions to revise prices after the product has been launched. However, one is also somewhat deterred from a marginalist characterization by the likelihood that complexity and technological considerations will ensure decision-makers in practice are arguing, with the aid of simplifying procedures, about discrete price/product combinations.

10.6 PRICING AND PRODUCT LIFE-CYCLES

Much of the literature in debates about marginalism has also overlooked the fact that the 'optimal' choice of a price/product combination is further complicated in strategic terms once one considers three areas in which there may exist scope for managing the dynamics of product life-cycles. First, firms can use variations in price to affect the rates of diffusion of their products, and inventory levels will need to be managed carefully if sales rates are to be compatible with changes in the willingness of buyers to make purchases. Second, substitutions between rival products may have an impact upon the pressure that manufacturers feel to get model replacements ready for the market (for example, in the European automotive industry in 1989, the continuing success of the BMW 3 Series and rally victory-led revival of Lancia Delta sales led their respective manufacturers to slow down the development of new models: see *Modern Motor*, 1989; and *Wheels*, 1989). Third, as sales accumulate for a particular model, costs may fall due to learning by doing, giving the manufacturer a choice between (a) taking a higher margin at the existing price, (b) lowering the price and expanding sales, (c) upgrading the product so that it offers better value for the same money, or (d) a mixture of (b) and (c).

If corporate strategists had a good knowledge of the likely responses of potential buyers and rival producers, they could formulate an optimization problem for a set of prices to apply during the life-cycle of each product, which would be implemented in conjunction with a plan concerning the upgrading of the product's specification to produce a particular net present value-maximizing time profile for inventories, costs and revenues. In reality, of course, any attempts at a dynamic pricing strategy are going to be experimental in nature, the more so the more that the product in question is breaking new ground within its market. It looks naive to employ the conventional normal cost rule in this kind of setting; here, the appropriate unit of analysis is not the individual product purchased by a customer, but the entire run of the product produced over its life-cycle. If a firm repeatedly earns supernormal overall profits on successive models in a particular product market, it is likely to attract potential competitors into its territory.

10.7   PRICING IN HISTORICAL CONTEXT

As methods of organization change in business, one would expect there to be changes in pricing practices. Hence it may be unwise to presume that empirical studies whose data sets stop well short of the present are anything more than contributions to economic history. The papers by Langlois (1989a, 1989b) must be viewed with some caution, for they use data only up to the end of 1979 and 1973, respectively, in attempting to build inventory targets into a marginalist analysis of pricing.

The automobile industry in the 1960s and 1970s certainly did work with substantial inventory holdings, embarking on major sales pushes when these got out of hand. Doubts about the wisdom of modelling inventory choices in optimizing terms seem in order in the case of Chrysler, given the fact that, at its peak (February 1969), the company's stock level was found to number 408,302 cars, much to the astonishment of senior executives (Moritz and Seaman, 1981, p. 109). But inventory considerations seem likely to play an increasingly unimportant part in pricing strategies. It is not merely that (a) when monetarist policies are applied to dampen demand, higher real interest rates make the costs of carrying stock so much higher; (b) that firms have also become aware of the damage to buyer goodwill that can result from fire sales of excess stock that destroy the second-hand values of their product; and (c) that Japanese-led trends toward shorter model-replacement cycles have enhanced the risk that vehicles held in inventories may become obsolete before they find buyers. Rather, the whole approach to the choice of what to produce and when to produce it is undergoing a fundamental change as a result of the application of computerized stock control systems, numerically controlled machine tools and computer assisted manufacturing.

These new production methods – whose significance was discussed at an early stage in Toffler (1980) and Piore and Sabel (1984) – mean that even final consumer goods are increasingly being built to order. Buyers who seek to individualize their purchases can do so by selecting appealing combinations of features from a menu of possibilities. To the extent that factory outputs are not linked directly to customer orders, it is still likely that manufacturers will only be producing output for which they have a definite dealer order: the experience of the Chrysler Corporation in the period 1967–79, shows how a policy of building products ahead of customer orders can be disastrous if the option preferences of buyers cannot be foreseen accurately (see Moritz and Seaman (1981, pp. 100–9; 244–4). As the 'design it yourself' philosophy takes hold (see *Economist*, 1989b), it becomes all the more imperative that firms in the West keep their input inventories under control by switching to the Japanese 'just-in-time' method of stock control. Unless they feel they can guess ultimate demand patterns better than their downstream customers, input suppliers, in turn, will wish only to produce to order, by dialling up the appropriate programme on their machine tools.

When very precisely specified inputs are produced to order with the aid of highly flexible computerized production systems, sellers are under pressure to quote prices and to meet quality and delivery schedules that are no worse than can be offered by current and potential producers of the products in question. In these markets the concept of the marginal revenue curve makes little sense and the logic of normal cost analysis is particularly compelling.

10.8   CONCLUSION

A behavioural perspective suggests that the forces which are likely to shape pricing decisions are much more complex than parties on either side of the debate over marginalism are usually willing to admit. Complexity may be expected to lead those who set prices to make use of simplifying decision rules and principles, but these may be expected to vary between different contexts, depending on what decision-makers regard as the key elements of the problem they are trying to solve. Hence the pricing behaviour of firms in a particular industry may be easy to explain in terms of a given pricing rule and yet difficult to reconcile with another rule that seems to match observations in other sectors or in the same sector at different points in time.

Catherine Langlois focused her contribution to the marginalism debate on the role of inventory targets and, regardless of how one construes the significance of her empirical analysis, we should be grateful for it. Her focus implicitly draws our attention to the possibility that, in industries in which it is expensive to vary the rate of production, price setters may take careful account of the impact of alternative prices on the time it takes to dispose of inventories. Despite their concern with the unfolding of economic events in historical time, Post Keynesians have tended to neglect this possibility because they have usually assumed, in their non-market-clearing view of pricing, that output rates can be adjusted easily to accommodate the pattern of sales. This is not always going to be a good assumption to make.

Economists involved in practical pricing decisions or antitrust investigations can deal with them on a case-by-case basis: they have little reason for favouring an absorptionist philosophy over a pluralistic one. Macroeconomists, however, face a major dilemma as they try to come up with something manageable to say about pricing that can be plugged into a larger model. Either they risk making mistakes or getting nowhere in attempts to construct more complex disaggregated models (for example, they might struggle to predict inflation via a model which portrayed some sectors as using a full-cost approach to pricing but others as allowing the pressure of demand to influence their prices); or they risk drawing inappropriate conclusions due to treating all firms as if their behaviour conforms to a particular rule. It would be unfortunate if the empirical success of Post Keynesian macroeconomic models built on simple full-cost pricing foundations led to a failure to recognize that full-cost models might have significant limitations in other analytical contexts.

11. Liquidity Preference, Marketability and Pricing

11.1 INTRODUCTION

Except when discussing rent and derived demands for human factors, price theory predominantly involves the prices of newly produced items considered in isolation from the workings of secondhand markets. The focus is on flow-prices and it seems to be taken for granted that prices of stocks of partly depreciated durable items are simply a matter of conditions of supply and demand related to physical rates of depreciation. This chapter, by contrast is an examination of some of the ways in which trade in secondhand markets affects behaviour in markets for current output and it emphasizes that rates of depreciation may have much more to do with speculation and reputation effects than with physical deterioration. In offering this analysis, I am reversing a criticism that Joan Robinson levelled at mainstream economics. She was never happy with attempts of economists such as Robert Clower to construct Walrasian microfoundations for Keynesian macroeconomics. Central to her dislike of such contributions was that 'all [brands of micro theory] share the characteristic of stressing exchange and neglecting production. Even the process of marketing commodities is not much discussed' (Robinson, 1977, p. 1321). As Robinson often said, neoclassical price theory may at best be a summary of the economics of a prisoner of war camp following the arrival of parcels from the Red Cross.

A recurring theme in the work of Robinson and other leading Post Keynesians such as Davidson (1978) and Shackle (1967, 1972) is that *poorly organized* spot markets make fragile the demand for durable goods, particularly specialized items of capital equipment. Hence, in focusing on the effects of having *relatively comprehensive* markets for secondhand durables, I may at first sight seem to be attempting something heretical in terms of Post Keynesian economics. A foreshadowing of the fact that I will be drawing on the work of leading Austrian economists, particularly Menger (1871) and Mises (1949), might give Post Keynesians further cause for concern about this chapter. However, it should gradually become apparent that the overall tone of the chapter is thoroughly in keeping with their work. Indeed, it displays the hallmark tendency of Post Keynesian scholars to feel at ease with a variety of seemingly incompatible ways of thinking about economic problems, that led to debate between Caldwell (1989) and Dow (1992).

In the Caldwell/Dow debate one example used as a focus was the work of Shackle (which questions the possibility of prediction) and Eichner (who was keen to make extensive use of empirical regularities as foundations for a Post Keynesian macroeconomic forecasting model). This chapter further displays the Post Keynesian's ease with contrasting perspectives by including an exploration of the relationship between a pair of contributions to the theory of value that receive attention in the literature of Post Keynesian economics. On the one hand, I employ the 'normal-cost' analysis of pricing, which portrays prices as typically being based on anticipated variable costs over a particular planning period plus a mark-up whose size is limited by the conjectures about the risk of encouraging additional sources of supply. Yet I also employ the view that it is appropriate to generalize, to durable goods at least, Keynes's analysis of the determination of the prices of money and financial assets with reference to the role of potentially unstable speculative expectations of changes in relative prices. The normal-cost perspective was considered at length in the previous chapter of this book. Its strongest statement is in the work of Andrews (1949, 1993), though it could also be read into Sraffa's (1960) analysis of prices without reference to demand or even traced back to Adam Smith's writings on 'natural prices' (see Kregel, 1990). The speculation-based position originated with Townshend's (1937) radical reading of, particularly, chapter 17 of Keynes's (1936) *General Theory* and was enthusiastically endorsed by Shackle (1967, 1972).

It is logical for me to begin with a 'chapter 17' perspective, but before I do so I think it is important to draw the attention of readers to one further source of inspiration which does not surface explicitly in the body of the chapter, namely Thompson's (1979) *Rubbish Theory*. This unusual (and unusually entertaining) work focuses from an anthropologist's standpoint on the changing values that people attach to durable items: on phenomena such as gentrification and the tendency for yesterday's kitsch to end up being sought after by collectors. What makes it especially interesting for those who study Keynes and uncertainty is that Thompson attempts towards the end of his book to use catastrophe theory to make sense of shifts in confidence in markets and faddish changes in social values.

11.2   OUTPUTS, CARRYING COSTS AND LIQUIDITY/RISK PREMIA

Keynes's (1936, chapter 17) discussion of portfolio choice can be exhausting to read because so much of it is rather abstractly couched in terms of own rates of (own) return, whereas normally we are used to thinking of expected yields of assets simply in terms of a money rate of return. But his two essential messages seem to be quite simple. The first is that how much money people are prepared to pay for a financial or physical asset depends on three things that determine the overall return to holding it. Keynes labelled as q the value they place on the flow of services they expect to get from it. From q is subtracted c, the costs they will incur whilst it is in their possession, generating these services. To $c - q$ is added l, the additional value (liquidity premium) they attach to it for its efficacy as a store of value. His second key message is that the ease with which an asset can be reproduced has a major role to play in determining how people will perceive it as a store of value.

There are striking similarities between these views of Keynes and the writings of Austrian economists, whose views of market processes often seem remarkably sophisticated. Streissler (1973), Hicks (1976, p. 139) and Negishi (1985, chapter 13) have already drawn attention to this in respect of the work of Menger. A flavour of the thinking of Mises (1949) may be given by the following extracts:

> As soon as an economic good is demanded not only by those who want to use it for consumption or production, but also by people who want to keep it as a medium of exchange and to give it away in a later act of exchange, the demand for it increases. A new employment for this good has emerged and creates an additional demand for it. As with every other economic good, such an additional demand brings about a rise in its value in exchange, i.e. in the quantity of other goods which are offered for its acquisition. The amount of other goods which can be obtained in giving away a medium of exchange, its 'price' as expressed in terms of various goods and services, is in part determined by the demand of those who want to acquire it as a medium of exchange. If people stop using the good in question as a medium of exchange, this additional specific demand disappears and the 'price' drops concomitantly. (Mises, 1949, p. 405)

> Consequently there emerges a specific demand for such goods on the part of people eager to keep them in order to reduce the costs of cash holding. The prices of these goods are partly determined by this specific demand; they would be lower in its absence. These goods are secondary media of exchange as it were, and their exchange value is resultant of two kinds of demand: the demand related to their services as secondary media of exchange, and the demand related to the other services they render. (p. 460)

The kinds of semi-money assets that Mises goes on to list include jewels, bank claims at short notice and widely held bonds which can be sold in *moderate* quantities without depressing their prices and, significantly for the purposes of this chapter, 'even commodities'.

Now, it is common to discuss $q - c + l$ with reference to money, bonds and investments in capital equipment. Thence one can show how nervousness about the prospective yield and resale value of plant and machinery can lead to an increased demand for money – which has the unfortunate characteristic, as far as employment generation is concerned, of being non-reproducible. A classic example of $q - c + l$ in relation to commercial projects is the Centrepoint office block in London during the early 1970s. This building, to the horror of many people, was left empty, earning no q but incurring c such as security costs, while its owners hoped to make a profit on it due to increases in its market value.

We may equally well apply $q - c + l$ to consumer durables, such as motor vehicles. The total cost of vehicle ownership may be dramatically affected by depreciation, rather than by the initial purchase price or interest charges, so motoring magazines are increasingly including in their road test informed guesses of the likely values of the test vehicles three years later. Reputations of rival brands for maintaining secondhand values will differ and tend to be self-reinforcing, as was noted in Chapter 8 in the discussion of the iconic status of brands such as BMW. The market for medium-size vehicles by mainstream manufacturers such as Ford collapsed at the turn of the twenty-first century as buyers opted for more prestigious brands. This compounded falls in secondhand prices associated with falling new-car prices. In late 2000 an unexpectedly sharp dive in used car values in the UK made it a struggle for manufacturers to achieve the minimum guaranteed future values that had been set three or five years earlier for personal contract purchases. As *Car Magazine* (2000) noted, this problem of negative equity was faced not merely by manufacturers, particularly Ford and Vauxhall, but also by 'creative leasing companies who put together longer-term packages of up to five years to ensure low monthly repayments. These vehicles are coming back to haunt them.' The same magazine subsequently introduced measures of depreciation and a 'depreciation disaster' category in its section of guidance for new-car buyers.

Keynes's equation also relates to the relative marketability of variants of a given car model. For example, compared with a standard model, a 'hot hatchback' or turbocharged variant may have a higher q (due to greater status and driving enjoyment, perhaps) and a higher c (more expensive to insure, finance and maintain). Given that buyers in the secondhand market are likely to be younger and face higher insurance costs on performance vehicles, these vehicles will tend to depreciate more rapidly unless they achieve some kind of cult status, as with the Volkswagen Golf GTi or Subaru Impreza Turbo. Similar problems of depreciation typically afflict top-end luxury variants whose initial prices often reflect price discrimination rather than merely the marginal cost of adding fancier trimmings (that may display its age relatively easily) and electronic gizmos (that later in life will become expensive to maintain). Hence the standard model is normally a better bet in terms of l. Sometimes vehicles are produced in deliberately limited numbers to give them instant classic status. This strategy is best known at the top end of the market for exotic sports cars (cf. Swann, 2001), but is also widely used in attempts to maintain demand towards the end of the life cycles of more mundane products. Expectations determining $q - c + l$ limit the prices that people will be prepared to pay for particular model types and brands and in turn shape the viability of producing them.

If one looks at patterns of demand from the perspective of Keynes's chapter 17, the scope for instability in sales and prices seems substantial, all the more so once the social nature of expectation-forming processes is incorporated. This was Townshend's key insight: Keynes himself had developed his consumption function analysis without adequately recognizing that all he had said about the fragility of demand for investment goods might be applied to consumer durables. The more affluent societies become, the more their expenditures are discretionary in nature, involving the replacement of durable items that were not worn out or broken beyond repair, and the more people may have access to credit. Aggregate demand is thus not a function of ability to spend so much as of willingness to part with liquidity (see Katona, 1960, for the most assertive statement of this idea, which is further discussed in the next chapter).

The underlying structure of demand may also display a fickleness that can be understood in terms of $q - c + l$. Once again the car market illustrates this in a down-to-earth way. Two examples will suffice. First, note the UK case of the Ford Sierra Cosworth in the late 1980s. Initially offered purely as a motor-sport homologation special, it became so sought after that it was refined and put into regular production. Despite being widely regarded as offering remarkable value for money, the model enjoyed an unexpectedly short life due to a collapse of sales that even a price cut of around 20 per cent could not stop. The trouble was that many owners were inconvenienced by thefts by joy-riders, reducing their expected or actual q. Insurance rates (c) soared to around a tenth of the new-car price for even the lowest risk drivers. This led to catastrophic rates of depreciation (which were not helped by the substantial price cut). Secondly, we may note how Mercedes-Benz reacted when faced with stocks of top-range S-class models worth over £850 million standing unsold at Bremerhaven docks in October 1992. The task of shifting these politically incorrect behemoths during a world recession posed a particularly difficult problem given that strong residual values had long been a major selling point of the marque. In the German market, where the marque is relatively ubiquitous, substantial discounting was used. In the US, however, the company offered a lease deal involving 2 per cent finance and a guaranteed residual, no doubt hoping that the market would have recovered by the time the 1992 cars came off their leases (see *Car Magazine*, 1993).

The view that the determination of current demand prices of durables may be significantly affected by speculation about future values would doubtless have troubled Dennis Robertson. He was worried that Keynes appeared to have used the idea of liquidity preference to construct what seemed to be a bootstraps theory of the price of money:

> [T]he rate of interest is what it is because it is expected to become other than it is; if it is not expected to become other than it is, there is nothing left to tell us why it is what it is. The organ which secretes it has been amputated, and yet it somehow still exists – a grin without a cat. (Robertson, 1940, p. 36)

In the case of consumer durables, liquidity premia unhitch valuations from the kinds of factors that modern, characteristics-based demand theories tend to focus upon, pointing to a need to integrate these theories with those from the literature on choices of financial assets.

In so far as there is an anchor (Robertson's cat) for prices it seems to have to come, as Townshend realized, from costs of production, particularly labour costs. However, workers have to speculate when assessing whether wage levels are acceptable. As Mises (1949, p. 576) observed, around twenty years before Alchian, Leijonhufvud, Friedman and Phelps drew attention to search-related aspects of unemployment and wage stickiness, 'The unemployed worker refuses to change his occupation or his residence or content himself with lower pay because he hopes to obtain at a later date a job with higher pay in the place of his residence and in the branch of business he likes best.' Furthermore, as will be discussed at greater length in section 11.7, conjectures about the size and variability of demand for new output affect the kinds of production arrangements that entrepreneurs are willing to make and thus affect their cost structures.

11.3   MARKETABILITY

Davidson (1978, pp. 62–3) notes that where spot markets for particular assets are poorly organized, assets will be held and used primarily for their anticipated ability to generate income (or, more generally, a flow of consumption services). In his terms, a well-organized market is one in which people can reasonably expect to be able to exchange a particular asset for cash at a price which differs little from well-publicized prices of previous transactions. It should be noted how this perspective relates entirely to the extent of variability in prices and has nothing to do with the existence of institutions concerned with facilitating trade in the type of asset in question. For example, in the market for used cars, there are many institutional devices that permit people to exchange their vehicles for spot cash or trade them in against other vehicles. Car dealers increasingly have to compete with car auctions in this role and the auction market for used cars is improving its standards of service by enabling would-be buyers to test vehicles prior to the auction. However, if auction prices or dealers' spot-cash offers for a particular class of car jump up and down markedly around some average figure, then we would not, if following Davidson, claim that the market for this vehicle is well organized.

If spot prices for assets are prone to jump around in this way, to differing degrees for different assets, it seems more appropriate to think of consumers not as if they add liquidity premia to $q - c$, but rather, as if they *subtract* risk premia, r, from the expected yields of assets, as in Kaldor's (1960) reformulation of Keynes's analysis, also favoured by Davidson. The degree of variance in auction prices provides some measure of the risk that a person takes when buying a particular asset: a measure of the unpredictability of its price in a *forced* sale. However, if the asset could be disposed of under less pressure the unpredictability would relate less to price and more to the carrying costs and marketing costs that would be incurred whilst waiting to achieve a particular price. Auction prices may tend to exhibit much greater variability than prices that dealers attach to items that they are holding in stock.

The factors that determine the variability of spot prices of assets or of the time it takes to sell an asset for a particular price must be investigated if we are to understand differences in liquidity premia or risk premia. For Menger (1871, pp. 241–56) and Kaldor (1960, p. 60) this was essentially a question about factors affecting marketability. As Streissler (1973, p. 170) points out, 'Liquidity, according to Menger, is above all due to the ubiquity of demand, the number of people dealing in a commodity, the continuity in time of demand, and the degree of speculation in the commodity in question.' Post Keynesians would accept the first three of Menger's factors but proceed cautiously in respect of the fourth. Suppose that speculation is based on expectations of price movements (as in Keynes, 1936, chapter 12) rather than inelastic views of supply and demand conditions (as in the classical theory). If so, assets that are subject to speculation may sometimes be prone to suffer precipitous price changes due to a flight of speculators from their markets. Post Keynesians such as Davidson (1978, pp. 67–8) have also emphasized that equities tend to be more marketable than building or machines owned by companies. This is because the former are more readily divisible, may not be attached to specific assets and can be transferred between owners without any need to turn off the flow of services from the asset. This perspective seems somewhat related to thinking in industrial economics (including not merely normal-cost theory but also the theory of contestable markets along with the markets and hierarchies literature) about the impact of asset specificity on the degree of competition. If capital were non-specific (like the mythical putty capital in neoclassical growth models) then questions of structural coordination would be unimportant – all that would matter would be the possibility of a general glut.

From the perspective of behavioural economics, there are two further points to make about differences in marketability. First, a rare and infrequently traded product has a major informational disadvantage to overcome: potential buyers may not have it on their agendas and not be actively looking for it. If introduced to it by a dealer they may have trouble sizing it up on the basis of reported experiences of others (for example, there may be considerable uncertainty over its reliability and maintenance costs). Furthermore, they may be concerned about problems in explaining/justifying their purchase to others in a social setting, quite apart from being worried about selling it at a later date.

Secondly, the literature on non-compensatory decision rules (see Earl, 1986, 1995) may help us understand why some products exhibit a much greater variance in the time it takes to sell them or the forced sale prices that they achieve. The $q - c + l$ or $q - c - r$ view of asset yields is very much in the compensatory spirit, when in fact buyers may be using decision rules that can be at odds with the principle of gross substitution. Some could be using a conjunctive rule (a kind of checklist approach involving a set of aspiration levels). Others might employ some kind of sequential rule (for example, elimination by aspects, where characteristic tests are applied randomly and brands that fail a test are debarred from further consideration, or characteristic filtering, where the victorious product is the one which passes most tests taken in a priority sequence). Goods that are prone to be rejected by most people's decision rules will have thin markets when new. In turn, they will be offered secondhand relatively infrequently because there are relatively few of them around. When they *are* offered for sale there may simply be no one around at all who is looking for that sort of product. Buyers who might have jumped at the opportunity had the products been available *when they were in the market* may have already bought something else. If so, they will probably be unable to afford the costs of changing over (particularly if what they bought is something similarly offbeat, which did not meet quite so many of their unusual requirements but seemed the least unsatisfactory option at the time). In general, it is important to get out of the neoclassical habit of proceeding as if people are active in all markets at all times. Instead, one should recognize that, due to costs of gathering information and the imperfect marketability of assets, people tend only to be active in and informed about a market when they have a particular problem to solve.

11.4   DEALERS AND PRICES

Any dealer, whether trading in new or secondhand goods, continually has to ask two questions. The first concerns which products it makes sense to order, accept as trade-ins or purchase on the wholesale market. Secondly, dealers need to ask themselves which of the products that they have in stock they should be trying to market more aggressively by price cuts or advertisements, and which ones should they be thinking of simply selling back to the wholesale market for whatever they will currently fetch. Wholesale markets range from formal auctions to nothing more than the use of cellular phones to ring around among other known dealers. These markets exist to facilitate adjustments of patterns of stock holding in line with diverse and shifting conjectures of dealers. As time passes, their assessments may change and meanwhile they face offers of trade-ins that – as a result of their customers' changing needs, incomes, perceptions and decision rules – are rather different from the kinds of items that they are known to specialize in selling.

Carrying costs loom large in attempts to answer these questions – not just in the form of working capital tied up in stock, but also in terms of opportunity costs. While a dealer with limited time and store space is trying to sell and display one set of commodities he or she is foregoing the chance to make money from stocking others. Consequently it is to be expected that, other things equal, the less marketable a product is seen as being, the higher will be the dealer's required mark-up on it. An upper limit will be implied to the price that the dealer is prepared to pay to acquire a particular product for stock. This will depend upon (a) the extent of carrying costs, (b) the dealer's conjectures about the chances of achieving particular prices over particular periods of time, and (c) the dealer's preferred strategy for pricing in terms of an opening gambit and subsequent rate of descent of the asking price. However, although a dealer's demand price is dependent on his or her conjectures about the likely population of potential buyers in the immediate and more distant future, the amounts offered for trade-ins may determine the prices that are acceptable to would-be buyers of existing stock. A buyer might, for example, be offering a highly marketable trade-in against something that has been sitting in stock for many months, or vice versa. In short, what a trade-in is worth will depend on what it is being traded for, as well as what it is.

In the light of this, we can begin to appreciate why the Austrian economists have come to write about market processes in words rather than in a style dominated by supply and demand diagrams. Menger went so far as to see all market transactions as one-off deals, isolated exchanges that were a form of bilateral monopoly. Very often, people are selling a single item and, at the time of sale, it may be the only one of its precise specification that is on offer. This limits the influence of large numbers as a force for producing uniformity in price offers, for although dealers may be competing with each other quite ruthlessly, their circumstances will differ. As Streissler (1973, p 169) notes, Menger even rejected completely the idea that a product would have a determinate market price. He did so not merely for secondhand goods but also for new items, not least of all for investment goods made to order. Streissler (1973, pp. 171–2) emphasizes that 'in durable consumption goods considerable downward price variation can be achieved by buying in periods of slack, by prompt payments, or by finding a trader not regularly dealing in the commodity in question but willing to take it on order as a sideline.' More generally, he sees Keynes's speculative motive as having at its root the idea that if one has immediate access to cash and can therefore close a deal promptly it may be possible to make capital gains in markets where prices are prone to variation. This will be particularly important as a recession looms and the frequency of distress sales increases.

Strategies that involve using price cuts to bring forward the timing of sales are inherently experimental. Price reductions may produce quick results in markets for frequently traded goods where buyers are able to compare similar products and then use price as a tie-breaker amongst those that emerge as satisfactory in terms of all the non-price criteria (determining which dealer gets the sale). Price reductions may also be effective where buyers fit into the conventional theoretical mould by being prepared to make compromises in non-price terms to get a better deal in terms of price (for example, buying a rather higher mileage car for a lower price). If a product of this kind is taking longer than average to sell, it may well be due to the dealer having allowed its price to get out of line with comparable offerings of rivals. If this is not the case, a better strategy than cutting its price might be to advertise its whereabouts more vigorously.

In thin markets, however, there may at present be no one around actively looking for the product in question. A price cut may be a means of discovering whether anyone is in the market and has been holding back because the product is outside his/her budget range. If no one bites on this bait, the original offer-price can be resumed or a yet lower price tried, depending on the risks the dealer is prepared to run. The trouble is, the dealer can never know whether a new potential customer is about to enter the market, willing to pay the gambit price. Moreover, a price cut on one of the dealer's products might do nothing more than signal, to those who are in the market for other products on the dealer's price list, that the dealer is prepared/able to make substantial mark-downs. It may thus encourage buyers to be more aggressive when haggling over prices of *other* products, now and in the future (cf. the analysis of bargaining offered by Shackle, 1970, pp. 143–7). In the long run, a strategy of standing firm may appear to have much to offer in a relatively thin market such as that for luxury cars. In this market, price is not a particularly decisive factor and buyers are business people who may be used to engaging in hard-nosed bargaining.

11.5 'TRICKLE-DOWN' INSTITUTIONS

If perfect secondhand markets existed for all durable assets, the tendency of pessimism to exert a depressing effect on aggregate demand would be much reduced. Consumers and firms could purchase durables without the fear that they would suffer capital losses out of all proportion to physical depreciation if they needed to sell them in the near future as a result of a change in circumstances. (Demands for ephemeral products of, say, the tourism and entertainment industries would still be vulnerable: people who were fearful that their jobs were shortly to be abolished would tend not to splash out on expensive holidays.) In practice, the state of development of secondhand markets varies quite considerably between different contexts.

The importance of secondhand markets for housing and motor vehicles is well recognized the world over, but it would be easy to underestimate the extent of dealing in other kinds of secondhand goods if one were accustomed to thinking of consumption in terms of the idea of a 'throwaway society'. Anecdotal evidence certainly suggests that in the most affluent societies (for example, Japan) it is possible to furnish an apartment and equip it with electrical durables without paying for anything; perfectly serviceable goods are often simply discarded in favour of those embodying the latest styles and technologies. However, in countries a bit further down the income per capita ranking, and particularly where relative prices of new manufactured goods have been inflated by import control policies, the recycling of durables between consumers is facilitated by a variety of institutions. These include:

1. classified advertisements in local newspapers;
2. pawn shops and other (often licensed) secondhand dealers; antiques stores;
3. Saturday morning garage sales;
4. auctions of effects of deceased states;
5. appliance, furniture and musical instrument retailers who accept trade-ins and (often after reconditioning them) resell them, either directly to consumers or via other dealers.

Whenever the purchase of a newly created good does not involve either the expansion of the market (through the entry of a first-time buyer of the good) or the replacement and consequent scrapping of a depreciated substitute by the purchaser, a whole sequence of 'trickle-down' effects may be triggered. Such sequences are particularly apparent in the car market, where average periods of ownership duration might be, say, three years and the average life-span of a car might be 18 years. Consider the purchase of one new vehicle in 1993, which is financed in part by, say, the trading in of a 1990 model. This, may sooner or later entail other buyers up-grading from vehicles made in 1987, 1984, 1981, 1978 and 1975, with the 1975 vehicle being dismantled for spares (another well-organized secondhand market!) and scrap. If such a process of trading up by half a dozen car buyers at each stage involves a dealer, then the income generated in the business of dealing will probably amount to a very significant fraction of the income generated in the process of manufacturing the new vehicle. As well as trickle down activity involving newly produced goods and older ones, we should note trade in secondhand goods alone, which arises due to sideways repositioning by consumers whose circumstances have changed. Examples here include a house sale due to job relocation, or a sports car being exchanged for a sedan due to the birth of a child.

If people are mostly trading up, a dealer's stock quality will get progressively devalued unless premium stock can be obtained on the wholesale market. The latter might come from more up-market dealers disposing of inferior trade-ins, or dealers who specialize in different niches disposing of trade-ins that do not fit their normal image. The avoidance of stock quality devaluation is important for two reasons. First, it helps to ensure that questions are not raised about the quality of more up-market fare. Secondly, it ensures there is no loss of the information advantages of being identified by buyers as having opted to deal in a particular market segment. To escape the transaction costs and quality uncertainty problems associated with using wholesale markets, it may pay an entrepreneur to create several operations, each specializing in different niches and masquerading as separate firms: this is very common in the business of car dealing.

11.6   THE SOCIAL ROLE OF SECONDHAND DEALERS

Although the disdain that the public has for used-car dealers and the like is sometimes justifiable, it is somewhat unfortunate that, following Akerlof's classic (1970) paper, economists seem to have focused their interest in the workings of such markets almost exclusively on problems due to informational asymmetries associated with quality uncertainty. Recognition of the interconnectedness of consumers' attempts to reshuffle their holdings of durables makes one aware of the social benefits arising from the presence of secondhand dealers. It also alerts us to the kinds of speculative dilemmas that they and their clients need to contend with even when they believe they have a good idea of what they are buying and selling. The willingness of dealers to buy durable goods today and hold them in the hope of selling them at a later date at a higher price allows consumers to trade up, down or sideways today. Consumers thereby escape feeling that they are part of a web of interlinked attempts at repositioning. In the absence of dealers, one cannot buy without simultaneously finding a buyer (and possibly accepting a trade-in). It may also be necessary to obtain bridging finance. Though dealers (usually) make a margin from acting as intermediaries, they enable buyers of durables to pay rather less attention to the resale potential (in other words, marketability/liquidity preference) of what they are buying than they would in an environment devoid of dealers.

This is something that is perfectly familiar to those who have found themselves caught in a 'chain' in the housing market. Unless first-time buyers are entering, or someone is willing and able to buy without first selling (for example, if assisted by an employer who has forced relocation upon them), a gridlock can develop. A favourable shift in liquidity preference may be a pre-requisite for breaking it: for example, would-be new entrants might become less nervous about losing their jobs or more fearful that property prices are going to start rising. Not only may they cease being the weak link as a result of becoming more willing to make a commitment, they may also give the market more degrees of freedom by becoming less fussy about which properties they buy or how much they borrow to pay for them. In times of buoyant expectations when property sales in general are moving with greater ease, more idiosyncratic homes may rise in value more rapidly than those that would normally be regarded as 'safe bets, easy to dispose of without undue loss if anything goes wrong'. The variance in their selling times may also narrow substantially.

The kind of gridlock observed in the housing market is a market failure that Austrian economists might expect entrepreneurs to step in and correct. Instead of the market being inadequately lubricated by real estate agents that merely act in the role of a broker, it might be better served by the emergence of used-house dealers who actually took title to property on a speculative basis. Of course, the dealers would also need finance. However, economies in transaction costs would mean that if they could not provide it from personal means they might be expected to be able to obtain large, rolling overdrafts from banks rather more easily than the owners might be able to obtain relatively small amounts of bridging finance.

What seems possible in principle seems rather rare in practice. The two examples with which I am familiar are both instructive. First, a colleague who had once worked for a large real estate agent group in the south of New Zealand mentioned that some of the most high-flying of his fellow estate agents managed to do so well because they were prepared to buy properties that were causing chains to develop. This was most likely where they stood to earn commissions from several sales if they could make the market move – enough to cover legal fees of buying and selling, the costs of bridging finance and of subsequently selling, whilst leaving a handsome margin for themselves. (This would be less viable in economies where substantial stamp duty charges are levied upon change of ownership.) Such actions would have positive externality effects for other agents involved in the chain. Bearing these in mind, we might imagine groups of agents involved in a chain clubbing together as consortium/partnership to purchase a property that was denying them all their commissions. The transaction costs might be higher, but regular activity of this kind could make matters more routine and deter free-rider behaviour.

A second type of used-house dealing was pioneered in the depressed UK property market in the early 1980s by Barratt Developments. This firm offered to take trade-ins of Barratt homes from those who were moving geographically or up-market by buying other Barratt homes (even ones in California!). Some common near-new designs that had been built by rival developers also seem to have been accepted on this basis. This was a quite remarkable strategy for improving the marketability of new Barratt homes, particularly when seen in the context of the firm's attempts to generate 'model' status for a limited range of designs that appeared on a wide range of real estate developments undertaken by the firm. In Scotland, they were named after Hebridean Islands and one might thus trade up successively from a St Kilda (one bedroom flat) to a Lewis or Raasay (two bedroom flat or house, respectively), and so on. In doing this, the Barratt client would usually receive a trade-in value in excess of what had nominally been paid for the property, though the next property would come at a corresponding premium. If one stayed loyal to the Barratt brand, one could apparently avoid the cognitive dissonance associated with exchanging houses on a depressed market where other recent purchasers could expect to have to take a loss if they sold. Even if one got the urge to move into something more distinctive, Barratt brand recognition would make a private, direct sale relatively easy: in other words, for risk averse buyers, a Barratt home seemed to have a built-in liquidity premium.

Given such entrepreneurial initiatives in the housing market, some comment appears in order about why they are not more widespread and why the chain problem remains a cause of misery for many people. The Barratt initiative certainly would not work well in, say, Australia or New Zealand where there is little sign of a willingness on the part of buyers to tolerate the uniformity of styles that characterized the UK housing market. But, then again, it would be less needed: if buyers commonly look for something distinctive, then designs that would seem risky in the UK may not seem to have a particularly thin market in Australasia. Differences in the extent of regulation in legal fees and estate agent commissions may also have implications for the costs of short-term house ownership. But a general deterrent in this area would seem to be the carrying costs associated with holding houses as stock. Although the portability of titles and mobility of sales personnel obviously means that 'used house dealers' might be able to avoid physically bringing homes together on a single plot of land for convenient inspection, geographical dispersion nonetheless renders difficult the task of policing against vandalism and squatters.[1] Unoccupied, empty houses may be harder to sell in any case due to difficulties prospective buyers have in imagining them furnished (another advantage for the Barratt strategy was the fact that the secondhand, empty houses were being sold close to similar new ones for which show homes were provided). With standardized units, particularly apartments in blocks with security entrances, some of these costs seem less of a worry. It should be added that since such difficulties arise even when homeowners can obtain bridging loans, they may prefer to forego such finance and stay put, incurring the costs of commuting or the risks of losing their desired property to someone else. The costs of relocating furniture and extracting adequate recompense from tenants who cause damage all limit the attractiveness of short-term renting as a means of overcoming these problems.

11.7   SPECULATION AND THE DETERMINATION OF MANUFACTURERS' LIST PRICES.

Although the analysis so far has been focusing mainly on speculative aspects of the pricing of secondhand goods, it appears also to be of relevance for understanding the recommended/list prices of new goods. Post Keynesian economists have grown accustomed to thinking of pricing in such cases as being dominated by manufacturers, not retailers, with the former setting cost-based prices and then adjusting their production rates to accommodate orders coming in from retailers. Even where resale price maintenance is an illegal practice, it would normally be assumed that manufacturers exert a good deal of influence over retail prices. This is because they are able to remove distribution franchises from those stores that sell at prices other than the manufacturer's recommended prices. This makes it dangerous for retailers to engage in discounting when trade is slow or to raise prices when a black market is tending to develop due to the inability of manufacturers to keep pace with orders.

As far as manufacturers are concerned, the issue of marketability is less of a problem than it appears to be for retailers. Individual retailers may be carrying a limited number or even a single unit of a product in the hope that someone, somewhere within their market territory, is a potential customer. In small towns, in country areas, orders from stores may be very infrequent for particular classes of products. However, taken together on a national or international basis, these erratic orders may provide a steady flow of business

---

[1]   In fact, I have noticed that 'used house yards' can be found in Australia and New Zealand, typically on low-grade land near airports, to which serviceable timber homes are taken on trucks from sites that are being redeveloped.

for the manufacturer. Prior to sinking any investment resources into the market, a manufacturer needs to guess the likely scale of these orders, at a price that will ensure an ongoing presence in the market by providing a satisfactory and at the same time not entry-inducing rate of return. Where the aggregate flow of orders for a product is prone to fluctuate, the manufacturer may have to weigh up the costs of changing the pace of production, versus the costs of producing at a steady rate and building up factory inventories in periods of slack sales.

Speculative elements are obvious in such decisions about how to make the flow of goods to retailers vary in line with final demand at a price based on normal costs. At the time of deciding which production method to use and what sorts of contract to agree with employees and other input suppliers, entrepreneurs should be considering the costs of flexibility in the light of their guesses about the variability in their future streams of orders. For example, if demand fluctuates sharply and carrying costs are high for inventories, a firm may achieve lower costs by breaking the production system up into a series of parallel modules that can be shut down one by one as demand contracts. As Stigler (1939) and Hart (1940) pointed out, this way of facing up to the vagaries of the market is likely to be more profitable than varying the output rate of machinery that is optimized for a particular constant rate of output. Likewise, an employment contract which gives the employer the right to lay workers off without pay will need to offer a premium rate of pay over one which (implicitly or explicitly) does not seem to entail such a risk to employees of disruption in their flows of income.

In some markets, sales rates and/or supply conditions for inputs may commonly exhibit a higher than normal degree of variance, yet flexibility and inventory buffering may be abnormally costly. Here, it would seem reasonable to expect to observe producers demanding risk premia in the form of higher than normal mark-ups or allowing their waiting lists to get unusually long in times of strong demand. In such circumstances, additional suppliers will not be attracted in unless they feel that incumbents are being unduly greedy or cautious.

To speak of 'variance' in demand is to use statistical terminology that, like probabilistic thinking, seems to presume advance knowledge of an overall pattern that *will* be generated if particular decision strategies are repeated in times to come. Normal-cost pricing, with the kinds of risk adjustments just discussed, seems conceptually well suited to 'mature' markets in which producers feel it safe to make such presumptions. When hitherto mature markets go into decline, it may initially be difficult for producers to judge whether they are looking at a temporary contraction or the onset of a terminal sales sickness. The former could make stock building and labour hoarding seem sensible, whereas the latter would make it timely to consider the kinds of strategies discussed in Harrigan (1980). Cognitive dissonance theory in psychology would predict a tendency for entrepreneurs initially to construe things in the former way. Thereby they would exacerbate the problems associated with making an orderly withdrawal: for example, normal-cost-based pricing is likely to be abandoned by a weak player seeking to dispose of inventories as a means of staving off a threat of being put into receivership. Such an attempt to go liquid imposes costs on other players in the market, and may even be counter-productive as a device for generating sales in the present if remaining would-be buyers of the product judge that further price cuts could be just around the corner.

Finally, we should note that pricing is inherently speculative in the early stages of a product's life, when entrepreneurs cannot be sure that it will even survive to a prolonged state of market maturity. Marketing theorists such as Joel Dean (beginning with his classic 1950 paper) have rather denied this by attempting to pin down the circumstances in which 'penetration' pricing strategy makes more sense than a 'skimming' one. Uncertainty arises because the initial price can have a major bearing on the subsequent development of demand and cost patterns via its impact on diffusion processes on the demand side and on the rate at which a firm achieves cost reductions through learning by doing. It may also affect the rate of investment in complementary products, as managers at Apple computers discovered to their cost after opting initially for a skimming strategy that led most software designers to focus their attention on the potential of the rival MS-DOS system.

The acceptance rate of a new product will be affected not just by the diffusion of information about its physical properties and reductions in its price, but also by consumer expectations about the pricing strategies of manufacturers and the prospect of quality improvements (cf. Bain, 1964). Those consumer who have lived in the age of microchip-based consumer goods are probably much more likely than their grandparents would have been to speculate that better deals will be available in the not too distant future. On the other hand, we might expect less socially confident (but strongly financially confident) consumers among the microchip generation to be strongly inclined to spend their discretionary income on new conspicuous consumption items, even if they anticipated that better value for money would be available at a later date. Such purchases may enable them to meet a need for social esteem of the kind canvassed by Maslow (1970) in his hierarchy of needs (for further discussion of economic implications of Maslow's work, see Lutz and Lux, 1979).

11.8 BILATERAL MONOPOLY VERSUS NORMAL COST ANALYSES OF PRICING

At first sight, the Austrian bilateral monopoly analysis emphasized in section 11.4 is totally at odds with the full-cost/normal-cost analysis of mark-up pricing considered in chapter 10 and section 11.7. Central to the latter theory, according to Lee (1984), is the idea that unit costs are based around estimated sales over a production planning period whose duration lies somewhere between conventional visions of the short run and long run. Catalogue prices that change relatively infrequently fit this perspective and entail capacity utilization rates (and hence daily or weekly average costs) that bob up and down with the ups and downs of sales rates, unless smoothing is achieved by inventory adjustments. However, such theorizing has been criticized (for example, by Silberston, 1970) with reference to the tendency of transaction prices to differ from catalogue list prices.

Despite these seemingly opposing points of view, it seems possible simultaneously to embrace normal-cost pricing *and* tendencies of transaction prices of identical products to diverge from list prices in a variety of ways varying with differences in trading circumstances. For a start, where trade-ins are involved, it is difficult to specify *the* price of either item. In this cases differences in 'change-over' payments required for a particular trade against a particular new item cannot be claimed to reveal anything about whether discounting is going on to move new goods from stock. Rather, they tell us that dealers see their opportunity costs differently. Rival dealers can be competing aggressively and nonetheless be willing to risk differently the loss of a particular deal by quoting different change-over prices because the deal carries different implications for them. They cannot be sure of what is going on in each other's heads, even if they can see what their rivals currently have on display. (If they are being kept busy seeing potential customers they may not even have time to get out and do some intelligence gathering.) As they would probably say, 'You win some, you lose some; the main thing is to win enough on terms good enough to enable you to earn a crust'.

In respect of the retailing of goods against which trade-ins are not made, it would be unwise to jump to the conclusion that differences in price amongst retailers of a particular product reflect differences in scope for exploiting, say, monopolistic location advantages. Commonly quoted 'recommended' prices provide a useful reference point for all market participants in judging whether a particularly keen price is being offered or whether one might have suspicions that a discount reflects corners being cut somewhere (for example, in respect of after-sales service). Certainly, if retailers are supplied with stock at identical ex-works prices, their decisions about whether to order are likely to be affected by these prices. However, this does not mean they will be similarly willing to stick to recommended retail prices, for here, too, their costs – what they feel they are giving up to win a particular deal – will vary depending on individual circumstances. For example, it may be perfectly rational to let some business slip away by refusing to budge on price if there is a good chance someone else will come along prepared to pay the full retail price. This is particularly likely in markets where carrying costs deter the holding of large inventories even though custom is reasonably steady. If stocks cannot be replenished overnight, the loss of a potential customer to a rival could mean that the rival will then go temporarily out of stock and be unable to serve the next would-be buyer that comes along.

11.9   CONCLUSION

A set of boundaries for prices in markets for both new and secondhand goods is provided by contracts that have previously been arranged with the factors of production, particularly those involving workers and suppliers of finance. For manufacturers, the nexus of contracts sets limits to the prices they can offer, and to how rapidly they can manufacture things, without facing insolvency or attracting undue attention from potential producers of rival products. But it would be wrong to say that such prices are fully determined by underlying demands for product characteristics and by supply conditions objectively implied by the nexus of contracts between entrepreneurs and the factors of production. The durability of goods provides scope for consumers to adjust the timing of purchases in the light of their conjectures about their chances of striking better or worse deals in the future. Such decisions about timing appear to have a crucial role in determining whether or not the market environment of firms can be treated as a 'normal' one in which firms adjust production and/or inventory levels in the face of changing sales, rather than revising also their prices and long-run market expectations.

12. Information, Coordination and Macroeconomics

12.1 INTRODUCTION

Claims that information problems underlie macroeconomic issues are common in the 'New Keynesian' branch of macroeconomics reviewed by Gordon (1990). It extends the reappraisal of Keynesian economics begun by Clower (in papers since collected in Walker, ed., 1984) and Leijonhufvud (1968) who sought to show how an economy lacking a Walrasian auctioneer may experience coordination difficulties when decisions are taken sequentially in a decentralized manner. The Clower–Leijonhufvud research programme is significant because it sets out the origins of unemployment and, latterly, the difficulties associated with high inflation (Heymann and Leijonhufvud, 1995) in terms of the dominant general equilibrium framework. Unfortunately, much of the literature it provoked concentrates mainly on failures of markets to clear because of informational barriers to price adjustments. Studies of a rich variety of 'market imperfections' by New Keynesians have enhanced our understanding of market processes at the cost of attention not being devoted to other potentially fertile areas that also entail information problems. My focus in this chapter therefore is primarily on features of modern economies whose significance has hardly begun to be recognized by the present generation of macroeconomists. Like Garretsen (1992), I emphasize the indeterminacy that becomes evident when one looks at the complexity of microeconomic interactions that generate macroeconomic data.

The chapter is divided up as follows. In section 12.2, I explore the origins of liquidity preference in developed economies and suggest that research on the consumption function needs to pay attention to George Katona's work on consumer confidence. In section 12.3, information problems associated with complex chains of transactions are examined. Sections 12.4 and 12.5 concern, respectively, the impact of intermediaries and speculation on aggregate demand. Interlinked investment decisions are the focus of section 12.6, which brings together ideas from G.B. Richardson, on investment coordination, and Hyman Minsky, on the origins of instability in multi-layered financial systems. Section 12.7 is a concluding discussion.

12.2   INFORMATION AND LIQUIDITY PREFERENCE

Keynes's (1936) vision of the roots of macroeconomic problems recognizes that people who perceive uncertainty in areas relevant to their decisions often opt to make choices that defer commitment to specific products until they have enough information to resolve the uncertainty, or they conclude that it will not become available soon enough ('In the long run we are all dead') and take a plunge one way or another on the basis of 'animal spirits' or by following a convention. Whilst waiting and exercising liquidity preference, decision-makers generate neither demand for current output nor information about future purchasing patterns required by firms for future production decisions. Consequently, firms may be reluctant to invest in current output, or may defer plans to invest in additional capacity. There is no automatic reason why firms should be bold enough to commission sufficient output to employ all those who wish to work, even at a somewhat lower money wage level than presently exists.

Keynes's emphasis on liquidity preference promotes a significantly different view of decision-making under uncertainty from that promoted by the Arrow–Debreu model. Decision-makers in the latter are forced, by the assumption that they are engaged in a once-and-for-all-higgle-haggle, to deal with problems of knowledge by placing bets: they purchase and/or supply commodities the delivery of which is contingent on the eventuation of particular states of world at particular future dates. Because the model collapses the future into the present, it leaves no place for waiting, liquidity or situations in which, to use a common expression, 'all bets are off'. It is a parable useful for thinking about insurance markets but in reality insurance-based strategies are normally disadvantaged by choosers' limited information processing and problem-solving capabilities, significant transaction costs, and the absence of, amongst other things, (i) a comprehensive set of markets, (ii) a complete list of possible states of the world, and (iii) a fixed technology set.

Boundedly rational consumers generally do not make advance purchases and instead opt to leave commitment until a time close to when they begin consuming what they buy (for example, many air tickets are paid for a few weeks before the journey starts, having only been reserved a few months earlier). As Richardson (1960, p. 178) pointed out, consumers and entrepreneurs who are aware of potential 'dislocation effects' will exercise liquidity preference – holding their wealth in adaptable forms (especially money and unused credit lines) – and avoid expensive physical assets involving the consumption of complementary goods. It was much later that economists trained in the Arrow–Debreu tradition recognized the choice between placing bets and waiting (see Jones and Ostroy, 1984, and Kreps, 1988); so far they have focused their attention on cases where required information does become available to those who wait and where a preference for liquidity will not cause chronic unemployment.

Although Keynes's arguments concerned the possibility of a persistent recession that money wage reductions would not necessarily cure, Post Keynesian economists should express greater delight than Davidson (1991, pp. 50–3) did when noting that neoclassical writers are trying, in their restricted manner, to analyse the economics of waiting. Regardless of whether a loss of nerve causes chronic unemployment or merely periodic temporary downturns, a reluctance to make commitments in the face of uncertainty causes the economy to go down a different path from the one it would have carved out if consumers and entrepreneurs had been more prepared to take a plunge and spend: More income would have been generated, which would have provided a basis for financing higher levels of future expenditure, and capacity would have been created for supplying higher levels of future output. In other words, hesitancy arising from temporary uncertainty can result, like chronic pessimism, in forever-lost opportunities in the present that have cumulating, momentum-sapping consequences in the future. Growth processes that falter via short-lived recessions should thus be a matter of concern to both Post Keynesian and New Keynesian economists if they observe anti-interventionist policies that use assumptions of rational expectations or rapid learning to deny path dependence and treat unemployment as an equilibrium phenomenon.

Even the majority of Post Keynesian critics of approaches to macroeconomics which downplay uncertainty appear unaware of how far their arguments can be pushed in complex and turbulent modern economies. Affluent consumers with considerable discretionary income can postpone much of their spending without greatly disrupting their lives, for existing consumer durables can continue to be used rather than upgraded so long as they are not damaged beyond repair. Liquidity preference may arise when people are speculating about:

(i)   Future income, such as: 'Will I have still a job next year and be able to keep up the repayments?', 'Will I get promoted?', 'What difference will the promised tax cuts make, if they materialize?'

(ii) Future circumstances, such as: 'Will I keep this relationship together?', 'Will a granny flat be necessary?', 'Will I have to make a big geographical switch to meet my employment goals?'

(iii) Future technologies that might outperform and render obsolete existing assets and replacements that might be bought today (see also section 9.3 above).

People whose circumstances change, can, of course, use secondhand markets to facilitate a reconfiguration of their wealth but such switches are often costly. Pecuniary rates of depreciation are poorly linked to functionality, largely for informational reasons: new goods have smaller risks associated with quality uncertainty and function more readily as status symbols. A newly perceived risk of a downturn in personal fortune might also make it desirable to limit current consumption involving expensive service products – a less lavish holiday is still a holiday and may be all the better for not being overshadowed by financial anxieties concerning potential dislocation. These considerations, along with budgetary flexibility implied by access to credit and discretion over repayment rates, lead to a revised view of consumption functions based not on trend/lifecycle/relative/current incomes but on *willingness* to spend, on consumer confidence and lack of worry about decisions possibly needing to be reversed or losses that might be avoided by waiting.

The significance of consumers' willingness to spend was asserted by Katona (1960) in the wake of the first post-war US recession and has been repeatedly supported by empirical work using indices of consumer confidence in many OECD countries (see, for example, Adams, 1964; Shapiro and Angevine, 1969; Katona, 1975; Smith, 1975; Pickering, 1977; and Williams and Defries, 1981). It nowadays finds support in the business and political press, too, as 'the feel-good factor'. Yet, within mainstream literature on the consumption function there is little sign of any recognition of the possible empirical significance of people 'putting things on hold' as they wait for information that will fundamentally affect their lives. This would have been more understandable if economists were modelling the behaviour of people in societies where people married to death did them part, rarely moved from the villages of their birth and did not have to contend with promotion ladders or possess specialized skills that made labour markets thin. It would also be less of an issue if decision-makers were only likely to go through short periods of spending hesitancy because the vital information about the future rapidly became available. But we are not modelling, say, farm labourers two centuries ago, who had little discretionary money income they could put aside during periods of uncertainty. An increasing proportion of consumers would seem better to approximate internationally mobile academics who have tenure tracks and the politics of promotion with which to contend and are part of a world in which the failure rates of human relationships are high. Such consumers may have to endure in some cases years of uncertainty before receiving information – for example, 'Will I get promoted *this* time or shall I have to move elsewhere?' – which enables them to reshape their lives with confidence.

It is perhaps understandable that Katona's perspective has been so little assimilated and extended even within the Post Keynesian research programme, given that it was presented as a challenge both to Keynes's suggestion that consumption is a function of income and to Galbraith's (1958) claims about the power of advertising. Yet it really deserves to be seen as a generalization, to the demand for consumer durables, of Keynes's view of the potential instability of investment decisions; indeed, Townshend (1937) foreshadowed it with reference to contemporary advertising copy that claimed the buyer of an Austin car was making an investment. The anti-Galbraith aspect of Katona's view of consumption is of potentially enormous significance to economies whose prosperity depends on sales of rapidly evolving, knowledge-based products such as personal computers and home fax machines: if most consumers anticipate product obsolescence and/or price decreases and hence forego state-of-the-art products in the hope of getting a better deal in future, they exert a *multiplied* downward pressure on both wages and the profits upon which the manufacturers depend for developing the next generation of products.

12.3   CHAINS AND MACROECONOMIC GRIDLOCK

Economists who study macroeconomics in a relatively disaggregated manner should think in terms of input-output systems in which multiplier processes work through complex webs of complementary production activities. Early on, Goodwin (1949) pioneered a matrix view of the multiplier. However, within the New Keynesian literature, Gordon (1981, 1990) has related the input-output perspective to informational issues by suggesting that the complexity of economies could cause price rigidities that produce quantity adjustments in response to aggregate demand shocks: because firms are not completely vertically integrated, their abilities to change their prices depend on their suppliers' abilities to change input prices, and so on, down the line to the primary sector, itself a user of manufactured goods. All face a problem of 'strategic complementarity' (Cooper and John, 1988). Even if all firms would benefit from simultaneously adjusting their prices and wages, major communication barriers hinder this, particularly when firms source their inputs internationally. Without global indexation, unilateral price reductions may be ruinous whereas output reductions may seem relatively safe responses to falling sales and enable managers to avoid costs of communicating with distant links in their supply chains and trying to push for changes in prices. A similar problem arises in labour markets if unions are organized at the level of the craft or firm rather than the industry.

Gordon's analysis is implicitly related to literature on the economics of vertical integration, in which it is recognized that internalization of sequential production stages in a single organization may lead to superior transmission of information about demand fluctuations and less of a tendency for signals to be obscured by changes in inventories. Inventory adjustments are deviation-amplifying, in the sense of Leijonhufvud (1968), when sales trend in a new direction as opposed to fluctuating around a normal level, for when the trend is eventually identified a larger production adjustment will be needed. However, vertical integration is incomplete since, as well as its coordination advantages, it too has costs, such as increased exposure to strategic inflexibility.

Questions need to be raised about the New Keynesian appeal to input–output complexity as a barrier to equilibrating price adjustments – not because such complexity is unlikely to inhibit price adjustments but because wage and price adjustments would not necessarily solve a problem of deficient real spending (as opposed to an inappropriate structural mix of demand) even if they occurred (see Keynes, 1936, chapter 19 and, for a numerical clarification, Earl, 1990, pp. 250–4). However, an alternative manifestation of the micro-complementarity problem is in markets where demand for new output is linked to trade in secondhand consumer durables. Affluent consumers may be willing to spend but be unable to do so owing to perceptions that their existing assets are illiquid rather than due to an absence of current income. The most significant example of this is expenditure on housing.

People seeking to change houses due to job transfers, and/or seeking to switch to properties in a different segment of the market, may first need to find buyers for their existing properties. Those they find face the same problem, unless the latter are entering the market for the first time. Hence a chain of frustrated buyers and sellers can develop, not because the prices being asked are unacceptable to all the pairs of would-be transactors but because the seller at the start of the chain cannot find a first-time buyer who can safely raise the finance to enter the market. If the person at the high-prices end of the chain – who may be more affluent and less financially constrained – initiated a price reduction it might trickle down to the first-time buyer. The end result might be that prices generally fell by similar amounts and no one in the chain had to raise additional finance. Unfortunately, the market signal is not that there is an absence of buyers at the top end, while anyone who initiates a price reduction is not guaranteed that others further down the chain will follow by similar amounts. Similar problems apply for anyone who might otherwise initiate price reductions from interior nodes in the chain except that the price reductions now need to trickle in both directions.

Until a first-time buyer comes in at the start of the chain, it is not merely a set of changes in ownership of existing houses that is being held up, but also the income generation process in terms of fees to lawyers and estate agents as well as expenditure on removers, home renovation products, carpets and furnishings. At the high-priced end of the chain there may be a new property to which a buyer cannot commit. Uncertainty probably also leads to a holding back in replacements of luxury durable goods: if housing sales are falling through all around, raising big question marks about whether or not it may be necessary to reduce offer prices in order to sell within an acceptable time horizon, it is a bold house-seller who uses up liquidity on a new car or makes other major purchases that could easily be postponed. The only winners when housing markets are bedeviled by chain problems are suppliers of real estate advertisements, but even they could find that the mere presence of these chains leads potential transactors not to put their homes on the market until there are reports that it is moving again with strong interest from first-time buyers.

Though most obviously caused by the lack of first-time buyers, chain problems can also arise due to missing links which might otherwise solve the selling problems of sets of would-be transactors further up-market and supply just the kind of properties being sought by people moving up from below who in turn have properties that would sell easily. Suitable 'missing link transactors' will only discover how easy it is to sell their existing homes and move up-market if they incur the costs of testing the market but they may be deterred from this by media reports of chain problems and real estate advertisements which suggest such problems by listing 'no chain involved' as a positive characteristic of particular properties.

12.4   INTERMEDIARIES AND AGGREGATE DEMAND

Research is now appearing on the existence of chains in housing markets (for example, Rosenthal, 1997) but attention has not yet focused on the significance for aggregate demand of market congestion problems that arise due to the dispersion of information about the whereabouts of potential buyers and sellers. Pending such work, macroeconomists might at least note that it would be a far greater problem without a variety of institutional arrangements that entrepreneurs have developed as means of earning profits whilst oiling the wheels of commerce: as Hodgson (1988) has argued, market institutions arise because of the transaction costs associated with bilateral exchange. The housing market attracts attention in respect of chain problems because real estate agents do not trade used houses in the way that used car dealers trade used cars by taking title to them and holding them in stock, sometimes for several months.

Traders in secondhand products increase the liquidity of the assets in which they deal as well as providing buyers with reduced transaction costs by enabling them to shop in centralized locations with institutional safeguards on quality that may not be available in private trades (Hodgson, 1988, provides excellent discussions of these reasons for the emergence of organized markets). Those who wish to trade up but cannot reach their goals by accepting trade-in values may opt to sell privately for a price somewhat nearer retail levels. Eventually they may succeed, after incurring a variety of marketing costs such as advertising and adapting their leisure activities to be available to communicate with potential buyers. Given the number of used cars or homes displayed for sale at any moment we can begin to see what might happen to aggregate demand if the intermediating services of car dealers and estate agents were not available: people who are spending their leisure hours as part-time used-car dealers are less able to get out and spend their money on other leisure activities. (It would be interesting to know the extent to which the availability of mobile telephones has to some extent diminished the use that people make of these intermediaries.) The presence of used-car dealers may encourage people to change their cars more often, and spend more money on motoring than they might have done. Even if this comes to some extent at the expense of other kinds of products there might be a net increase in spending if the ease of making a switch leads consumers to succumb to the temptation to live for the present by upgrading, rather than putting money aside for retirement.

Here we can see a conflict between, on the one hand, the Galbraithian vision of how the modern institutions of capitalism help prevent macroeconomic stagnation and, on the other hand, the emergence of more attractive means for deferring consumption and enabling consumers to bind themselves up – to become illiquid deliberately – to guard against weakness of will (cf. Thaler and Shefrin, 1981). Related both to self control and to liquidity is the role of dealer-provided finance as a means for making consumer budget constraints more elastic than they might have seemed had consumers not found themselves talking with sales personnel about products in rather more up-market budget ranges than they had in mind at the time they set out on their purchasing expeditions.

The margins that secondhand dealers extract as the price for facilitating liquidity can be avoided, though not the other costs of private marketing, with the aid of often-costly bridging finance. Compared with professional traders, private sellers lack competence by virtue of their infrequent forays into the market in question and may be poorly able to face up to what those with more experience would see as a need to cut their losses by selling more cheaply and avoiding carrying costs. Hence banks will prefer to supply working capital to professional traders than supply bridging finance to individuals.

Financial institutions have wider significance in mitigating macroeconomic congestion problems by reducing costs of bringing borrowers and lenders together (see also Earl, 1990, chapter 8). Like used-car dealers, banks solve information problems and provide flexibility at a price, enabling deals to be done sooner. A higher volume of business today need not come at the expense of business in the future if spare capacity exists today: at the very least, capacity is freed up in the future, but in some cases today's intermediated deals may entail purchases of physical assets such that the next period begins with higher total capacity than it would have done. Higher incomes today provide means for financing expenditure in the next period, so long as these funds can be mobilized, offsetting reduced demand coming from those whom the financial intermediaries have enabled to bring their borrowing forward. At the broadest level, money is an institution that has traditionally eliminated need for double coincidence of wants but modern information technology may make money superfluous if a satisfactory unit of account can be found. Eventually, 'smart cards' could store complete records of individuals' holdings of financial assets while electronic funds transfer terminals could be wired to share and unit trust registers. Payment could then involve scrolling rapidly along a wide-ranging menu rather than merely one pertaining to cheque or savings or credit card accounts, and corporate treasurers would then decide what to do with the portfolios of financial assets received in exchange for their firms' goods and services. With share trading on the Internet, we are close to this scenario already except for the need for portfolios to be shuffled into one's bank account before going shopping. In simplifying loan-broking and payments processes, information technology may also do much to eliminate the decongesting role of deposit-taking financial intermediaries and lead to wider use of direct financing and securitized lending.

12.5   SPECULATION AND AGGREGATE DEMAND

In terms of classical theories of speculation, the willingness of dealers to absorb stock would normally be seen as a device for maintaining aggregate demand at a steady level: prices for used commodities remain higher than they otherwise would have done, and hence the purchase of brand-new substitutes does not become as unattractive as it might have become. The willingness of dealers to run down their financial reserves and absorb stock *may* entirely offset the increased liquidity preference on the part of sellers of assets. But on other occasions the presence of well-organized secondhand markets can be a major cause of disruptions. Here I will give two examples based around the used-car market.

The first concerns the deregulation of motor vehicle imports into New Zealand. During much of the postwar era, until the late 1980s, New Zealand was notorious for having some of the toughest sets of controls of motor vehicle imports and consequently one of the oldest fleets of cars anywhere in the world. The very low depreciation rates during this era led many New Zealanders to feel relaxed about having quite a lot of their wealth tied up in motor vehicles. However, following the switch to free-market policies in 1984, a flourishing trade soon developed in the importation of low mileage used vehicles from Japan (mostly ones which had just reached the age of their first hideously expensive roadworthiness certification). Suddenly the prospect of a well-equipped, five or six year old Japanese vehicle came within the grasp of consumers who had been used to driving something antiquated, but owners of recent 'New Zealand new' vehicles found much of their equity wiped out overnight. New Zealand had imported Japanese depreciation rates and the consigning of old British and Australian designs to the scrap heaps would soon be followed by a similar fate for the ex-Japan vehicles that had initially seemed such a good buy. Those who were used to barely 10 per cent annual depreciation making it possible to trade up to something newer every couple of years had to consider whether it would be worth the sacrifice in an environment of 30 per cent annual depreciation. To the extent that they decided it would be, their funds would be diverted from other lines of expenditure in the longer term. Whatever happened to the new vehicles industry in the long term, in the short run it was in for a lean time if customers had to save up more and hesitated about the best strategy to adopt in this newly risky market environment.

The second case is from the other end of the market: the macroeconomic consequences of speculation in classic vehicles and new exotic models whose production runs have been declared to be limited by their manufacturers. Should we have worried in the 1980s about news reports of wildly fluctuating prices of used Porsches, and Ferraris that had had almost as many owners as they had covered miles? I think the answer must be in the affirmative: the great ups and downs that were observed in these markets in the late 1980s and early 1990s relate rather neatly (a) to what fundamentalist Keynesians regard as the two vital chapters of the *General Theory* (chapter 12, on casino-like behaviour and entrepreneurship, and chapter 17 on unemployment arising due to people demanding as stores of value commodities that cannot easily or legally be produced); (b) to Kaldor's (1983) critique of unregulated commodity markets; and (c) to Scitovsky's Fred Hirsch Memorial Lecture (Scitovsky, 1987), which highlights the status aspect of demand for difficult-to-reproduce durables.

Wild fluctuations in prices of used examples of particular kinds of products are symptomatic of a breakdown of classical mechanisms of speculation based on long-term views of supply and demand (in terms of consumption services), in favour of movement trading based on guesses about short-term changes in relative prices. Kaldor wrote about the efficiency of primary commodity markets as very largely depending on

> the traders' belief in the long run stability of the 'normal price' of each commodity. Once this belief is impaired or destroyed by the instability of *actual* prices, the trader's subjective appreciation of the risk incurred in holding stock is

increased, with the result that they require a higher expected compensation for any departure – upwards or downwards – from their normal commitments (their normal stock/turnover ratio). But this means, in turn, that any variation in the carry-over of stocks from period to period will be associated with an even greater variation in prices, which in turn will have further repercussions on the traders' willingness to take risks. Thus unregulated commodity markets, contrary to the generally held belief, represent a highly wasteful and primitive instrument for aligning the supply and demand for commodities. (Kaldor, 1983, p. 26, italics in original)

Now, if the prices of stocks secondhand exotic cars (and, of course, any other collectibles) are prone to fluctuate as a consequence of unstable beliefs held by speculators, the demand for the flow of newly produced examples will be difficult for their manufacturers to predict on a long-term basis. A strategy of reducing investment risks by keeping capacity levels below the trend in demand – even to the extent of having permanent waiting lists (the well-known policy of Morgan Cars in the UK) – obviously reduces employment associated with production of such durables in the short run. At the same time, if it is appropriate to apply Kaldor's line of thinking to this context, such a strategy serves to make the product all the more likely to be the subject of speculation in the long run.

Scitovsky suggests that speculative activity in markets for high-status, difficult-to-reproduce products may produce unemployment by diverting demand away from things that manufacturers would more willing and able to produce. How far such speculation does divert demand along these lines is difficult to assess because, for every buyer of a collectible, there has to be a seller, and the seller might well spend the money on newly produced output rather than holding it as a bank deposit or using it to finance the purchase of another asset for speculative purposes.

12.6   INVESTMENT COORDINATION

Reluctance or inability of consumers to signal spending intentions may make it difficult for entrepreneurs to form rational assessments of appropriate volumes of capacity or rates of output. But this is only one side of the problem of getting decentralized agents to have the confidence to generate enough aggregate demand to employ everyone who wants to work. Macroeconomists have almost completely ignored the investment coordination problem central to the work of Richardson (1959, 1960) – the fact that profitability depends not merely on the level of final demand but also on the level of competitive and complementary investment undertaken by other firms. Leijonhufvud (1968, pp. 69–70) has been almost alone in recognizing, in footnotes, the significance of his analysis for macroeconomics. As was explained in chapters 1 and 2, Richardson's work implies that even if entrepreneurs knew the vector of equilibrium prices implied by the underlying data of technology, preferences and initial endowments, they would have no basis for choosing output quantities unless they knew what the plans of other firms were. This barrier to forming, in Richardson's (1959, p. 233) terms, 'rational expectations' arises in both oligopolies and perfect competition: in the latter case, the point is that although an individual firm's output decision cannot affect the market price, the realized set of prices will depend on the aggregate volume of production of each product.

Richardson primarily considered the coordination problem at the level of the industry, suggesting that industrial structure affected its severity by facilitating or hindering opportunities for signalling and gathering intelligence about rivals' plans (in these terms perfect competition is vastly inferior to a concentrated oligopoly). He also noted the entry-restraining effects of a lack of entrepreneurial alertness or of necessary capabilities and considered (in Richardson, 1972) relational contracting and partial share-holdings as means of generating confidence in the availability of complementary goods and services without a need to resort to vertical integration. This takes us well away from the idea that the market mechanism would work better if less riddled with 'imperfections' and closer to perfect contestability: it makes one view the New Keynesian focus rather differently. However, Richardson's argument that 'imperfections' are vital for coordination is entirely consistent with Keynes's (1936, pp. 253, 269) views on the need for stable money wages as an anchor for the price level in a world in which contracts are based on nominal values. His work is also allied to Keynes's theory of asset pricing in stressing that price stability and an orderly business environment may depend on there being a mix of bullish and bearish expectations: if there is a very widespread belief that, say, ostrich farming is going to be very profitable then a 'bubble' episode awaits us in that sector. Keynes's analysis of asset prices and interest rates is based quite fundamentally on the notion that people differ in how they use information to assess future prices; it is when people use the same information sets and jump to the same conclusions about a piece of information that ragged macroeconomic performance is to be expected, for they cannot all get out of an asset without someone else wanting to buy it.

In a Keynesian setting, the 'Richardson problem' acquires an extra layer of complexity since the decisions that firms make to invest in current and future output contribute to aggregate demand as well as to aggregate supply – but not necessarily simultaneously (cf. the Harrod knife-edge problem in early Keynesian growth models). This is particularly apparent if Richardson's interests are integrated with Minsky's (1975) thinking on speculation and macroeconomic instability, which emphasizes the complementarity of financial choices. For example, consider a scenario in which there is a shortage of commercial office space during the early stages of a macroeconomic recovery. This promotes the formation of property companies trading in and leasing out existing buildings as well as commissioning new ones. With the formation of such companies comes an upturn in complementary activities such as banking, investment advice and share trading, all of which increase the demand for office space. Paper capital gains may be used as collateral for further borrowing, with the supply of funds being expanded as relatively inexperienced players try to get on the bandwagon by shifting money from their bank deposits to those of secondary financial intermediaries or subscribing to issues of shares in property companies. Choices involving new construction projects will add to supply several years hence and need ideally to be based on good information about both the patterns of complementarity and rival projects. There is considerable scope for gross over-building of new space, even though, once embarked upon, construction projects are very conspicuous. If such an excess of office space is supplied that property companies start to fail and drag financial institutions down too, a major implosion may result. This will be exacerbated the more that poor prices are achieved on forced sales of assets of failed developers as these will force downward revaluations of borrowers' collateral.

It is possible to view such boom–bust episodes – evident in London and Sydney in the 1970s and New Zealand in the 1980s (see, respectively, Reid, 1982; Daly, 1982; and Smith, 1995) – from the standpoint of mainstream rational expectations theory. If so, we might argue that decision-makers with a poor capacity to understand lag structures will get selected out by the market, so there is no ongoing problem of maverick agents. But this ignores the fact that those who emerge with fortunes from such episodes are not those who best understand the underlying fundamentals of supply and demand but those who successfully anticipate the turning points. With small differences in timing and different choices of business relationships, the pattern of gains and losses could have been radically different. For many speculators and entrepreneurs, the choice environment is one of crucial decisions (Shackle, 1972, p. 384) rather than repeated forays into a probabilistic arena: many who are bankrupted in one cycle find it hard to get a chance to prove in subsequent rounds that they were merely unlucky rather than lacking in judgment; those who make fortunes merely on the basis of luck may retire on the proceeds. It is thus difficult to learn anything inductively about precisely how to be a winner next time, when the set of players and circumstances will be different (cf. Boland, 1986).

The rational expectations philosophy also diverts attention from institutional design as a factor affecting the resilience of macroeconomic performances. Richardson's work highlights the importance of trade associations, planning bodies, networks and inside information for avoiding regretful choices. It also implies smaller risks of Minskian disasters in economies such as Germany where giant banks have a close involvement with the key decisions because bank finance rather than retained profits provides the major source of investment funds. Banks in such systems can get closer to the overall view of the strategic and balance sheet complementarity of the investment proposals with which they are presented. In highly concentrated banking systems it is easier to cross-reference client accounts on computers and thereby conduct in-house flow of funds analysis. Managers and auditors may thus be better able to spot potential defaults and uncover opportunistic activities that tend to thrive when booms are financed via many layers involving recently established secondary institutions with poorly developed control systems. The more dispersed the stock of information about the emerging matrix of financial claims and obligations, the less likely it is that credit rating agencies and central supervisory authorities will succeed in assembling the big picture and keeping abreast of innovative or guileful practices.

12.7   CONCLUDING THOUGHTS

Until the late 1960s, economists were accustomed to doing macroeconomics with very little attention to microfoundations and considerable reference to hydraulic circular flow analogies. Dangerous territory has awaited those who followed Leijonhufvud's invitation to think about macroeconomic problems as arising from coordination difficulties. Too much of a reductionist micro orientation has since made mainstream economists oblivious to Keynes's analysis of fallacy of composition problems entailed in supply and demand perspectives. Attempts to keep things simple by presuming that the world rapidly ends up populated by agents who have identical information sets and form conjectures in identical ways may result in simplistic or misleading policy advice.

Many of the points made in this chapter and the previous one lead me to doubt whether it is appropriate to focus on trends in macroeconomic *aggregates* as a basis for forming scenarios about the long run evolution of output and balance of payments outcomes. Often the arguments imply path dependence of economic systems of the kind emphasized in the work of Brian Arthur (1989, 1993) and his colleagues at the Santa Fe Institute. If it were possible to switch between one durable asset and other without hassle and without incurring capital losses that had little to do with rates of physical depreciation, then people could experiment without fear of being financially locked into their purchases. In practice, the costs of using markets make financial lock-in a significant issue, the more so the less conventional one's tastes in durables. A further complication likely to entail path dependence is that the results of experimental purchasing decisions are likely to be clouded cognitively by the kinds of dissonance-reducing ploys that people employ (Earl, 1992). This all sounds most unlike the neoclassical vision in which, even if the traffic is sometimes congested along the way, disturbances are prone to cancel out in the long run and economic agents eventually end up in states implied by the initial technology set, endowments and preferences.

Prediction seems unlikely if we recognize that people make decisions on the basis of idiosyncratic sets of information pertaining to their own hopes and fears, whose implications are construed according to the rules of the unique personal judgmental systems that underpin their individuality. The likelihood that we may only be able to describe processes is enhanced to the extent that a focus on information and individuals' dilemmas leads us to take a systems viewpoint and study macroeconomic outcomes in terms of complex and highly contingent networks of both parallel and sequential microeconomic exchanges.

Faced with Chaos, economists who wish to see macroeconomics in terms of problems of coordination might take as their analogy the management of traffic networks to avoid congestion and consider the following among their potential research strategies. First, they might follow Goodwin's lead with a good dose of Simon's (1969) thinking on the notion of system decomposability, and investigate the multiplier process from a matrix standpoint to discover the extent to which expenditure decisions produce localized stresses or dissipate in the broader system. Decision rules that embody check-list requirements for product characteristics and violate the axiom of gross substitutability seem likely to be relevant to understanding patterns of decomposability, as do financial ratios, patterns of corporate strategy, and flexibility of production systems. Secondly, and possibly in a collaborative venture with sociologists, they might undertake field research into networks of transactions in different kinds of contexts to ascertain how institutional differences that affect information flows and confidence contribute to or ameliorate tendencies towards inflation, slow growth or unemployment. A beginning would be case study work involving the tracing of networks of transactions and flow-on patterns of purchases in markets for cars and houses.

Bibliography

Adams, F.G. (1964) 'Consumer attitudes, buying plans and purchases of durable goods: a principal component time series approach', *Review of Economics and Statistics*, **46**: 347–55.

Adams, T.F.N. and Kobayashi, N. (1969) *The World of Japanese Business*, Tokyo, Kodansha International.

Adams, W.J. and Yellen, J.L. (1976) 'Commodity bundling and the burden of monopoly', *Quarterly Journal of Economics*, **92**, August: 475–98.

Adler, M. (1985) 'Stardom and talent', *American Economic Review*, **75**: 208–12.

Adler, N.J. (1986) *International Dimensions of Organizational Behavior*, Boston, Kent Publishing.

Akerlof, G.A. (1970) '"The market for lemons": quality uncertainty and the market mechanism', *Quarterly Journal of Economics* **84**: 488–500.

Akerlof, G.A. (1984) 'Exchange and efficiency-wage theory', *American Economic Review*, **74**: 79–83.

Alchian, A.A. and Allen, W.R. (1967) *University Economics: Elements of Inquiry*, Belmont, CA, Wadsworth.

Allen, G.C. (1959) *British Industries and their Organization* (4th edn), London, Longmans.

Andrews, P.W.S. (1949) *Manufacturing Business*, London, Macmillan.

Andrews, P.W.S. (1964) *On Competition in Economic Theory*, London, Macmillan.

Andrews, P.W.S. (1993) *The Economics of Competitive Enterprise: Selected Essays of P.W.S. Andrews* (F.S. Lee and P.E. Earl, eds), Aldershot, Edward Elgar.

Andrews, P.W.S. and Brunner, E. (1962) 'Business profits and the quiet life', *Journal of Industrial Economics*, **11**: 72–80 (reprinted in Andrews, 1993: 363–9).

Andrews, P.W.S. and Brunner, E. (1975) *Studies in Pricing*, London, Macmillan.

Aoki, M., Gustafsson, B. and Williamson, O.E. (eds) (1990) *The Firm as a Nexus of Treaties*, London, Sage.

Argenti, J. (1980) *Practical Corporate Planning*, London, George Allen & Unwin.

Armour, H.O. and Teece, D.J. (1978) 'Organizational structure and economic performance: a test of the multidivision hypothesis', *Bell Journal of Economics*, **9**: 106–22.

Arrow, K.J. (1962) Economic welfare and the allocation of resources for invention', in *The Rate and Direction of Inventive Activity*, National Bureau of Economic Research, Princeton, NJ, Princeton University Press.

Arrow, K.J. (1971) *Essays in the Theory of Risk Bearing*, Chicago, IL, Markham.

Arthur, W.B. (1989) 'Competing technologies, increasing return, and lock-in by historical events', *Economic Journal*, **99**: 116–31.

Arthur, W.B. (1993) 'Pandora's marketplace', *New Scientist* (Supplement), February: 6–8.

Assael, H. (1990) *Marketing: Principles and Strategy*, Hinsdale, IL, Dryden Press.

Augier, M. (2000) 'Interview with Herbert A. Simon', unpublished manuscript, Department of Economics, Stanford University.

Augier, M. (2001) 'Sublime Simon: the consistent vision of economic psychology's Nobel laureate', *Journal of Economic Psychology*, **22**: 307–34.

Australian Way (1990) 'Interview: Siimon Reynolds', *The Australian Way* (Trans-Australian Airlines In-flight Magazine), May.

Bain, A.D. (1964) *The Growth of Television Ownership in the United Kingdom*, Cambridge, Cambridge University Press.

Barkow, J., Cosmides, L. and Tooby, J. (eds) (1992) *The Adapted Mind: Evolutionary Psychology and the Generation of Culture*, New York, Oxford University Press

Barnard, C.I. (1938) *The Functions of the Executive*, Cambridge, MA, Harvard University Press.

Baudier, E. (1961) 'Review of G. Debreu's *Theory of Value*', *Econometrica*, **29**: 259–60.

Baumol, W.J. (1959) *Business Behavior, Value and Growth*, New York, Harcourt, Brace & World.

Baumol, W.J. (1982) 'Contestable markets: an uprising in the theory of industrial structure', *American Economic Review*, **72**: 1–13.

Baumol, W.J., Panzar, J.C. and Willig, R.D. (1982) *Contestable Markets and the Theory of Industrial Structure*, San Diego, CA, Harcourt Brace Jovanovich.

Becker, G.S. (1962) 'Irrational behaviour and economic theory', *Journal of Political Economy*, **70**: 1–13.

Beckett, A. (1996) 'Strategic management as a scientific research programme', pp. 288–305 of Earl, P.E. (ed.) *Management, Marketing and the Competitive Process*, Cheltenham, UK and Brookfield, US,

Edward Elgar.

Berger, L.A. (1989) 'Economics and hermeneutics', *Economics and Philosophy*, **5**: 209–33.

Bettman, J.R. (1979) *An Information Processing Theory of Consumer Choice*, Reading, MA, Addison-Wesley.

Blois, K.J. (1972) 'Vertical quasi-integration', *Journal of Industrial Economics*, **20**: 253–71.

Boland, L.A. (1986) *Methodology for a New Microeconomics*, Winchester, MA, Allen & Unwin.

Borch, K. (1973) 'The place of uncertainty in the theories of the Austrian school', in Hicks, J.R. and Weber, W. (eds), *Carl Menger and the Austrian School of Economics*, Oxford, Oxford University Press.

Boreham, T., Davis, M., Hely, S. and Shoebridge, N. (1989) 'The frenzy to grow bigger', *Business Review Weekly*, 16 June: 93-8.

Bovee, C.L. and Ahrens, W.F. (1982) *Advertising*, Homewood, IL, Irwin.

Boston Consulting Group (1975) 'Strategy alternatives for the British motorcycle industry', House of Commons Paper 532, London, HMSO.

Bowman, M.J. (ed.) (1958) *Expectations, Uncertainty and Business Behavior*, New York, Social Science Research Council.

Boyd, A. (1991) 'Westpac manager broke confidences', *Australian Financial Review*, 14 March: 19.

Browne, D. (1990) 'Agencies make a splash', *Australian Business*, 14 March: 52–65.

Buchanan, J.M. and Thirlby, G.F. (eds) (1973) *L.S.E.. Essays on Cost*, London, L.S.E./Weidenfeld & Nicolson.

Buckley, P.J. and Michie, J. (eds) (1996) *Firms, Organizations and Contracts*, Oxford, Oxford University Press.

Burker, W. (ed.) (1983) 'Special issue on organizational culture', *Organizational Dynamics*, Autumn.

Cable. J.R. and Dirrheimer, M.J. (1983) 'Hierarchies and markets: An empirical test of the multidivisional hypothesis in West Germany', *International Journal of Industrial Organization*, **1**: 43–62.

Caldwell, B.J. (1989) 'Post-Keynesian methodology: an assessment', *Review of Political Economy* **1**: 43–64.

Cann, K. (2000) 'Catalogue of the Shackle papers', pp. 368–418 of Earl, P.E. and Frowen, S.F. (eds) *Economics as an Art of Thought: Essays in Memory of G.L.S. Shackle*, London, Routledge.

Cantillon, R. (1755) *Essay on the Nature of Trade*, English version edited by H. Higgs, 1931, London, Macmillan.

Car Magazine (1987) 'In Britain', *Car Magazine*, June: 106–107.

Car Magazine (1989) 'Japan's careful move upmarket', *Car Magazine*, September: 36, 41.

Car Magazine (1993) 'Thousands of S-class unsold', *Car Magazine*, February: 11.

Car Magazine (2000) 'Equity scarred', *Car Magazine*, September: 30.

Carr, A.N. (1994) 'The "emotional fallout" of the new efficiency movement in public administration in Australia: a case study', *Administration and Society*, **26**: 344–58.

Chamberlin, E.H. (1933) *The Theory of Monopolistic Competition*, Cambridge, MA, Harvard University Press.

Chandler, A.D. (1962) *Strategy and Structure*, Cambridge, MA, MIT Press.

Channon, D.F. (1973) *The Strategy and Structure of British Enterprises*, London, Macmillan.

Christopher, M., Payne, A. and Ballantyne, D. (1991) *Relationship Marketing: Bringing Quality, Customer Service and Management Together*, Oxford, Butterworth-Heinemann.

Church, R. (1979) *Herbert Austin: The British Motor Car Industry to 1941*, London, Europa.

Clark, J.M. (1923) *Studies in the Economics of Overhead Costs*, Chicago, IL, University of Chicago Press.

Clarke, R. and McGuinness, T. (eds) (1987) *The Economics of the Firm*, Oxford, Blackwell.

Coase, R.H. (1937) 'The nature of the firm', *Economica*, **4** (new series): 386–405.

Coase, R.H. (1991) '1991 Nobel Lecture: The institutional structure of production', pp. 227–35 of Williamson, O.E. and Winter, S.G. (eds), *The Nature of the Firm: Origins, Evolution, and Development*, Oxford: Oxford University Press.

Cochoy, F. (1998) 'Another discipline for the market economy: marketing as a performative knowledge and know-how for capitalism', pp. 194–221 of Callon, M. (ed.), *The Laws of the Markets*, Oxford, Blackwell.

Contractor, F.J. and Lorange, P. (eds) (1988) *Cooperative Strategies in International Business*, Lexington, MA, Lexington Books.

Cook, P.L. (1964) 'Review of G.B. Richardson's *Information and Investment*', *Economic Journal*, **74**: 168–9.

Cooper, R. and John, A. (1988) 'Coordinating coordination failures in Keynesian models', *Quarterly Journal of Economics*, **103**: 441–63.

Cready, W.M. (1991) 'Premium bundling', *Economic Inquiry*, **29**: 173–9.

Cropley, S. (1986) 'Civic centre', *Car Magazine*, December: 106–9.

Cunningham, M.T. and White, J.G. (1974) 'The behaviour of industrial buyers in their search for suppliers of machine tools', *Journal of Management Studies*, **11**: 114–28.

Cyert, R.M. and March, J.G. (1955) 'Organizational structure and pricing behavior in an oligopolistic market', *American Economic Review*, **45**: 129–39.

Cyert, R.M. and March, J.G. (1956) 'Organizational factors in the theory of oligopoly', *Quarterly Journal of Economics*, **70**: 44–64.

Cyert, R.M. and March, J.G. (1963) *A Behavioral Theory of the Firm*, Englewood Cliffs, NJ, Prentice-Hall.

Daly, M.T. (1982) *Sydney Boom, Sydney Bust*, North Sydney, George Allen & Unwin.

Dalziel, P. (2002) 'New Zealand's economic reforms: an assessment', *Review of Political Economy*, **14**: 31–46.

Davidson, P. (1978) *Money and the Real World* (2nd edn), London, Macmillan.

Davidson, P. (1991) *Controversies in Post Keynesian Economics*, Aldershot, Edward Elgar.

Davies, J.E. and Lee, F.S. (1988) 'A Post Keynesian appraisal of the contestability criterion', *Journal of Post Keynesian Economics*, **11**: 3–25.

Davis, C.R. (1996) 'The administrative rational model and public organization theory', *Administration and Society*, **28**: 39–60.

Dawar, N. (1999) 'Brand equity', pp. 50–2 of Earl, P.E. and Kemp, S. (eds), *The Elgar Companion to Consumer Research and Economic Psychology*, Cheltenham, Edward Elgar.

Dean, J. (1950) 'Pricing policies for new products', *Harvard Business Review*, **28** (November–December).

Debreu, G. (1959) *Theory of Value*, New York, Wiley.

Dennard, L.F. (1995) 'Neo-Darwinism and Simon's bureaucratic anti-hero', *Administration and Society*, **26**: 464–87.

Desmet, P. and Feinberg, F. (2003) 'Ask and you shall receive: the effects of the appeals scale on consumers' donation behaviour', *Journal of Economic Psychology*, **24** (forthcoming).

Devine, P.J., Jones, R.M., Lee, N. and Tyson, W.J. (1976) *An Introduction to Industrial Economics* (2nd edn), London, George Allen & Unwin Ltd.

Devletoglou, N.E. (1973) 'Review of G.L.S. Shackle's *Expectation, , Enterprise and Profit* ', *Economic Journal*, **83**: 545–6.

Dickson, P.R. (1992) Toward a general theory of competitive rationality', *Journal of Marketing*, **56**: 69–83.

Dietrich, M. (1994) 'The economics of quasi-integration', *Review of Political Economy*, **6**: 1–18.

Dnes, A.W. (1992) *Franchising: A Case Study Approach*, Aldershot, Avebury.

Dobb, M.H. (1937) *Political Economy and Capitalism*, London, Routledge.

Dore, R. (1986) *Flexible Rigidities*, London, Athlone Press.

Douglas, M. and Wildavsky, A. (1982) *Risk and Culture*, Berkeley, CA, University of California Press.

Douglas, R. (1993) *Unfinished Business*, Auckland, Random House.

Dow, S.C. (1992) 'Post-Keynesian methodology: a comment', *Review of Political Economy* **4**: 111–13.

Downie, J. (1958) *The Competitive Process*, London, Duckworth.

Duck, S. (1983) *Friends, For Life: The Psychology of Close Relationships*, Brighton, Harvester Press.

Duhem, P. (1906) *The Aim and Structure of Physical Theory*, translated by P. Weiner, Princeton, Princeton University Press.

Dunn, S.P. (2000) 'Fundamental uncertainty and the firm in the long run', *Review of Political Economy*, **12**: 419–33.

Dunn, S.P. (2001) 'Galbraith, uncertainty and the modern corporation', pp. 157–82 of Keaney, M. (ed.), *Economist with a Public Purpose: Essays in Honour of John Kenneth Galbraith*, London, Routledge.

Dwyer, F.R., Schurr, P.H. and Oh, S. (1987) 'Developing buyer–seller relationships', *Journal of Marketing*, **51**: 11–27.

Earl, P.E. (1983a) 'A behavioral theory of economists' behavior', pp. 90–125 of Eichner, A.S. (ed), *Why Economics is Not Yet a Science*, Armonk, NY, M.E. Sharpe, Inc.

Earl, P.E. (1983b) *The Economic Imagination*, Brighton, Wheatsheaf.

Earl, P. E. (1984) *The Corporate Imagination: How Big Companies Make Mistakes*, Brighton, Wheatsheaf.

Earl, P.E. (1986) *Lifestyle Economics: Consumer Behaviour in a Turbulent World*, Brighton, Wheatsheaf.

Earl, P.E. (ed.) (1988) *Behavioural Economics*, Aldershot: Edward Elgar.

Earl, P.E. (1990) *Monetary Scenarios: A Modern Approach to Financial Systems*, Aldershot, Edward Elgar.

Earl, P.E. (1992) 'On the complementarity of economic applications of cognitive dissonance theory and personal construct psychology', pp. 49–65 of Lea, S.E.G., Webley, P. and Young, B. (eds), *New Directions in Economic Psychology*, Aldershot, Edward Elgar.

Earl, P.E. (1993) 'Epilogue: whatever happened to P.W.S. Andrews's industrial economics?', pp. 402–27 of Lee, F.S. and Earl, P.E. (eds), (1993) *The Economics of Competitive Enterprise: Selected Essays of P.W.S. Andrews*, Aldershot, Edward Elgar.

Earl, P.E. (1995) *Microeconomics for Business and Marketing: Lectures, Cases and Worked Essays*, Aldershot: Edward Elgar.

Earl, P.E. (1996) 'Contracts, coordination, and the construction industry', pp. 149–71 of Earl, P.E. (ed.), *Management, Marketing, and the Competitive Process*, Cheltenham, Edward Elgar.

Earl, P.E. (2001a) 'Introduction to Volume II', in Earl, P.E. (ed.), *The Legacy of Herbert Simon in Economic Analysis*, Cheltenham, Edward Elgar.

Earl. P.E. (2001b) 'Simon's travel theorem and the demand for live music', *Journal of Economic Psychology*, **22**: 335–58.

Earl, P.E. and Wicklund, R.A. (1999) 'Cognitive dissonance', pp. 81–8 of Earl, P.E. and Kemp, S. (eds), *The Elgar Companion to Consumer Research and Economic Psychology*, Cheltenham, Edward Elgar.

Economist (1986) 'Move over Arthur', 22 November: 68–70.

Economist (1989a) 'Advertising's big bang', 28 January: 61–2.

Economist (1989b) 'Design it Yourself', 29 July: 13–14, 57–8.

Economist (1989c) 'Berkeley Square takes on Madison Avenue', 17 September: 21–4.

Economist (1989d) 'The Saatchi brothers retreat', 9 December: 75–6.

Economist (1990a) 'The proof of the pudding: a survey of the advertising industry', 9 June.

Economist (1990b) 'Elegant Nippon', 8 December: 71.

Economist (1991) 'The flight of Icarus', 16 March: 67–8, 72.

Economist (1994) 'Shareholders' revenge', 24 December: 15

Economist (1995) 'It's people, stupid', 27 May: 67–8.

Edwardes, M. (1983) *Back from the Brink*, London, Collins.

Ehrenberg, A.S.C. (1988) *Repeat Buying* (2nd edn), London, Griffin/New York, Oxford University Press.

Eichner, A.S. (1976) *The Megacorp and Oligopoly*, Cambridge, Cambridge University Press, (reissued by M.E. Sharpe Inc., 1980).

Ellman, M. (1971) *Soviet Planning Today*, Cambridge, Cambridge University Press.

Ferry, J. (1990) 'Cutting Saatchis down to size', *Australian Business*, 7 February: 52–7.

Feyerabend, P.K. (1975) *Against Method: Outline of an Anarchistic Theory of Knowledge*, London, New Left Books.

Fishbein, M.A. and Ajzen, I. (1975) *Belief, Attitude, Intention and Behavior: An Introduction to Theory and Research*, Reading, MA, Addison-Wesley.

Ford, J.L. (1994) *G.L.S. Shackle: The Dissenting Economist's Economist*, Aldershot: Edward Elgar.

Foss, N.J. (1992) 'Theories of the firm: contractual and competence perspectives', *Journal of Evolutionary Economics*, **3**: 127–40.

Foss, N.J. (1994a) 'Cooperation is competition: George Richardson on coordination and interfirm relations', *British Review of Economic Issues*, **16**: 25–49.

Foss, N.J. (1994b) 'The two Coasian traditions', *Review of Political Economy*, **6**: 37–61.

Foss, N.J. (1996) 'Harold Malmgren's analysis of the firm: lessons for modern theorists?', *Review of Political Economy*, **8**: 349–66.

Foss, N.J. (ed.) (1997) *Resources, Firms and Strategies: A Reader in the Resource-Based Perspective*, Oxford, Oxford University Press.

Foss, N.J. and Loasby, B.J. (eds) (1998) *Economic Organization, Capabilities and Coordination: Essays in Honour of G.B. Richardson*, London, Routledge.

Foxall, G. (1997) *Marketing Psychology: The Paradigm in the Wings*, London, Macmillan.

Friedman, T. (1999) *The Lexus and the Olive Tree*, London, HarperCollins.

Fujimoto, T. (1995) 'Toyota motor manufacturing in Australia in 1995: An emergent global strategy', *Actes du Gerpisa*, no. 26: 37–62, http://www.univ-evry.fr/labos/gerpisa/actes/26/26-3.pdf.

Fulbrook, E. (ed.) (2002) *Intersubjectivity in Economics: Agents and Structures*, London, Routledge

Gabor, A. (1977) *Pricing: Principles and Practices*, London, Heinemann Educational Books.

Galbraith, J.K. (1958) *The Affluent Society*, London, Hamish Hamilton.

Galbraith, J.K. (1967) *The New Industrial State*, London, Hamish Hamilton.

Garretsen, H. (1992) *Keynes, Coordination and Beyond*, Aldershot, Edward Elgar.

General Motors (1996) 'GM and Toyota dissolve Australian joint venture', Press release, 15 March, available at http://207.37.252.232/io/releases/i906315b.htm.

George, K.D. and Joll, C. (1981) *Industrial Organisation* (3rd edn), London, George Allen & Unwin Ltd.

Gersick, C.J.G. (1991) 'Revolutionary change theories: a multilevel exploration of the punctuated equilibrium paradigm', *Academy of Management Review*, **16**: 10–36.

Goffe, W.L. (1994) 'Computer network resources for economists' *Journal of Economic Perspectives*, **8**: 97–119.

Goodhart, C.A.E. (1975) *Money, Information and Uncertainty*, London: Macmillan.

Goodwin, R.M. (1949) 'The multiplier as matrix', *Economic Journal*, **59**: 537–55.

Gordon, R.J. (1981) 'Output fluctuations and gradual price adjustment', *Journal of Economic Literature*, **19**: 493–530.

Gordon, R.J. (1990) 'What is New-Keynesian economics', *Journal of Economic Literature*, **28**: 1115–71.

Gould, S.J. (1991) 'The self-manipulation or my pervasive, perceived vital energy through product use: an introspective-praxis perspective', *Journal of Consumer Research*, **18**: 194–207.

Gould, S.J. (1995) 'Researcher introspection as a method in consumer research: Applications, issues and implications', *Journal of Consumer Research*, **21**: 719–22.

Grant, J. McB. (1962) 'Review of G.B. Richardson's *Information and Investment*', *Economic Record*, **38**: 125.

Greer, D.F. (1992) *Industrial Organization and Public Policy* (3rd edn), New York, Maxwell-Macmillan.

Hahn, F.H. (1961) 'Review of G. Debreu's *Theory of Value*', *Journal of Political Economy*, **69**: 204–5.

Hammerton, R. and Mellor, J. (1991) 'Toyota layoffs prepare for joint venture with Holden's', *The Australian*, 16 May: 22

Hampden-Turner, C. and Trompenaars, F. (1997) *Mastering the Infinite Game*, Oxford, Capstone.

Hanson, J.D. and Kysar, D.A. (1999a) 'Taking behavioralism seriously: the problem of market manipulation', *New York University Law Review*, **74**: 630–749.

Hanson, J.D. and Kysar, D.A. (1999b) 'Taking behavioralism seriously: some evidence of market manipulation', *Harvard Law Review*, **112**: 1420–572.

Harper, D. (1996) *Entrepreneurship and the Market Process: An Inquiry into the Growth of Knowledge*, London, Routledge.

Harrell, C. (1960) 'Review of G. Debreu's *Theory of Value*', *Southern Economic Journal*, **27**: 149–50.

Harrigan, K.R. (1980) *Strategies for Declining Businesses*, Lexington, MA, Lexington Books.

Harrigan, K.R. (1983) *Strategies for Vertical Integration*, Lexington, MA, Lexington Books.

Harris, L (1965) 'Review of G.B. Richardson's *Economic Theory*', *Economica*, **32**: 236–7.

Hart, A.G. (1940) *Anticipations, Uncertainty and Dynamic Planning*, Chicago, University of Chicago Press.

Hay, D.A. and Morris, D.J. (1979) *Industrial Economics: Theory and Evidence*, Oxford, Oxford University Press.

Hayek, F.A. von (1949) *Individualism and Economic Order*, Routledge & Kegan Paul

Hazledine, T. (1998) *Taking New Zealand Seriously: The Economics of Decency*, Auckland, HarperCollins.

Hearne, J. (1987) *Advertising Management*, Melbourne, Nelson.

Heiner, R.A. (1983) 'The origin of predictable behavior', *American Economic Review*, **73**: 560–95.

Heymann, D. and Leijonhufvud, A. (1995) *High Inflation: The Arne Ryde Memorial Lectures*, Oxford, Clarendon Press.

Hicks, J.R. (1939) *Value and Capital*, Oxford, Oxford University Press.

Hicks, J.R. (1976) 'Some questions of time in economics', in Tang, A.M., Westfield, F.M. and Worley, J.S. (eds), *Evolution, Welfare and Time in Economics: Essays in Honor of Nicholas Georgescu-Roegen*, Lexington, MA, Lexington Books.

Hirschman, A.O. (1970) *Exit, Voice and Loyalty*, New York, Norton.

Hoch, S.J. (1984) 'Hypothesis testing and consumer behavior: if it works don't mess with it', in Kinnear, T.C. (ed.), *Advances in Consumer Research 11*, Ann Arbor, MI, Association for Consumer Research.

Hoch, S.J., Bradlow, E.T. and Wansink, B. (1999) 'The variety of an assortment', *Marketing Science*, **18**: 527–46.

Hodgson, G. (1988) *Economics and Institutions*, Cambridge, Polity Press.

Hofer, C.W. and Schendel, D. (1978) *Strategy Formulation: Analytical Concepts*, St Paul, Minnesota, West Publishing Company.

Holbrook, M.B. (1995a) *Consumer Research: Introspective Essays on the Study of Consumption*, Thousand Oaks, CA, Sage.

Holbrook, M.B. (1995b) 'The four faces of the commodification in the development of marketing knowledge', *Journal of Marketing Management*, **11**: 641–54.

Holbrook, M.B. (2001) 'Times Square, Disneyphobia, HegeMickey, the Ricky Principle, and the downside of the entertainment economy: it's fun-dumb-mental', *Marketing Theory*, **1**: 139–63.

Horn, M.J. (1995) *The Political Economy of Public Administration*, Cambridge, Cambridge University Press.

Hunt, S.D. (1997a) 'Resource-advantage theory: an evolutionary theory of competitive firm behavior?' *Journal of Economic Issues*, **31**: 59-77

Hunt, S.D. (1997b) 'Resource-advantage theory and the wealth of nations: Developing the socio-economic research tradition', *Journal of Socio-Economics*, **26**: 335-57.

Hunt, S.D. and Morgan, R.M. (1995) 'The comparative advantage theory of competition', *Journal of Marketing*, **59**: 1–15.

Hurwicz, L. (1961) 'Review of G. Debreu's *Theory of Value*', *American Economic Review*, **51**: 414–17.

James, C. (1992) *New Territory: The Transformation of New Zealand 1984–92*, Wellington, Bridget Williams Books.

Jarillo, J.C. and Stevenson, H.H. (1991) 'Co-operative strategies – The payoffs and the pitfalls', *Long Range Planning*, **24**: 64–70

Jefferson, M. (1983) 'Economic uncertainty and business decision-making', in Wiseman, J. (ed.), *Beyond Positive Economics?* London: Macmillan.

Jelinek, M., Smircich, L. and Hirsch, P. (eds.) (1983) 'Organizational culture' (special issue), *Administrative Science Quarterly*, **28**: 331–499.

Jensen, M.C. and Meckling, W. (1976) 'Theory of the firm: managerial behavior, agency costs and ownership structure', *Journal of Financial Economics*, **3**: 305–60.

Jesson, B. (1999) *Only Their Purpose is Mad: The Money Men Take Over NZ*, Palmerston North, Dunmore Press.

Jones, R.A. and Ostroy, J.M. (1984) 'Flexibility and uncertainty', *Review of Economic Studies*, **51**: 13–32.

Kacher, G. (1987) 'Japan Strikes Trouble', *Car Magazine*, October: 128–37.

Kaldor, N. (1960) 'Keynes' theory of the own-rates of interest', pp. 58–74 of his *Essays on Economic Stability and Growth*, London, Duckworth.

Kaldor, N. (1972) 'The irrelevance of equilibrium economics', *Economic Journal*, **82**: 1237–55.

Kaldor, N. (1983) 'The role of commodity prices in economic recovery', *Lloyds Bank Review*, no. 149: 21–34.

Katona, G.A. (1960) *The Powerful Consumer: Psychological Studies of the American Economy*, New York, McGraw-Hill.

Kay, J.A. (1993) *Foundations of Corporate Success*, Oxford, Oxford University Press.

Kay, N.M. (1979) *The Innovating Firm: A Behavioural Theory of Corporate R&D*, London, Macmillan.

Kay, N.M. (1982) *The Evolving Firm*, London, Macmillan.

Kay, N.M. (1984) *The Emergent Firm*, London, Macmillan.

Kay, N.M. (1997) *Pattern in Corporate Evolution*, Oxford, Oxford University Press.

Keller, M. (1989) *Rude Awakening: The Rise, Fall and Struggle for Recovery of General Motors*, New York, Morrow.

Kelly, G.A. (1955) *The Psychology of Personal Constructs*, New York, Norton.

Kets de Vries, M. and Miller, D. (1988) 'Personality, culture and organization', pp. 81–99 of Albanese, P. (ed.), *Psychological Foundations of Economic Behavior*, New York, Praeger.

Keynes, J.M. (1936) *The General Theory of Employment, Interest and Money*, London, Macmillan.

Kilmann, R. H., Saxton, M. J. and Serpa R. (1986) 'Issues in understanding and changing corporate culture,' *California Management Review*, **28**: 87–94.

Kirzner, I.M. (1973) *Competition and Entrepreneurship*, Chicago, IL, University of Chicago Press.

Kleinman, P. (1989) *The Saatchi and Saatchi Story* (2nd edn), London, Pan.

Kogut, B. (1988) 'A study of the life cycle of joint ventures', in Contractor, F.J. and Lorange, P. (eds), *Cooperative Strategies in International Business*, Lexington, MA Lexington Books.

Kregel, J.A. (1990) 'Imagination, exchange and business enterprise in Smith and Shackle', pp. 81–95 of Frowen, S. (ed.) *Unknowledge and Choice in Economics*, London, Macmillan.

Kreps, D.M. (1988) *Notes on a Theory of Choice*, Boulder, CO, Westview Press.

Kuhn, T. S. (1962) *The Structure of Scientific Revolutions*, Chicago, University of Chicago Press.

Lachmann, L. (1976) 'From Mises to Shackle: an essay', *Journal of Economic Literature*, **15**: 54–62.

Lakatos, I. (1970) 'Falsification and the methodology of scientific research programmes', pp. 91–196 of Lakatos, I. and Musgrave, A. (eds.), *Criticism and the Growth of Knowledge*, London, Cambridge University Press.

Lamberton, D.M. (1965) *The Theory of Profit*, Oxford, Blackwell.

Lamberton, D.M. (ed.) (1971) *Economics of Information and Knowledge*, Harmondsworth, Penguin Books.

Lamfalussy, A. (1961) *Investment and Growth in Mature Economies: The Case of Belgium*, London, Macmillan.

Lancaster, K.J. (1966) 'A new approach to consumer theory', *Journal of Political Economy*, **74**: 132–57.

Langlois, C. (1989a) 'A model of target inventory and markup with testing using automobile industry data', *Journal of Economic Behavior and Organization*, **11**: 47–74.

Langlois, C. (1989b) 'Markup pricing versus marginalism: a controversy revisited', *Journal of Post Keynesian Economics*, **12**: 127–51.

Langlois, R.N. and Robertson, P.L. (1989) 'Explaining vertical integration: lessons from the American automobile industry', *Journal of Economic History*, 49: 361–75.

Langlois, R.N. and Robertson, P.L. (1995) *Firms, Markets and Economic Change*, London, Routledge.

Latsis, S.J. (1976) 'A research programme in economics', pp. 1–41 of Latsis, S.J. (ed.), *Method and Appraisal in Economics*, Cambridge, Cambridge University Press.

Lazonick, W. (1990) *Competitive Advantage on the Shop Floor*, Cambridge, MA, Harvard University Press.

Lazonick, W. (1991) *Business Organization and the Myth of the Market Economy*, Cambridge, Cambridge University Press.

Lee, F.S. (1984) 'Full cost pricing: a new wine in a new bottle', *Australian Economic Papers* 23: 151–66.

Lee, F.S. (1993) 'Philip Walter Sawford Andrews, 1914–1971', pp. 1–34 of Lee, F.S. and Earl, P.E. (eds), *The Economics of Competitive Enterprise: Selected Essays of P.W.S. Andrews*, Aldershot, Edward Elgar.

Leibenstein, H. (1950) 'Bandwagon, snob and Veblen effects', *Quaterly Journal of Economics*, **64**: 183–207.

Leibenstein, H. (1966) 'Allocative efficiency vs. X-efficiency', *American Economic Review*, **56**: 392–415.

Leibenstein, H. (1976) *Beyond Economic Man*, Cambridge, MA, Harvard University Press.

Leibenstein, H. (1978) 'X-ineffieciency X-ists – reply to an Xorcist', *American Economic Review*, **68**: 203–11.

Leijonhufvud, A. (1968) *On Keynesian Economics and the Economics of Keynes*, New York , Oxford University Press.

Levitt, T. (1983) 'The globalisation of markets', *Harvard Business Review*, May–June: 92–102.

Lewis, P. and Norris, K. (1997) 'Recent changes in economics enrolments', *Economic Papers*, **16**, March: 1-13.

Linder, S.B. (1970) *The Harried Leisure Class*, New York, Columbia University Press.

Littlechild, S.C. (1981) 'Misleading calculations of the social costs of monopoly power', *Economic Journal*, **91**: 348–64.

Littlechild, S.C. (1982) 'Controls on advertising: an examination of some economic arguments', *Journal of Advertising*, **1**, pp. 25-37.

Littlechild, S.C.. (2000) 'Disreputable adventures: the Shackle papers at Cambridge', pp. 323–67 of Earl, P.E. and Frowen, S.F. (eds), *Economics as an Art of Thought: Essays in Memory of G.L.S. Shackle*, London, Routledge.

Loasby, B.J. (1967) 'Management economics and the theory of the firm,' *Journal of Industrial Economics*, **15**: 165–76.

Loasby, B.J. (1976) *Choice, Complexity and Ignorance*, Cambridge, Cambridge University Press.

Loasby, B.J. (1986) 'Competition and imperfect knowledge: the contribution of G.B. Richardson', *Scottish Journal of Political Economy*, **33**: 145–58.

Loasby, B.J. (1989) *The Mind and the Method of the Economist*, Aldershot, Edward Elgar.

Lodge, D. (1989) *Nice Work*, Harmondsworth, Penguin Books.

Lorsch, J.W. (1986) 'The invisible barrier to strategic change', *California Management Review*, **28**: 95–109.

Love, J.F. (1986) *McDonald's: Behind the Arches*, New York, Bantam Books.

Lutz, M.A. (1999) *Economics for the Common Good*, London, Routledge.

Lutz, M.A. and Lux, K. (1979) *The Challenge of Humanistic Economics*, Menlo Park, CA, Benjamin/Cummings Publishing Company.

MacKie-Mason, J.K. and Varian, H. (1994) 'Economic FAQs about the Internet', *Journal of Economic Perspectives*, **8**: 75–96.

Magnet, M. (1986) 'Saatchi and Saatchi will keep gobbling', *Fortune International*, 23 June: 43–6.

Mahoney, J. T. and Pandian, J.R. (1992) 'The resource-based view within the conversation of strategic management', *Strategic Management Journal*, **13**: 363–80.

Maital, S. (1982) *Minds, Markets and Money*, New York, Basic Books.

Malmgren, H.B. (1961) 'Information, expectations and the theory of the firm', *Quarterly Journal of Economics*, **75**: 399–421.

March, J.G. (1988) *Decisions and Organizations*, Oxford, Blackwell.

March, J.G. and Olsen, J.P. (1976) *Ambiguity and Choice in Organizations*, Bergen, Norway, Universitetsforlaget.

Mariti, P. and Smiley, R.H. (1983) 'Co-operative agreements and the organization of industry', *Journal of Industrial Economics*, **31**: 437–52

Marketing News (1985) 'AMA adopts new marketing definition', *Marketing News*, **19**, no. 5, 1 March: 1.

Marks, L. and Kleinman, P. (1987) 'The rise and rise of Saatchi and Saatchi', *Australian Business*, 14 October: 76–9.

Marris, R.L. (1964) *The Economic Theory of 'Managerial' Capitalism*, London, Macmillan.

Marshall, A. (1890) *Principles of Economics*, London, Macmillan.

Martin, J.P. (1978) 'X-inefficiency, managerial effort and protection', *Economica*, **45**: 273–86.

Martin, S. (1993) *Advanced Industrial Economics*, Oxford, Blackwell.

Maslow, A. (1970) *Motivation and Personality*, New York, Harper & Row.

Mason, R.S. (1981) *Conspicuous Consumption*, Farnborough, Gower Publishing.

Massey, P. (1995) *New Zealand: Market Liberalization in a Developed Economy*, London, Macmillan.

McCracken, G. (1989) 'Who is the celebrity endorser? Cultural foundations of the endorsement process', *Journal of Consumer Research*, **16**: 310–21.

McQueen, D. (1994) 'On re-reading Samuelson: a teacher's perspective', *Challenge*, March/April: 39–45.

Mellor, J. (1988) 'News comment: Holden/Toyota Marriage,' *Car Australia*, February: 41–43

Menger, C. (1871) *Grundsatze der Volkwirtschaftslehre*, Wien, Wilhelm Braumuller (later translated as *Principles of Economics* by J. Dingwall and B.F. Hoselitz, New York, New York University Press and Institute for Humane Studies, 1976; references to translation).

Miles, C. (1968) *Lancashire Textiles: A Case Study of Industrial Change*, Cambridge, Cambridge University Press/NIESR.

Miller, C.M., McIntyre, S.H. and Mantrala, M.K. (1995) 'Toward formalizing fashion theory', *Journal of Marketing Research*, **30**: 142–57.

Miller, D. (1982) 'Evolution and revolution: A quantum view of structural change in organization', *Journal of Management Studies*, **19**: 131–51.

Miller, G.A. (1956) 'The magic number seven plus or minus two: Some limitations on our capacity for processing information', *Psychological Review*, **63**: 81–97.

Minsky, H.P. (1975) *John Maynard Keynes*, New York, Columbia University Press.

Mises, L. von (1949) *Human Action: A Treatise on Economics*, London, William Hodge & Co.

Modern Motor (1989) 'BMW delays new 3-series', *Modern Motor*, **36**, 4,

September: 29.

Moritz, M. and Seaman, B. (1981) *Going for Broke: The Chrysler Story*, New York, Doubleday.

Morris, M. (1993) 'Things to do with shopping centres', pp. 295–319 of During, S. (ed.) *The Cultural Studies Reader*, London, Routledge.

Muth, R.F. (1961) 'Rational expectations and the theory of price movements', *Econometrica*, **29**: 315–35.

Negishi, T. (1985) *Economic Theories in a Non-Walrasian Tradition*, Cambridge, Cambridge University Press.

Nelson, R.R. and Winter, S.G., Jr (1982) *An Evolutionary Theory of Economic Change*, Cambridge, MA, Harvard University Press.

Newstead, A. (1986) 'Review of *Towards a Cashless Society*, by the Technological Change Committee of the Australian Science of Technology Council, Canberra, AGPS', *Prometheus*, **4**: 399–401.

Nightingale, J. (1997) 'Anticipating Nelson and Winter: Jack Downie's theory of evolutionary economic change', *Journal of Evolutionary Economics*, **7**: 147–67.

Nightingale, J. (1998) 'Jack Downie's competitive process: the first articulated population ecology model in economics', *History of Political Economy*, **30**: 369–412.

Olins, R. (1990) 'Selling with star billing', *Sunday Times*, 17 June, Arts section: 9.

Olshavsky, R.W. and Granbois, D.H. (1979). 'Consumer decision making – fact or fiction?' *Journal of Consumer Research*, **6**: 93–100.

O'Reilly, D. (1986) 'Advertising's doublespeak', *Management Today*, November: 76–7, 144.

Overy, R.J. (1976) *William Morris, Viscount Nuffield*, London, Europa.

Packard, V. (1957) *The Hidden Persuaders*, London, Longmans.

Penrose, E.T. (1959) *The Theory of the Growth of the Firm*, Oxford, Blackwell.

Phlips, L. (1988) *The Economics of Imperfect Information*, Cambridge, Cambridge University Press.

Pickering, J.F. (1973) *Industrial Structure and Market Conduct*, London, Martin Robertson.

Pickering, J.F. (1977) *The Acquisition of Consumer Durables: A Cross Sectional Investigation*, London, Associated Business Programmes.

Piore, M.J. and Sabel, C.F. (1984) *The Second Industrial Divide: Possibilities for Prosperity*, New York, Basic Books.

Polanyi, M. (1958) *Personal Knowledge*, London, Routledge & Kegan Paul.

Porter, M.E. (1980) *Competitive Strategy: Techniques for Analyzing Industries and Competitors*, New York, Free Press.

Porter, M.E. (1985) *Competitive Advantage*, New York, Free Press.

Power, J.H. (1961) 'Review of G.B. Richardson's *Information and Investment*', *American Economic Review*, **51**: 761–2.

Potts, J. (2000) *The New Evolutionary Microeconomics: Complexity, Competence and Adaptive Behaviour*, Cheltenham, Edward Elgar.

Prahalad, C.K. and Bettis, R.A. (1986) 'The dominant logic: a new linkage between diversity and performance', *Strategic Management Journal*, **7**: 485–501.

Prais, S.J. (1973) 'Review of D.S. Ironmongers *New Commodities and Consumer Behaviour*', *Economic Journal*, **83**: 578–80.

Press (1997) 'Top compaigners to M&C Saatchi', *The Press* (Christchurch, New Zealand), 12 April.

Quine, W. van O. (1951) 'Two dogmas of empiricism', *Philosophical Review*, reprinted as pp. 20–46 of Quine, W. van O. (1961) *From a Logical Point of View*, New York, Harper & Row.

Radley, K. (1990) 'Honda going multi-national hints new boss Kawamoto', *Car Magazine*, December: 24–25.

Rappaport, E.D. (1999) *Shopping for Pleasure: Women and the Making of London's West End*, Princeton, NJ, Princeton University Press.

Ratchford, B.T. (19975) 'The new economic theory of consumer behavior: an interpretive essay', *Journal of Consumer Research*, **2**: 65–75.

Reid, G.C. (1987) *Theories of Industrial Organization*, Oxford, Blackwell.

Reid, M. (1982) *The Secondary Banking Crisis, 1973–75*, London, Macmillan.

Remenyi, J.V. (1979) 'Core demi-core interaction: toward a general theory of disciplinary and subdisciplinary growth', *History of Political Economy*, **11**: 30–63.

Richardson, G.B. (1959) 'Equilibrium, expectations and information', *Economic Journal*, **69**: 223–37.

Richardson, G.B. (1960) *Information and Investment*, Oxford, Clarendon Press (2nd edn, 1990).

Richardson, G.B. (1964a) *Economic Theory*, London, Hutchinson.

Richardson, G.B. (1964b) The limits to a firm's rate of growth', *Oxford Economic Papers*, **16**: 9–23.

Richardson, G.B. (1965) 'The theory of restrictive trade practices', *Oxford Economic Paper*, **17**, 432–49.

Richardson, G.B. (1966) 'The pricing of heavy electrical equipment: competition or agreement?', *Bulletin of the Oxford University Institute of Economics and Statistics*, **28**: 73–92.

Richardson, G.B. (1967) 'Price notification schemes', *Oxford Economics Papers*, **19**: 355–65.

Richardson, G.B. (1969) *The Future of the Heavy Electrical Plant Industry*, London, BEEMA.

Richardson, G.B. (1971) 'Planning versus competition', *Soviet Studies*, **22**: 433–47.

Richardson, G.B. (1972) 'The organisation of industry', *Economic Journal*, **82**: 883–96.

Richardson G.B. (1975) 'Adam Smith on competition and increasing returns', in Skinner, A.S. and Wilson, T. (eds) *Essays on Adam Smith*, Oxford, Oxford University Press.

Richardson, G.B. (1998) *The Economics of Imperfect Knowledge: Collected Papers of G.B. Richardson*, Cheltenham, UK/Northampton, MA, Edward Elgar.

Ricketts, M. (1987) *The Economics of Business Enterprise: New Approaches to the Firm*, Brighton, Wheatsheaf Books (3rd edn, Cheltenham, Edward Elgar, 2002).

Ries, A. and Trout, J. (1981) *Positioning: The Battle for Your Mind*, New York, McGraw-Hill.

Ritzer, G. (2000) *The McDonalization of Society*, Thousand Oaks, CA, Pine Forge/Sage.

Robertson, D.H. (1940) 'Mr Keynes and the rate of interest', in his *Essays in Monetary Theory*, London, P.S. King & Son.

Robinson, J.V. (1953) '"Imperfect Competition" Revisited', *Economic Journal*, **63**: 579–93.

Robinson, J.V. (1954) 'The impossibility of profits', in Chamberlin, E.H. (ed.), *Monopoly and Competition and their Regulation*, London, Macmillan.

Robinson, J.V. (1977) 'What are the questions?', *Journal of Economic Literature*, **15**: 1318–39.

Robinson, P. (1987) 'Merger! Holden and Toyota to form a new company', *Wheels*, December: 8–9.

Robinson, R. (1971) *Edward H. Chamberlin*, New York, Columbia University Press.

Rook, D.W. (1999) 'Impulse buying', pp. 328–33 of Earl, P.E. and Kemp, S. (eds), *The Elgar Companion to Consumer Research and Economic Psychology*, Cheltenham, Edward Elgar.

Rosenthal, L. (1997) 'Chain-formation in the owner-occupied housing market', *Economic Journal*, **107**: 475–88.

Sabbagh, K. (1989) *Skyscraper: The Making of a Building*, London, Macmillan/Channel 4.

Saul, J.R. (1993) *Voltaire's Bastards: The Dictatorship of Reason in the West*, Toronto, Penguin Books.

Scherer, F.M. and Ross, D. (1990) *Industrial Market Structure and Economic Performance* (3rd edn), Boston, Houghton Mifflin.

Schmalensee, R. and Willig (eds) (1989) *Handbook of Industrial Organization, Volume 1*, Amsterdam, North-Holland.

Schumpeter, J.A. (1934) *Theory of Economic Development*, Oxford: Oxford University Press.

Schumpeter, J.A. (1939) *Business Cycles*, New York: McGraw-Hill.

Schumpeter, J.A. (1943) *Capitalism, Socialism and Democracy*, London, George Allen & Unwin (reprinted 1992, London, Routledge).

Scitovsky, T. (1985) 'Pricetakers' plenty: a neglected benefit of capitalism', *Kyklos*, **38**: 517–36.

Scitovsky, T. (1987) 'Growth in the affluent society', *Lloyds Bank Review*, no. 163: 1–14.

Scitovsky, T. (1990) 'The benefits of asymmetric markets', *Journal of Economic Perspectives*, **4**: 135–48.

Selznick, P. (1957) *Leadership in Administration*, Evanston, IL, Harper & Row.

Shackle, G.L.S. (1938) *Expectations, Investment and Income*, Oxford: Oxford University Press (2nd edn, 1968).

Shackle, G.L.S. (1959) 'Review of H.A. Simon's *Models of Man*', *Economic Journal*, **69**: 547–9.

Shackle, G.L.S. (1961) *Decision, Order and Time in Human Affairs*, Cambridge, Cambridge University Press.

Shackle, G.L.S. (1967) *The Years of High Theory: Invention and Tradition in Economic Thought, 1926–1939*, Cambridge, Cambridge University Press.

Shackle, G.L.S. (1970) *Expectation, Enterprise and Profit*, London, George Allen & Unwin.

Shackle, G.L.S. (1972) *Epistemics and Economics*, Cambridge, Cambridge University Press (republished 1992, Transaction Publishers, New Brunswick, NJ).

Shackle, G.L.S. (1974) *Keynesian Kaleidics*, Edinburgh: Edinburgh University Press.

Shackle, G.L.S. (1979) *Imagination and the Nature of Choice*, Edinburgh, Edinburgh University Press.

Shackle, G.L.S. (1985) 'Review of H.A. Simon's *Reason in Human Affairs*', *Economic Journal*, **95**: 246.

Shackle, G.L.S. (1988) *Business, Time and Thought* (edited by S.F. Frowen), London, Macmillan.

Shapiro, H.T. and Angevine, G.E. (1969) 'Consumer attitudes, buying intentions and expectations', *Canadian Journal of Economics*, **2**: 230–49.

Shoebridge, N. (1990) 'How ad dollars make Mitchell a media power', *Business Review Weekly*, 8 June: 86–9.

Silberston, A. (1970) 'Surveys of applied economics: price behaviour of firms', *Economic Journal*, **80**: 511–82.

Silver, M. (1984) *Enterprise and the Scope of the Firm*, Oxford, Martin

Robertson.

Simon, H.A. (1945) *Adminitrative Behavior*, New York, Macmillan/Free Press.

Simon, H.A. (1957) *Models of Man*, New York: Wiley.

Simon, H.A. (1959) 'Theories of decision-making in economics and behavioral sciences', *American Economic Review*, **49**: 253–83.

Simon, H.A. (1969) *The Sciences of the Artificial*, Cambridge, MA, MIT Press.

Simon, H.A. (1976) 'From substantive to procedural rationality,' pp. 129–48 of Latsis, S.J. (ed.), *Method and Appraisal in Economics*, Cambridge, Cambridge University Press.

Simon, H.A. (1982) *Models of Bounded Rationality*, Cambridge, MA, MIT Press.

Simon, H.A. (1983) *Reason in Human Affairs*, Oxford, Blackwell.

Simpson, R. (1989) 'Going for brokers', *Marketing*, 5 January: 35–6

Singer A.E. (1996) 'Metatheory, hyperstrategy and ultragames', pp. 329–51 of Earl, P.E. (ed.), *Management, Marketing and the Competitive Process*, Cheltenham, Edward Elgar.

Skinner, A.S. (1983) 'E.H. Chamberlin: the origins and development of monopolistic competition', *Journal of Economic Studies*, **10**: 52–67.

Smith, C.A. (1995) 'Minsky's financial instability hypothesis in a New Zealand context', unpublished M.C.M dissertation, Lincoln University, Canterbury, New Zealand.

Smith, R.P. (1975) *Consumer Demand for Cars in the USA*, Cambridge, Cambridge University Press.

Smyth, R.L. (1967) 'A Price-minus theory of costs', *Scottish Journal of Political Economy*, **14**: 110–17.

Sraffa, P. (1960) *Production of Commodities by Means of Commodities: Prelude to a Critique of Economic Theory*, Cambridge, Cambridge University Press.

Steer, P.S. and Cable, J.R. (1978) 'Internal organisation and profit: an empirical analysis of large companies, *Journal of Industrial Economics*, **27**: 13–30.

Stewart, M. (1967) *Keynes and After*, Harmondsworth, Penguin Books.

Stigler, G.J. (1939) 'Production and distribution in the short run', *Journal of Political Economy*, **47**: 305–27.

Stigler, G.J. (1968) 'A note on block booking', in his collection *The Organization of Industry*, Homewood, IL, Irwin.

Stigler, G.J. (1976) 'The Xistence of X-inefficiency', *American Economic Review*, **66**: 213–16.

Stigler, G.J. (1982) *The Economist as Preacher* Oxford, Blackwell.

Streissler, E.W. (1973) 'Menger's theory of money and interest', in Hicks, J.R.. and Weber, W. (eds), *Carl Menger and the Austrian School of*

Economics, Oxford, Oxford University Press.

Swann, G.M.P. (2001) 'The demand for distinction and the evolution of the prestige car', *Journal of Evolutionary Economics*, **11**: 59–75.

Taylor, B. and Wills, G. (eds) (1969) *Pricing Strategy:Reconciling Customer Needs and Company Objectives*, London, Staples Press.

Teece, D.J. (1981) 'Internal organization and economic performance: an empirical analysis of the profitability of large firms', *Journal of Industrial Economics*, **30**: 173–200.

Thaler, R. and Shefrin, H.M. (1981) 'An economic theory of self control', *Journal of Political Economy*, **89**: 392–406.

Thompson, M. (1979) *Rubbish Theory*, Oxford, Oxford University Press.

Thompson, S. (1983) 'Internal organisation and profit: a note', *Journal of Industrial Economics*, **30**: 201–12.

Tirole, J. (1988) *The Theory of Industrial Organization*, Cambridge, MA, MIT Press.

Toffler, A. (1980) *The Third Wave*, London, Collins.

Townshend, H. (1937) 'Liquidity premium and the theory of value', *Economic Journal*, **47**: 157–69.

Treisman, A. (1988) 'Features and objects', *Quarterly Journal of Experimental of Psychology*, **40**: 201–37.

Treisman, A. and Gelade, G. (1980) 'A feature-integration theory of attention', *Cognitive Psychology*, **12**: 97–136.

Tricker, R.I. (1984) *Corporate Governance*, Aldershot, Gower Publishing.

Underhill, P. (1999) *Why We Buy: The Science of Shopping*, New York, Simon & Schuster.

Uttal, B. (1983) 'The corporate culture vultures', *Fortune*, **108**, no. 8 (October 17): 66–72.

Utton, M.A. (1982) *The Political Economy of Big Business*, Oxford, Martin Robertson.

Wagner, L. and Baltazzis, N. (eds) (1973) *Readings in Applied Microeconomics*, Oxford, Oxford University Press.

Walker, D.A. (ed.) (1984) *Money and Markets: Essays by Robert W. Clower*, Cambridge University Press, Cambridge.

Ward, D. (1990) 'Rover-Honda shares swap', *Car Magazine*, June: 17.

Wheels (1986) 'Nissan know-how a Holden no-no', *Wheels*, June: 8.

Wheels (1988) 'Farewell to Honda Sterlings and Rover Legends', *Wheels*, June: 29.

Wheels (1989) 'Delta success delays launch,' *Wheels*, October: 26.

Williams, B.R. (1949) 'Types of competition and the theory of employment', *Oxford Economic Papers*, **1** (new series): 121–44.

Williams, R. (1993) 'Advertising: the magic system', pp. 320–36 of During, S. (ed.), *The Cultural Studies Reader*, London, Routledge.

Williams, R.A. and Defries, L. (1981) 'The roles of inflation and consumer sentiment in explaining Australian consumption and savings patterns', *Journal of Economic Psychology*, **1**: 105–20.

Williamson, O.E. (1964) *The Economics of Discretionary Behavior*, Englewood Cliffs, NJ, Prentice-Hall.

Williamson, O.E. (1970) *Corporate Control and Business Behavior*, Englewood Cliffs, NJ, Prentice-Hall.

Williamson, O.E. (1975) *Markets and Hierarchies: Analysis and Antitrust Implications*, New York, Free Press.

Williamson, O.E. (1985) *The Economic Institutions of Capitalism: Firms, Markets, Relational Contracting*, New York, Free Press.

Wilson, T. (1984) *Inflation, Unemployment, and the Market*, Oxford, Clarendon Press.

Wiseman, J. (1989) *Cost, Choice and Political Economy*, Aldershot, Edward Elgar.

Wool Textile EDC (1969) *The Strategic Future of the Wool Textile Industry*, London, HMSO.

Young, A. (1928) 'Increasing returns and economic progress', *Economic Journal*, **38**: 527–42.

Young, W. and Lee, F.S. (1993) *Oxford Economics and Oxford Economists*, London, Macmillan.

Index of Names

Index of Subjects